Placemaking Fundamentals for the Built Environment

Dominique Hes · Cristina Hernandez-Santin
Editors

Placemaking Fundamentals for the Built Environment

palgrave
macmillan

Editors
Dominique Hes
Place Agency, Faculty of Architecture,
Building and Planning
University of Melbourne
Parkville, VIC, Australia

Cristina Hernandez-Santin
Thrive Research Hub and Place Agency,
Faculty of Architecture, Building
and Planning
University of Melbourne
Parkville, VIC, Australia

ISBN 978-981-32-9623-7   ISBN 978-981-32-9624-4   (eBook)
https://doi.org/10.1007/978-981-32-9624-4

© The Editor(s) (if applicable) and The Author(s), under exclusive license to Springer Nature Singapore Pte Ltd. 2020

This work is subject to copyright. All rights are solely and exclusively licensed by the Publisher, whether the whole or part of the material is concerned, specifically the rights of translation, reprinting, reuse of illustrations, recitation, broadcasting, reproduction on microfilms or in any other physical way, and transmission or information storage and retrieval, electronic adaptation, computer software, or by similar or dissimilar methodology now known or hereafter developed.

The use of general descriptive names, registered names, trademarks, service marks, etc. in this publication does not imply, even in the absence of a specific statement, that such names are exempt from the relevant protective laws and regulations and therefore free for general use.

The publisher, the authors and the editors are safe to assume that the advice and information in this book are believed to be true and accurate at the date of publication. Neither the publisher nor the authors or the editors give a warranty, expressed or implied, with respect to the material contained herein or for any errors or omissions that may have been made. The publisher remains neutral with regard to jurisdictional claims in published maps and institutional affiliations.

Cover credit: © Alex Linch/shutterstock.com

This Palgrave Macmillan imprint is published by the registered company Springer Nature Singapore Pte Ltd.
The registered company address is: 152 Beach Road, #21-01/04 Gateway East, Singapore 189721, Singapore

*To all those who are working on strategies to connect people to place.
We hope this book helps you with your journey.*

Foreword

While the placemaking movement has flourished in the last decade or two, the notion of place is not new. Placemaking is connected to practices that have been living for thousands of years as well as to new contemporary initiatives that thrive in our present-day culture. In *Placemaking Fundamentals for the Built Environment*, the knowledge, experience and ideas of many academics, professionals and communities working in this field are shared with a view to expanding practice, furthering our understanding and enabling others through capacity building. While not a comprehensive account of an increasingly diverse and complex field, it does attest to the investment and energy engaging with place at all levels.

Placemaking can be understood as an intentional process of situating, revealing and creating meaningful environments. Places are diverse; they can be vibrant urban streets that come alive with neighbourhood gathering; stretches of wilderness for reflective walking; a residual space commandeered from under a bridge that serves as a meeting place or highly intentional creative endeavours like public squares that create a heart for a city. What is clear from the chapters in Placemaking Fundamentals for the Built Environment is that place is about people's engagement with environments, with ecologies, and with each other.

For me, the key outcome of placemaking, whether it has been intentional or through happenstance, is the sense of attachment we can feel to the place. Places enable connections; sometimes these are intense and formative to our sense of ourselves, and at other times, our attachment may be momentary and quickly dissipate. This place attachment, is what makes us feel that we are part of a place and that we belong. It gives us a desire to live in it, invest in it and share that experience with others.

Even though there is an increasing interest in place and in placemaking, there is no consensus on its definition. For some, placemaking is about fleeting events that disappear as quickly as they were made, and for others, placemaking is about permanence, materiality and transcendence across time. Perhaps, this ambiguity is placemaking and place's greatest strength. Although we cannot agree that place is one thing, there is a shared energy that placemaking is a valuable contribution to the lives lived in cities, neighbourhoods and rural areas.

The case studies, frameworks and methods for and about placemaking presented here attest to a broad engagement with place across industry, creative professionals, institutions and governance. The collaboration and contributions are part of a momentum and a desire to be connected to where we live, work and play, to feel included in the places we inhabit. The contributions in this book are an invitation to reflect on how you might make your own place.

Cristina Garduño Freeman
The University of Melbourne, Parkville, Australia

Preface

Acknowledgement to First Nations

We acknowledge the First Nations People of the places where we work and live. We acknowledge how critical it is to engage with and listen to their voices and respect the knowledge and contribution that elders past, present and emerging have to develop thriving places.

> "We are here now and telling our stories, the Narinya (Living Dreaming) and the Garuwanga (Ancestral Dreaming). But is anyone listening? So many decisions are being made, projects developed and Country cleared (still) that it appears to local Sydney Aboriginal people that, no, no-one is listening".
> Shannon Foster
> Sydney D'harawal Knowledge Keeper

Introduction to This Book

This book aims to support the competency in both graduates and placemakers in the world in the knowledge, art and practice of placemaking. It came from research done in 2016 with 35 educators across Australia. They identified that graduates were coming out of university with the theoretical knowledge, that is the case studies, research and theories of placemaking but not the engagement skills. One student said: "we keep being told engagement is so important, but this is the first time we actually got to work with community, to engage". Although community, government and industry see the importance of connecting communities to their places and give them agency to care for place, they do not often have all the skills or understanding of how to facilitate this to its potential.

The basis for the content of this book was developed over a two-day workshop with 55 academics and industry practitioners (30–31st of October 2017) where the current needs were identified and then the topics that would fill these needs. From this workshop, 300 capabilities and capacities were gathered, and from these, 62 skills of creating places were identified while the rest were areas of understanding that needed to be fostered. These were aggregated into 13 themes, which form the basis of this book. As it is the intention of this book to be both rigorous and tacit, the chapters contain both the latest theory, thinking, literature, case studies and practical aspects.

The book has been written by academics from eight universities around Australia: The University of Melbourne, Curtin University, the University of Queensland, the University of Technology Sydney, the University of Adelaide, the University of Notre Dame, the University of New South Wales, the University of Tasmania; as well as an academic from Hong Kong Polytechnic University.

As part of the development of this book, the team produced associated teaching materials including curriculum, slides, readings, activities and videos. These are aimed at giving students the ability to learn the competencies required to be able to carry out placemaking so as to facilitate agency in communities and other stakeholders of a place.

A Brief Outline of the Book

The book begins in Chapter 1 with the fundamentals of placemaking, outlining the key concepts thinkers and approaches of placemaking, while Chapter 2 proposes a 5P framework (people, process, product, programme and place evaluation) reflecting on current practice of placemaking. One of the critical aspects that are often missing in the placemaking discourse and practice is the role of the non-human in place. This book, therefore, places emphasis on this aspect through outlining the many benefits and practices of integrating the non-human (plants, animals, insects, etc.—see Chapter 3) in placemaking. Humans need nature to be mentally and physically at their best; thus, this chapter explores strategies to incorporate nature into placemaking activities.

The next chapter of the book (Chapter 4) builds on the acknowledgement of First Nations contribution to the idea of place. They had what this book is advocating: agency over their places. Past and present First Nations People continue to have a sense of responsibility and care for Country. They see themselves as much part of the country as the grass, trees, soil, rain, flora and fauna yet with greater agency for its care and thriving. They are part of the land in a mutually reciprocal relationship. This chapter is a wonderful narrative and conversation between a traditional knowledge holder and placemaking academic.

The book continues with Chapter 5, which explores community engagement as a critical aspect of the placemaking process. The chapter outlines community engagement tools and methods. Deep engagement is the pivotal point where agency is invited or repelled; thus, it should be planned and delivered with care and transparency while seeking deep communication. However, engagement often requires us to interact with those in power. Chapter 6 introduces the voice of placemakers who work within government, private and community sectors discussing the value of placemaking. This is done through two engaging cases studies and through the voices of the stakeholders.

Following on, when conducting best-practice placemaking, the product being designed should be adaptable and flexible to ever-changing conditions. In Chapter 7, the application of adaptive design thinking is explored in the context of rapid urban change. It examines strategies which can be put in place and how placemaking initiatives can assume a substantial role in urban design, to respond to the complex challenges posed by urban transformations.

A critical aspect of placemaking is how the financial argument is being presented. Chapter 8 outlines the ways economics is applied to placemaking using standard well-known approaches with worked examples to ensure there is a basic level of literacy of these aspects. As placemaking becomes part of the narrative of built environment projects, evaluating its performance not just economically but holistically is argued in Chapter 13 that chapter also challenges placemaking to engage stakeholders in continuous evaluation and reflection processes to support its ability to adapt and evolve.

The role of the 'place maker' is explored through three projects of different scales in Chapter 9. These roles are explored within the placemaking approach outlined in Chapter 2 around people, project, place, process, product and programme. Chapter 10 outlines the leadership aspects needed to carry out placemaking and argues for a decentralised distributed approach through case studies and interviews of successful placemaking projects. This rolls into Chapter 11 which outlines governance approaches to ensure placemaking occurs and continues to thrive beyond the first investment. The book ends looking to the future of placemaking, digital technology (Chapter 12) and art (Chapter 14).

Parkville, Australia   Dominique Hes

Acknowledgements

We would like to acknowledge the privilege we have to be living on the land of the oldest continuing culture on earth and its lessons to how to be with this Country. We would also like to acknowledge The Myer Foundation for having the insight of the importance of creating agency in our communities for their places and their funding of the Place Agency collaboration. Lastly, we acknowledge and thank the industries and practitioners for their input in guiding this book and the adjacent education programme into this book and the whole programme. This includes the following organisations: Place Leaders Asia Pacific, CoDesign Studio, Village Well, Here Studio, 226 Strategic, Place Design Studio, John Mongard Landscape Architects, ASPECT Studios, City Collective, Oxigen, PIDCOCK—Architecture + Sustainability, Place SA, TPG + Place Match, MRA, Jensen + and EcoUrban.

Contents

1 **Fundamentals of Placemaking for the Built Environment: An Introduction** 1
Dominique Hes, Iderlina Mateo-Babiano and Gini Lee

2 **People in Place: Placemaking Fundamentals** 15
Iderlina Mateo-Babiano and Gini Lee

3 **Nature in Place: Placemaking in the Biosphere** 39
Judy Bush, Cristina Hernandez-Santin and Dominique Hes

4 **There's No Place Like (Without) Country** 63
Shannon Foster, Joanne Paterson Kinniburgh and Wann Country

5 **Community Engagement: What Is It?** 83
Melissa Nursey-Bray

6	**Local Governments and Developers in Placemaking: Defining Their Responsibilities and Capacities to Shape Place** *Robyn Creagh, Courtney Babb and Holly Farley*	107
7	**Design for Change: An Adaptive Approach to Urban Places in Transformation** *Elisa Palazzo*	129
8	**Economics of Place** *Neil Sipe*	157
9	**Project Implementation** *Sébastien Darchen, Laurel Johnson, Neil Sipe and John Mongard*	177
10	**Leadership in Placemaking** *Lara Mackintosh*	201
11	**The Systems of Place Agency: Adaptive Governance for Public Benefit** *Jillian Hopkins*	227
12	**DigitalXPlace** *Andrew Toland, Melissa Cate Christ and Julian Worrall*	253
13	**Place Evaluation: Measuring What Matters by Prioritising Relationships** *Dominique Hes, Cristina Hernandez-Santin, Tanja Beer and Shih-Wen Huang*	275
14	**The ART of Engagement Placemaking for Nature and People in Cities** *Melissa Nursey-Bray*	305

Notes on Contributors

Courtney Babb is a Lecturer in urban and regional planning at the School of Design and Built Environment, Curtin University. He teaches in transport planning and research methods and design for urban planning. His research activities focus on children's geographies, planning for walking and cycling and the governance of urban redevelopment.

Dr. Tanja Beer is an early career researcher with extensive experience in transdisciplinary research in the field of sustainability. Her research integrates built environments, urban ecology, performance studies (particularly through ecoscenography), positive psychology, systems thinking and Indigenous knowledge to inform our capacity as humans to thrive in today's changing climate.

Dr. Judy Bush is a Postdoctoral Research Fellow with the Clean Air and Urban Landscapes Hub at the University of Melbourne. Her research is focused on urban green space governance in a changing urban landscape. Her research investigates innovative governance arrangements that address multifunctional and participatory approaches, to link policy domains and to facilitate green space management and evidence-based policy processes.

Melissa Cate Christ is a Research Assistant Professor of Design at Hong Kong Polytechnic University, a registered landscape architect (Canada), and the founding director of transverse studio. She has also taught at the University of Hong Kong and the University of Toronto and has worked at Gustafson Guthrie Nichol Ltd. and DuToit, Allsopp, Hillier. Melissa has a Master of Landscape Architecture from the University of Toronto and a Bachelor of Liberal Arts from St. John's College.

Wann Country in Chapter 4, the authors refer to the land as a living entity that speaks to the community and their cultural practice. Wann is Country that speaks to Shannon Foster and Joanne Paterson Kinniburgh through their project.

Robyn Creagh is a Senior Lecturer in Architecture in the School of Arts and Science at the University of Notre Dame Australia, in Fremantle. Her research and creative practice explores the interaction of sense of place, embodied experience and built environment design.

Sébastien Darchen is a Senior Lecturer in Planning at the School of Earth and Environmental Management (SEES), UQ. He holds a Ph.D. in Urban Studies obtained in 2008 from INRS—Urbanisation, Culture et Société (Montreal). Dr. Darchen studies the political economy of the built environment with a focus on the strategies of urban stakeholders involved in the provision of the built environment. His main research areas are urban regeneration of city centres and creative economy policies in cities.

Holly Farley is an ethno-architecture researcher and practitioner. Her research explores socio-culture spatial use patterns and the intersection of first nations culture and the built environment. Before undertaking her Ph.D., Holly completed a Master of Architecture at Deakin University and trained and worked as an architect.

Shannon Foster is a D'harawal Saltwater Knowledge Keeper, academic and artist working on Country in War'ran (Sydney). Shannon is currently completing her doctorate at the Centre for the Advancement of Indigenous Knowledges, University of Technology Sydney, where she collaborates with Joanne Paterson Kinniburgh.

Cristina Hernandez-Santin has achieved a Master of Environment, Melbourne University, and a Bachelor of Biology, Universidad de las Americas. Combined with her qualifications within the field of ecology, she has extensive experience working across disciplines and utilising her expertise in Landscape Design and Participatory Design practice. Convinced of the critical role that nature plays in ecological and human health, she is particularly interested in the topics of Biodiversity Sensitive Urban Design and bridging the gaps between place-practice and ecology-practice.

Dominique Hes received degrees in science engineering and architecture. Her key research questions are: Why, when we have been 'doing' sustainability for so long, are we having an ever-increasing impact? Why is it so difficult to be a thriving part of the earth's systems? Her conclusion is we don't have the narrative right about who we are in the world and the contribution we can have. She believes placemaking is central to re-connecting people to place and re-reaction of this narrative.

Jillian Hopkins is a registered architect and academic. At the University of Technology Sydney, she teaches architectural design studios around urban resilience, social agency and rights to the city. Her academic research focuses on the public value of design and the governance systems that support it. In 2015, she was awarded a Byera Hadley Travelling Scholarship to investigate youth participation in construction. She currently works as a senior design advisor for the Government Architect NSW.

Shih-Wen Huang (Jenny Huang) currently a student of the University of Melbourne is interested in environmental governance, vegetation management, risk mitigation and urban planning. To further her work as an interdisciplinary student and researcher, she engaged with Place Agency through a 3-month internship which triggered further work into the relationship-based framework for project evaluation. She was supervised by Dr. Dominique Hes and Cristina Hernandez-Santin.

Laurel Johnson is a national award-winning urban, regional and community planner with over 25 years of experience in education. She is an academic at the University of Queensland. She has ample experience designing experiential learning opportunities embedding community engagement and planning into design practice, public realm activation and implementation strategies.

Gini Lee is a landscape architect, interior designer and pastoralist and is Professor of Landscape Architecture at the University of Melbourne, Australia. Her academic focus in research and teaching is on cultural and critical landscape architecture and spatial interior design theory and studio practice, to engage with the curation and postproduction of complex landscapes. She is a registered landscape architect and contributes to the strategic planning, design and practice of urban and educational landscapes in Melbourne and beyond.

Lara Mackintosh is a Senior Lecturer in Architecture in the School of Arts and Science at the University of Notre Dame Australia in Fremantle. Her research on transformative architectural education informs her teaching practice. As a practising architect, Lara focuses on learning environments and school design.

Iderlina Mateo-Babiano is a Senior Lecturer at the University of Melbourne. An architect, urban planner and transport planner by training, she teaches undergraduate and postgraduate subjects, including Placemaking Studio, *Urban Design for People and Places*, and *Place Making for The Built Environment*. Her research is concerned with improving our understanding of how people interact with place, creating unique challenges but also opportunities for positive place-based change. She has also advanced a significant body of knowledge in streets as places, active transport, gender and transport, with theory and policy implications within the Australasian setting.

John Mongard is a placemaker based in Brisbane. John Mongard Landscape Architects have undertaken major public space commissions throughout Australia, with an emphasis on cultural development at a whole-of-town level. John has facilitated community planning in over fifty Australian towns, where he has pioneered placemaking through his interactive 'set up shop' community design process that often involves hundreds of people. John has published widely, and his current areas of research are placemaking in public space and the design of self-sustainable living places.

Melissa Nursey-Bray works as an Associate Professor in the Department of Geography, Environment and Population, at the University of Adelaide. Her research focuses on how to engage communities in environmental decision making. She has worked with Indigenous peoples, local governments, state government and non-government organisations across Australia. She is particularly interested in how to enjoin people to connect to nature in cities, in placemaking and urban ecologies.

Elisa Palazzo is an urban landscape architect with broad international experience in both academia and practice. Her Ph.D. in urban design, regional and environmental planning examined the role of landscape architecture in urban design to achieve more equitable and environmentally sound cities. Elisa's research work focuses on adaptive and transdisciplinary design strategies to address environmental change specifically exploring the role of water and bio-cultural diversity in the regeneration of urban and rural socio-ecological systems.

Joanne Paterson Kinniburgh has a passion for research-based methods that counter colonised accounts of place. Jo (West African Ngāti Pākehā) is committed to educating and to practising in a way that is respectful of the Aboriginal (hi)stories, cultures, languages and knowledges of country. With over a decade of architectural practice experience in Aotearoa/New Zealand, she embraces the negotiation between cultural protocols of different world views to find productive modes of Indigenous/Non-Indigenous collaboration. She brings this passion to her role as Lecturer in the School of Architecture at the University of Technology Sydney (UTS) and to her collaborations with Shannon Foster.

Neil Sipe is a Professor of Planning in the School of Earth and Environmental Science at the University of Queensland and serves as the editor of Australian Planning. His research interests include transport and land use planning; natural resource management; and international comparisons of planning systems.

Andrew Toland is a Lecturer in landscape architecture at the University of Technology Sydney. He has also taught at the University of Hong Kong and the National University of Singapore. His research addresses the relationship between landscape and architectural design practices and infrastructural imaginaries and aesthetics, including technological infrastructures, as well as landscape regulation and technical performance metrics. His work has appeared in scholarly edited collections, as well as journals such as *Cabinet*, *Scapegoat*, and *Architecture Australia*.

Julian Worrall is a Professor of Architecture at the University of Tasmania. An architect and scholar, with a Ph.D. from the University of Tokyo, his research is broadly concerned with the construction of 'alternative modernities' in architecture and urbanism, particularly as seen through the lens of the East Asian metropolis. Widely published, including the book *21st Century Tokyo* (Kodansha International, 2010), he has contributed to numerous institutions and exhibitions of architecture culture globally, including *A Japanese Constellation* (New York, MoMA, 2016).

List of Figures

Fig. 2.1	Sandbox narratives. Left: Modelling in groups off-site. Centre: Re-imagining the lane. Right: A place for ideas by ThinkCity (Photos by Gini Lee, 2018)	31
Fig. 4.1	**Wann Country** (Image by Shannon Foster and Joanne Kinniburgh)	69
Fig. 4.2	Left: **Dahl'wah,** Yongliang Lio Chen, Luyiyang Louis Yuan and Rick Tian with Shannon Foster, Joanne Paterson Kinniburgh, Daniel Beasly and Tran Dang. Right: **Dahl'wah seed pod** (Photos by Joanne Kinniburgh, 2018)	76
Fig. 4.3	Left: **Wugan**, by Tiffany Kuo, Jesse Del Valle and Kevin Chen with Shannon Foster, Joanne Paterson Kinniburgh, Daniel Beasly and Tran Dang. Right: **Wugan Detail**, showing the work of bull ants to move pieces, and unfired tiles melting back into the earth a month after installation (Photos by Joanne Kinniburgh, 2018)	79
Fig. 6.1	Inaugural Town teams conference (*Source* Town Team Movement (2018b) Engagement summary report)	111
Fig. 6.2	The Town Square during an Inglewood on Beaufort Night Market event (Photo by Rebecca Stone)	123

List of Figures

Fig. 7.1	Cooks River to Iron Cove GreenWay masterplan and coordination strategy (*Source* GCSWG, 2009, p. 20)	135
Fig. 7.2	The GreenWay timeline and incremental process (Image by Elisa Palazzo based on McGregor/Coxall [2018], Legacy and van den Nouwelant [2015], Jennifer George [2018])	144
Fig. 7.3	The Lords Road mural and the Hawthorne Canal community mosaic projects in August 2018 (Photo by Elisa Palazzo)	147
Fig. 7.4	Long-term objectives and evolving project (*Source* GreenWay Masterplan 2018 [McGregor/Coxall, 2018])	148
Fig. 9.1	Placemaking methodology for public place projects (*Source* John Mongard Landscape Architects, Place Practice Procedures [2018])	178
Fig. 9.2	Chris Trotter's kangaroo sculpture in George Street, Brisbane (Photos by Neil Sipe, 2019)	185
Fig. 9.3	Brolga Lakes, aerial view of site adjacent to Ramsar Wetlands (*Source* EcoUrban, 2018)	192
Fig. 9.4	Brolga Lakes masterplan, commons and living areas (*Source* John Mongard Landscape Architects, February 2018)	194
Fig. 10.1	Leadership in placemaking reflective tool (Image by Lara Mackintosh, 2018)	210
Fig. 12.1	Andorra Living Lab interactive model by the MIT Media Lab (*Source* Ariel Noyman, City Science group, MIT Media Lab [Creative Commons BY-SA 4.0])	258
Fig. 12.2	Hong Kong Stair Archive Map (HKSA) online map, April 2019 (*Source* Melissa Cate Christ)	263
Fig. 12.3	An overview of the headline event of *Lean Means*, the 2016 iteration of FESTA Christchurch (Photo by Julian Worrall)	268
Fig. 13.1	Four dimensions of place framework for relationship-based evaluation (Image by Cristina Hernandez-Santin)	281
Fig. 13.2	Sample of analysis of existing tools and their ability to measure relationship. Y = yes, N = no. This was a preliminary desk-based analysis and will be tested in the field through the Rating Place Project (Box 13.1) which is currently being developed with industry	282

Fig. 13.3　TLP place evaluation framework. The image specifically shows the first four steps of the suggested process to develop your place evaluation framework (Image by Cristina Hernandez-Santin)　293

List of Tables

Table 3.1	Nature in place framework: guidelines for embedding nature in placemaking	49
Table 5.1	Summary of engagement approaches	92
Table 7.1	A theoretical framework for adaptive design of changing urban places	136
Table 7.2	Summary of placemaking strategies and urban design approaches deployed to respond to urban transformation in the GreenWay project	152
Table 8.1	Estimated costs and benefits of the Renew Newcastle project. Estimations based on data from Flanagan and Mitchell (2016, p. 42)	161
Table 8.2	Example placemaking project characteristics	164
Table 8.3	Simple cost–benefit analysis	165
Table 8.4	Cost–benefit analysis using net present value with a 10% discount rate	166
Table 8.5	Cost–benefit analysis using net present value with a 5% discount rate	166
Table 8.6	Cost–benefit analysis using internal rate of return	167
Table 9.1	Stakeholders in placemaking	181

Table 9.2	Roles of placemakers	198
Table 13.1	TLP evaluation summary on input, output, outcome and legacy	297

List of Boxes

Box 3.1	Connecting with nature in place: *facilitating* reflections on nature in place	50
Box 3.2	Designing and implementing habitat and biodiversity: *co-designing* with nature in place	52
Box 3.3	Adaptive governance for placemaking: *maintaining* nature in place	54
Box 3.4	Nature stewardship: *monitoring, evaluating and caring* for nature in place	55
Box 13.1	Rating Place Project (https://placeagency.org.au/rating-place/)	291

1

Fundamentals of Placemaking for the Built Environment: An Introduction

Dominique Hes, Iderlina Mateo-Babiano and Gini Lee

Introduction

This chapter sets the scene for this book by introducing placemaking through its (hi)story, outlining the benefits and the issues faced by a practice of engaging people in creating places. Specifically, it looks at the issues of place masking and place wash, where 'engagement' and community consultation is used to just drive development without long-lasting benefits. It also presents and discusses the aspect of place-making that can result in gentrification. Lastly, it concludes by listing the social, ecological and economic benefits of engaging in placemaking practices.

D. Hes (✉) · I. Mateo-Babiano · G. Lee
Faculty of Architecture, Building and Planning,
University of Melbourne, Parkville, VIC, Australia
e-mail: dhes@unimelb.edu.au

I. Mateo-Babiano
e-mail: imateo@unimelb.edu.au

© The Author(s) 2020
D. Hes and C. Hernandez-Santin (eds.), *Placemaking Fundamentals for the Built Environment*, https://doi.org/10.1007/978-981-32-9624-4_1

The Story Behind Making Places

This section will explore the most common definitions and frameworks used to conceptualise placemaking, including its limitations and propose the four dimensions of place framework as opportunities to identify the relationships necessary to achieve long-term impact.

What Is Placemaking?

Spaces shape us, yet we also contribute to the shaping of these spaces through placemaking. Placemaking is fundamentally a continuous process. It is a way of shaping spaces to create meaningful experiences (in, of and for) people (Wyckoff, 2014). Indeed, Lefebvre in his seminal work *The Production of Space* posits that space is produced and reproduced through people's intentions in how they plan to live (Lefebvre & Nicholson-Smith, 1991). Therefore, at the individual level, placemaking is a mundane way of asserting our claim on everyday life (Lefebvre, 1996). This is evident in how activities manifest in our daily spatial practices, and reflecting who we are as individuals, such as the way we arrange our furniture (Marcus & Francis, 1998). Yet Harvey (2003) argues that the claim to a (city) space should go beyond the individual, and in fact is a collective exercise to reshape space. So, beyond the four walls of our home, we claim the right to space through the social interactions that we make in public spaces; it is also played out in political struggles for space, revealing who is 'in-place' and who is 'out-of-place' (Cresswell, 1992); or even the way street traders ply their wares on the footpath to appropriate space. Yet no matter how many times we assert our claim to space, each time that we do, we embed our own unique pattern in creating a rhythm of life, which Lefebvre (2004) refers to as rhythmanalysis. These rhythms ultimately contribute to the way we humanise space, which is core to placemaking (Friedmann, 2007).

The Placemaking (Hi)story

Placemaking or the shaping of places is guided by people's needs and aspirations, and so, is vital to our existence and our culture. Although the shaping of places is as old as time, it was only in the 1970s that the term placemaking came into vogue and was used mainly by practitioners and those who theorised about place. Placemaking is said to have evolved from the Urban Design discipline (Carmona, 2019), yet placemaking as a movement was mainly a response to the monotony of modernist design and architecture for public space. Modernism was perceived to be more concerned with the form of these spaces rather than how these spaces were being used. Many perceived that most design approaches have resulted in buildings and places that were isolating rather than connecting.

The Project for Public Spaces (PPS) is known to have played an important role in advancing the placemaking movement in the United States, and more recently, globally. Spearheaded by Fred Kent, along with Kathy Madden and Steve Davies, PPS started as a three-year demonstration project in 1975. The trio transformed public spaces into places for people, to show the vital role of spaces in creating thriving public life in cities such as New York. But more importantly, their collaborative projects advocating awareness-raising engagement and capacity-building activities over the past forty years were instrumental to expose placemaking dialogue to the global stage, making place and placemaking a key component in the New Urban Agenda. Adopted in 2016 during the Habitat III in Quito, Ecuador, the New Urban Agenda represents a shared vision among cities and nations to create a better and more sustainable future for people.

Placemaking as a movement in the United States has been inspired by concepts introduced by Jane Jacobs (1992) such as her 'eyes on the street', William Whyte's (1980) the need to shape 'social life in our public spaces' and then later with Jan Gehl's claim that cities should first have '…life, then spaces, then buildings, as the other way would not work' (see Gehl 2004a, 2004b, 2010). These urban thinkers played an instrumental role in stirring alternative ideas for urban designers, planners, landscape architects and architectures to design public spaces that primarily cater for the needs of people, arguably over the needs of non-human participants.

Placemaking as a discipline is often referred to as a concept that grew from some Western societies, yet the shaping and making of places are also very much present in the design and planning of places in Eastern societies such as Edo period Tokyo. For instance, the concept of *Artful naturalness* was used in the design of gardens during the Edo period. This garden design approach imitated the natural environment by borrowing scenery or *shakkei* (Pregill & Volkman, 1999). Employing vistas such as distant rolling mountains adds to the impression of a natural landscape (Wada, Sadao, & Miho, 2003) as clearly displayed in the design of the sixteenth-century *Katsura* Imperial Villa in Kyoto (Pregill & Volkman, 1999). Also, the concept of view planning or the way streets are designed and oriented to align in the direction of natural elements and landmarks reflect the importance of natural elements in (Edo period) Tokyo's public life. This was a common planning practice during the Edo period where streets in the *Shitamachi* area or the commoner's district were oriented towards the famous Mount Fuji, the Sumida River, Mount Tsukuba, among others. Indeed, natural views virtually became synonymous with the Edo townscape (Jinnai, 2004). Edo period Japan believed in the sacredness of nature, articulating the key role of the natural environment in creating and recreating the sociology of street life. Nature had been part and parcel of the Japanese psyche, an element which is often limited if not outright lacking, in the current narrative about place and placemaking.

Australia's placemaking story began in the early 1990s when design professionals and community groups started to engage in the activation of under-utilised public spaces to create better places. At the helm of the placemaking movement was Village Well, a creative placemaking firm launched in 1992 by its founder Gilbert Rochecouste. Village Well contributed significantly to the activation of Melbourne's now-iconic laneways (Village Well, n.d.) through blueprints that helped revive inner-city activities laneways. At that time, organising a festival was an important placemaking initiative which brought like-minded individuals together and empowered them to advocate for change in Melbourne's laneways, mobilising a series of actions and bringing placemaking to a strategic level of engagement. The 'people' element is core in the placemaking process. At around the same time, Penny Coombes collaborated with PPS to setup People for Places and Spaces, a firm which transforms places to enhance city liveability (PPS, 2016). It also began placemaking masterclasses delivered by PPS in collaboration with several placemaking professionals, including David Engwicht and his Creative Communities and Kylie Legge of Place Partners. Like Village Well, Place Partners also recognised that community participation is crucial to shaping great places. Beyond 'people', Place Partners espoused two other key goals; place character and economic revitalisation (Legge, 2015). More recently, Placemaker Lucinda Hartley's Neighbourhood project is aimed at creating impact on three areas of innovation of 'Place, People and Process' placed emphasis on the social architecture of place (The Neighbourhood Project, n.d.). Village Well's 5P lens which focuses on Physical, Product, Programme, People and Planet serve as the key guiding principles to the placemaking process that Village Well advocates. Mr. Rochecouste believes there is value in understanding the "DNA" of a place as a process of '(re) connecting people with place'. The frameworks which guide placemaking in Australia have a strong focus on people, 'people in place' are enshrined in how practitioners have defined and practised placemaking, which is further expounded in Chapter 2.

Placemaking—Place Wash, Gentrification and the Importance of a Term

> Placemaking 'is political and challenging, it can be used as a quick fix and it can be fake if there is no empowerment. Placemaking should be strategic and multi-disciplinary. It should involve skills such as brokering and negotiating. It should be dynamic and synergistic when subversive actions change the processes'. (Carolyn Whitzman, personal communication, February 17, 2019)

It is well known that placemaking is seen as a particular school of thinking, and that this has led to some unintended consequences. It is not the intention that this book is an argument for the term; it is instead a vehicle to communicate the importance of creating agency and citizenship in our communities. Placemaking is a term used by many to describe this process, but there are other terms, and in fact, as our acknowledgement of First Nations peoples and practices that started this book demonstrates, it is an idea practised over thousands of years using many different words and languages. The key remains engendering responsibly, care and connection for place. For more on the First Nations perspective on this, see the wonderful narrative and experience of Chapter 4.

Where possible this book has identified other schools of thought and approaches to achieving this same aim. It has also focused on the issues of place wash/place masking identified limitations and dangers of placemaking (see Chapters 2, 3, 4, 12 and 13). A summary of the key issues found in practice and in the literature is provided below, with links to further reading.

While Placemaking is oftentimes seen as a positive process, it also is critiqued as a practice of place destruction, or what Jamie Kalven calls as place(un)making. For him, the practice of substituting an existing place with one that is perceived to be a better version of it is, in fact, a process that may assault the identities of residents of the place and subsequently exclude them (Kalven, n.d.); transformation contradicts the very essence of placemaking. This contradiction is also evident in how 'placemaking' by dominant cultures in Australian cities persistently marginalises Aboriginal people (McGaw, Pieris, & Potter, 2011), while study of Polish migrants in Brooklyn (United States) illustrates the impact of gentrified areas in the everyday placemaking abilities and experience of migrants. Their continued loss of agency and freedom was a result of the production of new public spaces that threatened their everyday ability to confirm their lived places (Stabrowski, 2014).

Gentrification as a negative outcome is most commonly talked about in placemaking workshops where the questions of 'how to we ensure this work we are doing doesn't force property prices up so that we can't live here anymore?' might be raised. Yet gentrification is not an outcome of connecting people to place and designing for the thriving of those people and their environment. Juliet Khane from Projects for Public Spaces writes:

> [gentrification] is the result of the complex and often hidden movement of capital, as well as the uneven production and consumption of urban space. Public space development and improvement does not directly cause gentrification, and should not suffer the blame for forces that are much greater than a few small-scale updates that can add considerably to the overall health and vitality of a neighborhood. (Kahne, 2015, paragraph 6)

In fact, gentrification is the opposite of the intention of placemaking, which values and celebrates community diversity and sees diversity as critical to the ability for a place to have the niches, the quirkiness, the uniqueness that gives it a 'sense of place'. PPS go on to write in the same article on gentrification that if places are developed as just a physical outcome, without community agency, what results is '"placelessness".... This is not Placemaking… These physical attributes are important, but they are the means, not the end. If you're not building social capital in the community where you're working, you're not Placemaking; you're just reorganizing the furniture' (Kahne, 2015, paragraph 11).

Researcher and commentator Kate Shaw (2008), in her work on placemaking and social equity, talks about the importance of creating places for all communities, all socio-economic groups, all ethnicities. Together Fincher, Pardy and Shaw introduce the concept of place masking in their 2016 paper on three case studies in Australia looking specifically at the outcomes of placemaking initiatives and social justice. They looked at issues of displacement, where placemaking is designed for future residents, rather than current low-income residents. Fincher, Pardy, and Shaw (2016) argue that place masking occurs particularly when cities prioritise economic development while socio-spatial equity becomes secondary (or even irrelevant) in the process, resulting in gentrified neighbourhoods. The reality is that gentrifying processes design certain groups of people out, despite those displaced being often the original residents (Shaw, 2008). Often these privatised public spaces transform into larger social problems reinforcing inequality while also advancing critical placemaking as a tool to support the development of more inclusive, participatory and democratic communities (Toolis, 2017). One of the key conclusions from Fincher et al. (2016) is:

> What is evident from these interviews is that social equity is not identified as a priority, and nor are professionals with expertise in social questions closely involved in the design-oriented place-making process. Rather, planning and design-driven place-making appears to actively close down opportunities for decreasing disadvantage by masking the place of the lowest-income existing residents in only too familiar patterns of gentrification. (Fincher et al., 2016, p. 529)

So, what does this mean for future placemaker? Firstly, it is critical to integrate ideas of social justice and create opportunities not just for engagement of all the stakeholders but the authors (Fincher et al., 2016) suggest it is critical to ensure there is representation of experts on social justice in the decision-making process. Secondly, they also conclude that the most successful placemaking projects are small and micro-local, and that it is more difficult to achieve the aims of placemaking when doing it at a large scale, especially for highly commercial projects. Here the placemaker needs to work harder to ensure the outcomes are authentic and meet social and ecological potentials.

Many of these negative outcomes were not intended or anticipated. Some of the societal impacts include promoting seclusion, displacement, gentrification and social inequality through marginalisation. Yet in all cases, it is not the placemaking that is advocated for in this book, that of engaging all stakeholders with the development of their place. Many occur because of the complex system that is a place and working on the improvement of the amenity of the place (see, for example, Blokland, 2009; Peck, 2005, 2010; Sarimin & Yigitcanlar, 2012; Solnit, 2014; Stehlin, 2016). There are also often many negative impacts that are ecological; we argue in this book that this is because the natural and non-human environments have not been seen as an integral part of the placemaking process. Further, if they are considered it is often in how they benefit people and not as one of the key outputs of placemaking for their own thriving (see Chapter 3).

It is our intention that this book will help with minimising the negative outcomes of placemaking. We argue that a good way to avoid some of the pitfalls that can be associated with placemaking is to evaluate place outcomes and impacts based on relationships (see Chapter 13). This requires leadership (Chapter 10), effort, time, money and the skills in the placemaker to engage, listen, connect and often re-establish trust with stakeholders. This is helped by an adaptive decision-making process (see Chapter 11) to help create a more resilient and adaptive approach to placemaking and management. Chapter 12 outlines the opportunities of digital placemaking to support more widespread engagement and innovation, which can reduce the outcomes of placemaking being skewed to particular community groups.

Placemaking Benefits

Concluding this chapter, we will briefly outline the benefits of creating places; this is extended on in throughout the book. A recent study by Carmona (2019) reviewed 271 studies of place and its benefits; this study has the most comprehensive list of benefits some of which are listed below and liked to chapters in this book which elaborate on them.

Benefits of placemaking have been shown to be varied, interrelated and connected and often not just in one category, but for the purpose of this introduction they have been divided into social, ecological and economic:

Social Benefits include improved civic pride, inclusiveness, social integration, vitality and sociability, fewer accidents, improved educational outcomes (Carmona, 2019), reduced crime and vandalism in association with green spaces (Carmona, 2019; Kuo & Sullivan, 2001), improved social connectedness and sense of belonging, resulting in improved health (Hystad & Carpiano, 2012), reduced depressions (Carmona, 2019; Semenza, March, & Bontempo, 2007) and general well-being through benefits to physical, psychological, social, health, spiritual and aesthetic benefits (Carmona, 2019; Frumkin,

2003), recreational benefits, improved urban resilience (see Chapter 6) and improved sense of place (Frumkin 2003). For more details, see Chapters 2, 6, 7, 8, 11 and 14.

Ecological Benefits include improved ecological outcomes—biodiversity, health, resilience, ability to adapt, reduced impact on waterways, cleaner air, reduced ecological vandalism, increased participation in community in supporting ecosystem functions and reduced energy use, adaptable use of building, local exchange network, reduced heat stress, reduced waste, reduced pollution, working with nature, increased diversity (Carmona, 2019); interestingly, most of the benefits in this section of the Carmona research is based on the benefits to people of nature not really the ecological benefits themselves. For more information, please refer to Chapters 3 and 6 or see Carmona (2019).

Economic Benefits include increased footfall visitation and length of visit (time spent on site), reduced public expenditure (Carmona, 2019), improved economic outcomes such as increased revenue, job creation or skill development, high cost-benefit ratio (Chapter 8 and Carmona, 2019) reduced public expenditure (Carmona, 2019) and increased property value (Robinson et al., 2017). For more details on economic benefits and how to build a cost-benefit analysis, please refer to Chapter 8.

Conclusion

The story of placemaking is a complex one. The myriad use of the term, which is often implied to be a positive process, can also be negative, placing emphasis on the sometimes confusing and contradictory nature of space production and construction. Yet Harvey (2003) contends that placemaking is a social process of trying to find momentum, meaning and political-economic implications. So much information is available to explain what placemaking is, resulting in perplexing and cumbersome conversations for placemakers to undertake. Critical to considerations for restructuring and shaping places is the need to gain an understanding of projects where placemakers have successfully shaped places that communities value to guide finding ways to inform placemaking decisions.

Key Lessons from This Chapter Are

- There is a long history of placemaking, from First Nations People, to the rich history of Europe and Asia.
- Placemaking can have unintended outcomes and these need to be thoughts about as a project seeks to move forward.
- There are many benefits of creating great social, green and vibrant spaces that are shared by the community and invested in by all stakeholders.
- Key to it all is that placemaking is not done to a place or community, it is co-created, co-managed and shared.
- A place is something that evolves and changes over time, and the key is to give stakeholders the agency and support to be involved.

References

Blokland, T. (2009). Celebrating local histories and defining neighbourhood communities: Place-making in a gentrified neighbourhood. *Urban Studies, 46*(8), 1593–1610.

Carmona, M. (2019). Place value: Place quality and its impact on health, social, economic and environmental outcomes. *Journal of Urban Design, 24*(1), 1–48.

Cresswell, T. (1992). *In place-out of place: Geography, ideology, and transgression* (Vol. 2). Minneapolis: University of Minnesota Press.

Fincher, R., Pardy, M., & Shaw, K. (2016). Place-making or place-masking? The everyday political economy of "making place". *Planning Theory & Practice, 17*(4), 516–536.

Friedmann, J. (2007). Reflections on place and place-making in the cities of China. *International Journal of Urban and Regional Research, 31*(2), 257–279.

Frumkin, H. (2003). Healthy places: Exploring the evidence. *American Journal of Public Health, 93*(9), 1451–1456.

Gehl, J. (2004a). *Lively, attractive and safe cities, but how? Cities for people as design challenge.* Centre for Public Space Research, School of Architecture, The Royal Danish Academy of Fine Arts. Paper presented at the Stockholm Conference "New Urbanism and Beyond", 4–8 October 2004, 42.

Gehl, J. (2004b). *Towards a fine city for people: 'Public space public life' study in London 2004*. London: Transport for London and Central Partnership.

Gehl, J. (2010). *Cities for people*. Washington, DC: Island Press.

Harvey, D. (2003). The right to the city. *International Journal of Urban and Regional Research, 27*(4), 939–941.

Hystad, P., & Carpiano, R. M. (2012). Sense of community-belonging and health-behaviour change in Canada. *Journal of Epidemiology and Community Health, 66*(3), 277–283.

Jacobs, J. (1992). *The death and life of great American Cities*. New York: Random House. Retrieved from https://www.buurtwijs.nl/sites/default/files/buurtwijs/bestanden/jane_jacobs_the_death_and_life_of_great_american.pdf. Accessed 26 Mar 2019.

Jinnai, H. (2004). Edo the original Eco-city. *Japan Echo, 31*(1), 56–60.

Kahne, J. (2015). *Does placemaking cause gentrification? It's complicated*. Project for Public Spaces. Retrieved from https://www.pps.org/article/gentrification. Accessed 12 Apr 2019. Paragraph 11.

Kuo, F. E., & Sullivan, W. C. (2001). Environment and crime in the inner city: Does vegetation reduce crime? *Environment & Behavior, 33*(3), 343–367.

Lefebvre, H. (1996). The right to the city. In E. Kofman & E. Lebas (Eds.), *Writings on cities*. Cambridge, MA: Wiley-Blackwell.

Lefebvre, H. (2004). *Rhythmanalysis: Space, time and everyday life*. London: A&C Black.

Lefebvre, H., & Nicholson-Smith, D. (1991). *The production of space* (Vol. 142). Oxford: Blackwell.

Legge, K. (2015). Guest editorial: The evolution of placemaking—What's next? *The New Planner, The Journal of the New South Wales Planning Profession* (104), 4–5. Retrieved from https://www.planning.org.au/documents/item/6981. Accessed 26 Mar 2019.

Marcus, C. C., & Francis, C. A. (1998). *People places: Design guidelines for urban open space* (2nd ed.). New York: Van Nostrand Reinhold.

McGaw, J., Pieris, A., & Potter, E. (2011). Indigenous place-making in the city: Dispossessions, occupations and implications for cultural architecture. *Architectural Theory Review, 16*(3), 296–311.

Peck, J. (2005). Struggling with the creative class. *International Journal of Urban and Regional Research, 29*, 740–770.

Peck, J. (2010). *Constructions of neoliberal reason*. Oxford: Oxford University Press.

PPS. (2016). *Research: The case for healthy places*. Retrieved from https://www.pps.org/article/pps-releases-new-report-the-case-for-healthy-places-how-to-improve-health-through-placemaking. Accessed 12 Apr 2019.

Pregill, P., & Volkman, N. (1999). *Landscapes in history: Design and planning in the Eastern and Western traditions*. New York: Wiley.

Robinson, S., Barkham, R., Carver, S., Gray, H., Siebrits, J., Holberton, R., … Marini, R. (2017). *Placemaking: Value and the public realm*. CBRE Consulting.

Sarimin, M., & Yigitcanlar, T. (2012). Towards a comprehensive and integrated knowledge-based urban development model. *International Journal of Knowledge-Based Development (IJKBD), 3*, 175–192.

Semenza, J. C., March, T. L., & Bontempo, B. D. (2007). Community-initiated urban development: An ecological intervention. *Journal of Urban Health, 84*(1), 8–20.

Shaw, K. (2008). Gentrification: What it is, why it is, and what can be done about it. *Geography Compass, 2*(5), 1697–1728.

Solnit, R. (2014). *Resisting monoculture*. Retrieved from www.guernicamag.com/daily/rebecca-solnitresisting-monoculture. Accessed 9 Sept 2016.

Stabrowski, F. (2014). New-build gentrification and the everyday displacement of Polish immigrant tenants in Greenpoint, Brooklyn. *Antipode, 46*(3), 794–815.

Stehlin, J. (2016). The post-industrial shop floor. *Antipode, 48*, 474–493.

The Neighbourhood Project. (n.d.). *About the neighbourhood project*. Retrieved from https://theneighbourhoodproject.org/about-tnp/. Accessed 20 Apr 2019.

Toolis, E. E. (2017). Theorizing critical placemaking as a tool for reclaiming public space. *American Journal of Community Psychology, 59*(1–2), 184–199.

Village Well. (n.d.). *Our story*. Retrieved from http://www.villagewell.org/. Accessed 20 Apr 2019.

Wada, S., Sadao, T. S., & Miho, T. (2003). *Discovering the arts of Japan: A historical overview*. Tokyo: Kodansha International.

Whitzman, C. (2019, February). Personal interview.

Whyte, W. H. (1980). *The social life of small urban spaces*. Washington, DC: Conservation Foundation.

Wyckoff, M. A. (2014). Definition of placemaking: Four different types. *Planning & Zoning News, 32*(3), 1.

2

People in Place: Placemaking Fundamentals

Iderlina Mateo-Babiano and Gini Lee

> *The most memorable cities I have visited are those which allow me to connect to place.*
> Iderlina Mateo-Babiano

Introduction

Placemaking is the continuous process of shaping, experiencing and contributing to 'place'. 'Place' itself is a multidimensional construct, referring to a locality but also the relationships that occur within the locality, including the socio-economic reality, ecological conditions and political standpoint. Placemaking places people at its core, either by employing a participatory process to public space design, gaining an understanding of residents' perceptions and aspirations or responding

---

I. Mateo-Babiano (✉) · G. Lee
Faculty of Architecture, Building and Planning, University of Melbourne, Parkville, VIC, Australia
e-mail: imateo@unimelb.edu.au

through projects/programmes, which generate positive relationships in/to/with place. Placemaking is a process that creates the capacity for people to invest space with meaning.

This chapter introduces the fundamentals of place and placemaking. It begins by exploring the most common definitions of place. It then presents Place Agency's 5P framework of placemaking, which deliberates a more systematic way of shaping places. By recognising that placemaking is purpose-driven, it engages in a focused discussion on why the shaping of places matters, and introduces several placemaking strategies, supported by examples in Australia and internationally. The chapter culminates with the Placemaking Sandbox workshop delivered during the World Urban Forum in 2018, which presented a placemaking as a capacity-building strategy to harness the power of community in shaping and transforming places in Kuala Lumpur (Malaysia).

What Is Place? How Are Places Made?

For each of us, the idea of what place is depends upon our cultural, spatial and emotional intelligence and literacy, demonstrated by our geographical footprints and reinforced by familiarity with a particular locale. In an increasingly globalised and multicultural world, historical understandings of generic place, increasingly challenged through cultural lenses that may be shared or distinctive, may provoke either comfort or distress in public places. Recognising the cues to understanding an idea of place and how it manifests in the physical and everyday spaces that multiple publics traverse and occupy is essential to the practices that the placemaker/designer must employ in scripting and creating places of well-being in the urban realm. Place comes from the root Latin word *Loc*, which means place or location, which does not also include an assumption that location is also enacted in time and space. Place is a multidimensional concept, referring to a geographical area or locality but also the habitual relationships that occur within the setting, including socio-economic reality, ecological condition, political standpoint and, most critically, cross-cultural spatial awareness and attachment.

Concepts of the Meaning of Place: A Brief Review

Of the multiple theories and spatial practices that revolve around gaining an understanding of place, there is only space in this chapter for a few fundamental references that can provide underpinning concepts upon which to operate in creating/making successful places for people.

Edward Relph's classic writing over some forty years on the nature of place and placelessness (1976) is a useful introduction into the symbiotic relationship between place, involving spatial and personal relationships which are located identifiably somewhere, and the sense of placelessness which is increasingly recognised as being situated anywhere. The concept of being in place anywhere is expressed in Marc Auge's examination of the non-places appearing in an increasingly globalised environment such as airports and supermarkets (Augé, 2009). Relph confirms that these concepts are relational rather than oppositional, as all places have some degree of distinctiveness and standardisation represented not only by their physical characteristics but also in the ways they are materialised and performed. Yet place philosopher Jeff Malpas opines on place and singularity stating that 'every place is singular, having a character that is proper to it alone' (Malpas, 2015, p. 65).

Notions on place identity such as genius loci, the 'spirit of place' and 'sense of place' are examined by many theorists including the urban phenomenologists Christian Norberg-Schulz (1980) and Yi-Fu Tuan (2001). Their writings elaborate upon ideas of place that are embedded in the environmental and social structures of human relationships and more intangible and temporal conditions. For Norberg-Schulz, the 'environmental character... the essence of a place resides in its "atmosphere"'.

> A place is therefore a qualitative, total phenomenon, which we cannot reduce to any of its properties, such as spatial relationships, without losing its concrete nature out of sight. (Norberg-Schulz, 1980, p. 8)

Appreciation of individual connection to identity through sight, hearing, smell, movement, touch, imagination, purpose and anticipation is a characteristic definition towards apprehending sense of place.

Such awareness is gained through observation and experience of spaces, regions and the activities that occur in them over time. Edward Casey's writings on place introduce the concept of the place-world and the multiplicity of experiences that contribute to the recognition of the power of place as an idea and as activation. To help to reduce the tendency to a developing uniformity of place across territories, he advocates for a return to common experiences to uncover the local or regional (Casey, 1997, p. xiii). Such perspectives are also espoused by Lucy Lippard in the *Lure of the Local: Senses of Place in a Multicentered Society*, where she relates returning to familiar places to promote an insider perspective of place beyond landscape. 'Space defines landscape where space combined with memory defines place' (Lippard, 1997). Through examining art practices made for place, she discusses the qualities and values of site specificity in design and intervention in a localised site and how these works contribute to communicating place sensibility to both locals and outsiders.

> Place-specific art would be an art that reveals new depths of a place to engage the viewer or inhabitant, rather than abstracting that place into generalisations that apply just as well to any other place. (Lippard, Part V: Chapter 1)

Returning to Relph, who offers a number of qualities for place that may be regarded as self-evident, confirms an ongoing concern in most place writers to connect place to the community, to values and to mediating complexity inherent in human to human and human to environment relationships. Importantly, place enables identity and attachment to be practised through designed interaction with space, materiality and narrative.

> Place is differentiated by values, qualities, stories, shared memories;
> Place is named;
> Place fuses culture and environment, activity and sharing;
> Place corresponds with community and locality across scale;
> (and conversely)
> Placelessness corresponds with inequality (Relph, 2008, pp. 311–323)

In order to comprehend and promote sustainable action towards negotiating present and future challenges, Relph commends developing perspectives and approaches to a pragmatic sense of place. He defines this concept as

> a locally based, yet outward-looking attitude that combines an appreciation of the complex unity of a particular place with an understanding of the diffuse global character of the social and environmental processes that affect it. (Relph, 2017, paragraph 2)

Built into this perspective is the acceptance that ongoing negotiation between the specific local and the global dynamics that affect place stability and economy is necessary. Pragmatic approaches

> … blend an appreciation of place identity with other place knowledge together with an understanding of connectivity from the local to the global, and seek appropriate local courses of action reflective of an openness to external considerations, to deal with emerging social and environmental challenges and injustices, both local and global' paraphrasing. (Relph, 2008, p. 321 revised in 2019)

The extent to which mobility as a way of life is increasingly facilitated by global economies and population dynamics, including the influences of climate change, migration and multicultural adoption of unfamiliar places, also affects peoples' attitudes to place and identity. The tendency to embrace small spaces as the real site of place identity and relationships is both accepted and challenged by John Friedmann's review of concepts of place in relation to placemaking in China. He reminds us that places can be sites of inclusion as much as they are sites of resistance and that they are shaped by planning, rules and regulations, as much as by community occupation, memory and local experience and activity. Places are also evidence of change over time, with the juxtaposition of historic places of great permanency and memory, as much as they may house moments of temporary and perhaps illegal occupation (Friedmann, 2007).

Place and Sustainable Development Goals

Relph opens up the concept of pragmatic attitudes to place as the necessity for the local to embrace the global, and vice versa, in order to face current and future challenges to place identity and occupation. Goal 11 of the Sustainable Development Goals confirmed by the United Nations 2030 Agenda for Sustainable Development supports the concept of Sustainable Cities and Communities to 'address the global challenges we face, including those related to poverty, inequality, climate, environmental degradation, prosperity, and peace and justice. Making safe, accessible and enjoyable places for people is critical to sustainable city living and working' (UN, 2017, paragraph 1).

To support the strengthening and endurance of place-based strategies in an increasingly urbanised world, where space is ever more at a premium, Goal 11's principles promote inclusivity, sustainability, participation and investment in urban planning and management. It specifically supports accessibility for the vulnerable and minorities, for people of all ages through sustainable programmes for more liveable urban environments, based on balancing ecological, cultural and economic programmes that will deliver real on-the-ground benefits to communities.

The New Urban Agenda (NUA), adopted after the United Nations sponsored Habitat 3 meeting in Quito in 2006, seeks to provide a road map towards the provision of basic services for everyone (UN Habitat, 2018). The NUA prompts us to ask, how can place-based thinking, alongside ecosystems knowledge, support open space and public place agendas for the city? In part, the answer is to improve urban planning and design, finance and support, yet it also proposes greater regulation and rules-based approaches. It is up to planners and designers to embrace the principles and values of place thinking to devise programmes cognisant of community and the dynamics of physical, environmental, social, political and economic change. The types of actions necessary to support place-based thinking and beneficial outcomes must embrace new opportunities to reduce inequality and discrimination and be respectful of peoples' rights to open space, programmes for cleaner and more resilient cities in the face of more intensive climatic and population forces, energy efficient with reduction in pollutants and waste and supportive of green-ing initiatives alongside effective water supply and conservation programmes.

What Makes a Great Place?

Considerations into the qualities, values and benefits of places that might be regarded as great are a widely researched, debated and practised topic. Many researchers have offered diagrams that seek to visualise the various components of a system for promoting place as a destination, a panacea for disconnection from the lifeworld and an opportunity for well-being and creativity to be experienced. These diagrams engage with the tangible; space, scale, object, audience, material and haptic environments and the intangible; activities, atmospheres, relationships and temporal projections. What is consistent across most of these models is the need to summarise all the variety of data, observations, aesthetics and experiences into key themes. For instance, Project for Public Spaces proposes four key elements for a great place: (1) sociability, (2) uses and activities, (3) comfort and image and (4) access and linkages. What placemaking frameworks have in common is that they privilege people and their human experience as the central driver for ideal place concepts. Arefi (2014) uses Lefebvre's conceptual triad to highlight the key determinants of building emotional connection to place, which include how the place is conceived (created and recreated to fit community values), lived (the activities occurring) and perceived (understanding and knowledge of the place).

In the introduction chapter, the (hi)story of placemaking described ways in which places in the past were purposefully shaped, including discussion on the key aims of placemaking, which highlights the focus on relationship building between the community and place, yet largely ignores other elements such as nature.

The 5P: A Place Agency Placemaking Framework

Place Agency's 5P framework—People, Process, Product, Programme and Place evaluation—refers to the five elements—or building blocks—of placemaking. These elements can easily be understood but also universally applicable in most place-shaping activities and situations. Each element encompasses sub-elements, which are a collective suite of possible options that are made available to interested placemakers aiming for gaining better understanding of how different elements interact and combine to generate different placemaking strategies. The 5P framework's elements and sub-elements have been inspired by the ideas, concepts and experiences drawn from best-practice cases and frameworks shared by key placemaking professionals in the field, including Village Well, Co-Design Studio, Project for Public Spaces and Place Partners amongst others. By also critically reviewing scholarly work, theoretical underpinnings associated with placemaking and the different conceptual models of placemaking evident in the 5Ps.

What is distinct in the 5P framework is a systematic way of making sense of the different placemaking approaches, tactics, techniques and tools that are already available and in use by communities and practitioners. The 5P proposes how five components, when creatively combined, can shape different placemaking strategies, in interactions and combinations, to better assist understanding of how these strategies are shaped by specific forces which drive decisions for placemaking. More importantly, the framework enables purposeful facilitation of 'bespoke placemaking strategies' (Village Well, 2019, paragraph 1), to effect easy adoption of techniques leading to positive community outcomes.

People

Placemaking has evolved as a community-led approach in shaping places, with 'people' as fundamental agents of place-led change. The 'people' component is three-pronged:

First, 'People' refers to place leadership. The shaping of place can be championed by a single actor, a community group or any type of associated entity. In placemaking, 'people' band together with the single purpose of influencing place-based change to the places they love. This may refer to a teacher using the 'Take your Place tool'[1] to build awareness in the classroom, particularly on the role of placemaking to enable place sustainability and livability; to the New York resident duo David and Hammond[2] (2011) championing the transformation of a derelict elevated railway in New York; or even a loose group of community members advocating the temporal re-purposing of under-utilised neighbourhood streets into 'play streets'.[3]

Second, 'People' is about the people's level of engagement and participation in place and placemaking. The 'People' element refines placemaking 'for' the community by importantly articulating the nature of involvement, the level of engagement and the types of relationships created in placemaking 'with and by' the diverse communities which placemakers serve. This affirms how people as agents of place and place change can leverage the ambiguities and opportunities of governance to effect socio-spatial transformation, which is further discussed in Chapter 11.

Third, 'People' is about understanding what the community needs which may manifest as a single issue or as a group of thematically based issues. Different actors and agencies bring with them their own values, needs, hopes, aspirations, experiences and relationships, which are formed by their cultural backgrounds and ethnicities, often influencing their own perspectives of place. Hence, placemaking is a pluralistic exercise, which aims to understand how 'multiple publics' relate to and claim public space (Iveson, 2007).

Placemakers uphold the 'People' element with the following principles: (1) create a setting in which wider community involvement is

---

[1] Place SA's developed a tool for teachers teaching place and liveability that gets your students involved in a fun and exciting experience while in the classroom. Refer to http://www.placesa.com.au/about/.

[2] Robert Hammond and Joshua David led the transformation of the High Line with community members. Read more about this in their book titled *The Inside Story of New York City's Park in the Sky*.

[3] Refer to Play streets Guide. https://www.playstreetsaustralia.com/.

encouraged to explore place-based change; (2) facilitate a platform to empower community members to voice and discuss their perspectives of place in a dynamic, democratic and collaborative process; (3) support pathways to create and strengthen relationships with self and others; and (4) help strengthen their connection with the places they (the community) share (see, e.g., PPS, 2008), including both relationships with the built and the natural environment.

Process

Placemaking is fundamentally a continuous social process of influencing place-based change. If Harvey argues that place construction is about 'receiving, making and remaking' (Harvey, 2003, pp. 29–34) of place, then placemaking emerged as primarily a bottom-up, assets-based, purpose-driven process which has increasingly informed top-down principles and policies.

Bottom-up, it employs ways of mobilising people from the grassroots to lead change. It is a process which encourages involvement, engagement and co-design with and by the community. In Chapter 5, Community Engagement, Nursey-Bray describes different modes to engage with and by community.

Assets-based, it capitalises upon and taps into local community assets, wisdom, inspiration and potential to shape the physical and relational characteristics of neighbourhoods, towns, cities or regions (Kretzmann & McKnight, 1996), drawing from local residents, associations and community groups, including its material resources and respecting the unique qualities of each location and cultural mores (Potter, 2012). A methodology to incorporate Indigenous perspectives of place is found in Chapter 4, where Foster and Kinniburgh offer new ways of spatially encountering first people's knowledge of site within a colonial context.

Purpose-driven, placemaking is undertaken for a specific purpose. The next section in this chapter, 'Places in the Making: strategies and case studies', details the different purposes communities have in transforming places or undertaking specific placemaking.

As a unique or a series of cooperative activities delivered within a given timeframe and finite resource, placemaking is a dynamic, democratic and iterative future-focused process.

Dynamic, activities do not finish when the place is built but continue to prepare the 'people' to proactively respond to place-based **change**.

Democratic, providing agency to people to shape the places they love. The shaping of places can take on different approaches to suit different situations and conditions. For instance, activities may be small-scale, short-term experiments or large-scale strategic processes involving formal to informal practices and interactions.

Iterative, the process is often not linear and straightforward. It can be incremental, sequential, cyclical, parallel or holistic. For instance, the process can start by identifying the key issues of place drawn through multiple ways of listening to different voices beyond those traditional methodologies of observation—street life studies, household surveys in communities or towards posing a great question about place and to gaining local ideas to aid the design thinking processes.

Futures-focused, approaches that best respond to present and future challenges. While futures-focussed, the tactics can both be reactive to quickly respond to a place-based issue as exemplified from PPS' (2007) 'Lighter, Quicker, Cheaper (LQC)', or proactive to shape places for multiple futures. Places must be co-designed and envisioned as flexible, adaptable and sustainable environments, with long-term positive impact on the community.

The placemakers' role is to collaboratively devise placemaking processes that facilitate continuous listening to and understanding the voices of our multiple publics, to recognise the key values, needs and hopes identified in the 'People' element/component and to purposefully shape positive affective bonds of people and place.

Product/Project

Placemaking leads to transformative change. This change can be represented as outputs, outcomes and impacts. The 'Product' of placemaking which was traditionally considered as an ingredient for economic growth has now evolved into the collective outcomes drawn from the wisdom of the community about their own place.

The 'Product' of placemaking may be described as:

An **output** manifesting at different scales. It can be large-scale intervention, medium-scale neighbourhood placemaking events, street scale pop-ups or a community capacity-building design thinking workshop.

The **physical outcomes** of the production of space, hence, it is tangible. 'Tangible' assets can be temporal or fixed. When fixed, it can be a short-, medium- or long-term place implementation or installation. That was designed in step two. For instance designs, strategies or plans. Or the implementation of forms of art, festivals and celebrations.

Its **relational outcomes** to enhance social environments in forms that strengthen people's connections to and use of place, hence, these take on intangible forms. Intangible assets are reflected in increased awareness to place advocacies, stronger community bonds (i.e. social cohesion), igniting the love of place (topophilia) and extends this love to expressing the importance of nature (biophilia) (Kellert & Wilson, 1995; Tuan, 1974).

The **multidimensional benefits and impact on the wider community** is further discussed in Chapter 13 on place evaluation.

As placemakers, the central challenge is to facilitate the co-production of place that seeks to continuously nurture the community's love of place to fuel the larger goal of creating and re-shaping inclusive places for all.

Programme

Programming is vital to generating enduring connections between people and with place. Temporary events have found a role within the placemaking literature for their ability to revitalise and activate an area to enhance social bonding across communities (Richards, 2017). Each connection evokes a placemaking story. Programming is creating the continuous, yet iterative story of shaping places, narrated and curated across time, space and themes, with the sole purpose of creating meaning in place, and this narrative is different depending on the culture and circumstances of the specific community embedded in this place. Hence, meaningful programming is important for placemaking to be effective (Coghlan, Sparks, Liu, & Winlaw, 2017; Richards, 2017).

Placemaking programming is the mechanism which glues seemingly discrete activities into a holistic, continuous (hi)story of place. It is also the thread that integrates placemaking initiatives undertaken by different and sometimes competing entities belonging to the private, public and community spheres.

Placemaking programming is based on a specific purpose or a series of purposes. It can be a strategic vision to shape place experience or a locally initiated projects to inject life into ignored places. It can take the form of a long-term suite of interventions to create positive place legacy, or it could be short term, incremental, small scale, with the intent of 'acupuncturing' to catalyse place-led change.

Programming is about maintaining and sustaining the 'Product' that was created. Dempsey and Burton (2012) refer to this as placekeeping. Placekeeping is a vital component of place programming because it guarantees that social, economic and environmental values and benefits of place are maintained and continually enjoyed through time. It is more than the development of a series of activities, but integrates the management and governance strategies that continue to build and re-build relationships to re-engage the community, connecting them to other local residents, associations and institutions, yet the challenge is often ensuring adequate funding and resources are available for placekeeping. As placemakers, our role includes assisting the community to plan and manage structures and processes to ensure continuity and positive legacy.

Place Evaluation

Place evaluation is critical to the ability to continually understand place values, the outcomes of initiatives and assess when it is time for a new iteration of the placemaking process. However, one should ask, what is it that we are evaluating? There are countless tools and frameworks to assess the quality of urban spaces or that aim to quantify livability of a particular area; however, if placemaking is about developing meaningful relationships, then the place evaluation should incorporate strategies to assess if these relationships were achieved.

Place evaluation is about critically appraising the efforts to achieve positive physical and relational outcomes. It is about drawing insightful lessons learned from placemaking successes and failures. It is enabling ways to iteratively, dynamically transform places to respond to change.

Chapter 13 presents a relationship-based evaluation model based on four interacting dimensions: the self, the community, the man-made environments and the natural environments.

Summary

The cyclic, iterative nature of Place Agency's 5P framework helps us to understand the social processes involved in placemaking. Fundamentally, placemaking is a complex, continuous, place-shaping **Process** to develop affective bonds between **People** and place, or topophilia, and through **Programming**, creates a shared meaning and common sense of purpose, to achieve positive place-based outcomes—love of place, empowerment, social inclusion and cohesion, improved health and overall sustainability. These outcomes will emerge through **Place evaluation**.

This section discussed the 5P framework as the building blocks of placemaking. The purpose was to establish a systematic, holistic approach to the shaping of people's place-based experiences, as a means to create 'the affective bond between people and place or setting' (Tuan, 1974, p. 4). Research has long recognised the importance not only of our constructed places but also of our natural environments in shaping people's love of place. Kellert and Wilson (1995) used the term biophilia to describe our innate affinity for the natural world. The field of environmental design acknowledges the paramount role of nature in designing places for restoration and healing (Hartig & Staats, 2003) while the empirical study conducted by Ogunseitan (2004) presented people's ubiquitous preference for natural over built environments. While we recognise the vital role of nature in achieving love of place, this is beyond the scope of this chapter. Our discussion of 5P has deliberately focused on the architecture of placemaking. Strategies to incorporate 'Nature in Place' are discussed in Chapter 3.

Places in the Making: Strategies and Case Studies

There are many types of placemaking processes defined based on the specific tactics or strategies applied. This includes tactical placemaking, strategic placemaking, green placemaking, creative placemaking, place branding, regenerative placemaking amongst many others. Depending on which type you apply, the level of impact to the place may differ. However, when you understand placemaking as the process to invest meaning, you may need to apply different placemaking tactics. Thus, the most important thing is that placemaking is at its core is <u>purpose-driven</u>. In the sections below, we demonstrate this by introducing strategies and case studies leading to purposeful discussion on ways to shape places through placemaking by design.

Placemaking as an empowering strategy. Community-led placemaking, bottom-up placemaking or community-driven placemaking are several approaches which refer to creating installations on and re-purposing public space that emerge from and are championed by grassroots communities. One example is PARK(ing) Day. Coombs (2012) explains how an urban intervention became a global phenomenon by empowering people's capacity to temporarily re-purpose (parking) spaces into other uses such as parks, plazas and green spaces for the benefit of communities. Case study examples are also articulated in Chapters 11 and 14 (Governance and the ART of engagement, respectively).

Placemaking as a governance strategy. As a governance tool, placemaking can be a pathway for social inclusion justice and creating a voice for the voiceless, through government policy and programmes. Yet it can also be party to the antagonisms brought about by the impact of placeless architecture in our public places. Strategic placemaking is an example of a policy-led, strategic approach to creating places. Examples include the Placemaking Framework of the City of Greater Dandenong and the City of Adelaide's 2014–2015 Placemaking Strategy. Case studies are introduced in Chapter 11.

Placemaking as an acupuncturing strategy. is an interventionist approach which uses puncture points in public spaces to catalyse long-term positive change (Lerner, 2014). Some examples of place acupuncturing are 'tactical placemaking', 'pop-up', 'guerrilla' or 'DIY' urbanism. These approaches are typically characterised as community-generated, low-cost and often temporary as opposed to top-down, capital-intensive and bureaucratically sanctioned urban change (Talen, 2015).

Placemaking as a reclaiming strategy. The desire to repossess public spaces to encourage urban encounters and facilitate exchange continues to drive placemaking. For instance, Engwicht (1995) engages communities and activists to create safer transport environments.

Placemaking as an experiential strategy. The way we experience a place is afforded through our different senses—our sense of smell, sight and sound gives a place its unique significance. Henshaw (2013) promotes urban smellscapes whilst Beer explores the role of ecoscenography in creative approaches to shaping of places (Beer, Lanxing, & Hernández-Santín, 2018).

Placemaking as a place-storytelling strategy. Our interest in a place is based on the meaning we derive from the place—about loss and recovery or even about character and transformation. These little histories of the world also constitute our own self-identity, which help us increase our own knowledge of the place (Friedmann, 2007). CoCreate Cremorne's strategy employs listening to, amplifying and giving value to the people whose stories are embedded in the place. Stories have the power to tell not only about who we are, but also what we do and what we can be.

Placemaking as a capacity-building strategy. Everyone is and can be a placemaker. We all have the ability to shape the places we live, visit and work in. Building capacity in placemaking is an important goal for Place Agency. Place Agency's Placemaking Sandbox Studio is about 'creating the capacity for people to invest space with meaning'. The Placemaking Sandbox aims to deliver a capacity-building tool not only to train existing professionals and 'experts' in the field but, more importantly, aims to empower the emerging workforce, including grassroots women's movement inclusion of girls and children. Place Agency has developed a programme that brings together the range of approaches from both academic and placemaking practitioners to guide placemaking for public space through synthesising methods that are informed through on-the-ground case studies. One such example is the Placemaking Sandbox workshop conducted during the World Urban Forum in 2018.

Placemaking Sandbox Workshop

Placemaking Strategy: Placemaking as a capacity-building strategy
Location: Kuala Lumpur, Malaysia, Asia-Pacific
Scale: Public Square, Lane

The World Urban Forum 9 in Kuala Lumpur (2018) provided the venue to engage with diverse communities on placemaking theory and practice (Fig. 2.1). Building upon the placemaking definition 'the collaborative craft to co-create neighbourhoods that respond to local needs for emotional and meaningful connection and experience', we used the Sandbox placemaking methodology as a capacity-building strategy to purposefully develop tactics and ways for people to invest meaning in spaces. This was followed by a practical example in a laneway in old Kuala Lumpur near the Medan Pasang Central Market area.

Fig. 2.1 Sandbox narratives. Left: Modelling in groups off-site. Centre: Re-imagining the lane. Right: A place for ideas by ThinkCity (Photos by Gini Lee, 2018)

People

A critical component in developing the Placemaking Sandbox involved on-the-ground coordination with key people and organisations. We worked with local people and also people with expertise in global conditions that affect people in public space. We partnered with nine local and international organisations.[4] The workshop attracted about 70 participants from 30 countries showing the international draw of placemaking. One of our partners was ThinkCity. They helped transform an inhospitable public square into a green, sustainable place through contemporary pop-up design, in only a few months, to coincide with the World Urban Forum.

Process

Method and Intended change. Placemaking sandbox employed participatory learning strategies to engage people across cultures and ages through group collaboration in an intensive workshop. To demonstrate the practical application of placemaking in a real-world site, people and site-specific strategies were developed for an unused community space.

Provocation. A provocation was posed to incite scenarios for (practical) place transformation in line with SDG 11 principles. Firstly, the Placemaking Sandbox sought to create green and accessible public spaces for all, with special attention to persons with disabilities and older persons, to grassroots women and to provide a safe and playful place for young people in a space where they like to gather after school or work. Secondly, in identifying the multiple publics involved in the Placemaking Sandbox workshop, we allowed the convenors to develop a range of tools for engagement to include a diverse range of ages,

---

[4]Our placemaking partners included: Place Agency, Melbourne Sustainable Society Institute, Thrive Hub, University of Melbourne, Joyati Das, Sudeshna Chatterjee (Action for Children's Environments), Jinaping Lee (ThinkCity), Joanne Taylor (Place Leaders Asia Pacific) and SDI (Slum/Shack Dwellers International).

languages, placemaking knowledge and connections to their home places and the city which we were seeking to immerse them in.

Posing a Great Question established a mindset for the project to frame imagining scenarios for placemaking as a concept beyond place. We asked 'how does a place where young people/women can have fun, feel safe, and make new friends' look like? This immediately placed the audience in an insider/outsider position in the groups they were asked to form to brainstorm ways of addressing the question. The children and women present could imagine their ideal conditions while reflecting upon the current issues which contribute to their familiar places being not so great—how great could things be if they were designed differently? The consultants and academics needed to apply their theory and practice to the everyday and pragmatic examples drawn from diverse cultural and geographical backgrounds to collaborate in coming to a range of general ideals.

Design thinking exercise. To facilitate this thinking, a series of sub-questions were framed as a game followed by a dynamic, democratic and iterative future-focused exercise to **Negotiate, Design + Build** and **Synthesise**, through utilising simple children's model making materials to make a spatial maquette for a great place.

- How do you make friends?
- What do you do to have fun?
- What makes nature enjoyable?
- What makes public space fun?

Product

Visual models of ideal places as outputs. This practical activity was undertaken utilising the floor as the available space for activity provided a lively, iterative and immersive activity where strangers and friends contributed alike and produced, as simple 'outputs' but often compelling functional and spatial models to convey possibilities for their ideal space.

Sharing of ideal places as outputs. Assigned spokespeople **Shared** their 'outputs' as ideal place requirements resulting surprisingly in very similar ideals that were easily translated into strategies for community design in public space for women and children, applying also to those with disabilities and older people. Reinforcing there are some universal needs which apply locally and globally across diverse groups.

Physical and relation outcomes. The 5 ideal outcomes for places for women and young people should embrace:

- Safety and accessibility,
- Nature and particularly trees,
- Water in all its healthy forms,
- Shelter and a place to rest,
- Playful space and activity.

To test these ideals in a real place, many agreed to undertake a **Journey-to-Place** travelling along a route including walking and train travel through the city passing by shops, markets, car parks, the river, busy roads, the pop-up green park and finally gathering in the Lorong (lane) which the locals hope to transform from a service road to a gathering place. ThinkCity had already made a temporary installation in a corner of the public lane, providing a space to help to make this place great including a blackboard inscribed with 'I wish my Lorong is…' to invite people to chalk their thoughts. Our groups were armed with the 5 ideals gleaned from the session plus tools to draw the potential for transformation applied in situ, with a collective willingness to apply placemaking principles to make a new place for the elderly, women and children, achieving inclusive places for all.

As this was a capacity-building process, knowledge about place programming was limited to key takeaways from the sessions. Most of these ideas were expressed during the place evaluation session.

Place Evaluation

Importantly, time was made to **Evaluate** the programme over refreshments to reflect upon what tools might have been learnt and to critique and suggest useful and practical methods to iteratively and dynamically transform places to respond to change. Participants were asked to note down what is your biggest 'aha' moment? Over the course of the day. The opportunity to put strategies into tactics for performative practice, moving from the 'classroom' into the 'site for action', was regarded as a most useful activity. One such response commented on the creation of place as not confined to gender stereotypes.

> when we went out of the Pasar and directed towards to square we were wondering what is place was created for and then we realised it's a public space – also we were surprised it was done by women.
> Workshop participant

And

> It's not just an internal workshop, but also it has a tour to see a great example of implementing what we had discussed in the workshop.
> Workshop participant

Conclusion

For facilitating effective places subject to continuous making and remaking, placemakers need to pose the following questions: Have we created a place that is accessible for all, both human and non-human creatures? Have we shaped places that cater for place-based needs but also empower capabilities for stewardship? Can we formulate place values and capacities that strike the balance between sustainability and liveability? How does the 5Ps framework, People, Process, Product, Programme and Place evaluation, enable working strategies for community engagement and relationship building for place design?

The Sandbox placemaking workshop sought to demonstrate how capacity-building exercises can enable designers, facilitators and users to collaboratively respond to complex space situations, combine theoretical and strategic learning with practical and performative activities and always promote the participation of diverse audiences in the game of making place. In developing the placemaking toolkit based on the 5Ps framework, and in evaluating learning gained from the workshop exercises, we included participant feedback and observations made during the two forms of delivery, formulating strategies in groups and participatory testing on site. The interconnections made between the people involved, the demonstration of their collaborative thinking through modelling a place type, in this case for women and children, resulted in a project that reinforced place identity, the clear articulation of design strategies and the opportunity to test ideas on site to confirm the efficacy of the participatory consultation programme.

For new urban development, it is clear that initiatives for local action from the ground up are necessary to enable the hoped-for success of more universal agendas. If place identity is critical to the protection of existing ideal places, alongside the promotion of new places reflective of a more mobile society in changing environments, then the principles and practices of placemaking are a critical strategy to support community-focused and place-driven ways to reaffirm the power of place in society. One does not need to be a designer to be a placemaker, yet working with designers can lead to a more holistic space-based, cultural/ecological collaboration with the community.

References

Arefi, M. (2014). *Deconstructing placemaking: Needs, opportunities, and assets.* Routledge.

Augé, M. (2009). *Non-places: Introduction to an anthropology of supermodernity* (new ed.). London, UK: Verso Books.

Beer, T., Lanxing, F., & Hernández-Santín, C. (2018). Scenographer as placemaker: Co-creating communities through The Living Stage NYC. *Theatre and Performance Design, 4*(4), 342–363.

Casey, E. (1997). *The fate of place: A philosophical history*. London and Berkeley: University of California Press.

Coghlan, A., Sparks, B., Liu, W., & Winlaw, M. (2017). Reconnecting with place through events: Collaborating with precinct managers in the placemaking agenda. *International Journal of Event and Festival Management, 8*(1), 66–83.

Coombs, G. (2012). Park(ing) day. *Contexts, 11*(3), 64–65.

David, J., & Hammond, R. (2011). *High line: The inside story of New York City's park in the sky*. New York: Farrar, Straus and Giroux.

Dempsey, N., & Burton, M. (2012). Defining place-keeping: The long-term management of public spaces. *Urban Forestry & Urban Greening, 11*(1), 11–20.

Engwicht, D. (1995). Reclaiming our cities & towns: Better living with less traffic/Review. *Alternatives Journal, 21*(3), 41.

Friedmann, J. (2007). Reflections on place and place-making in the cities of China. *International Journal of Urban and Regional Research, 31*(2), 257–279.

Hartig, T., & Staats, H. (2003). Guest's editors' introduction: Restorative environments. *Journal of Environmental Psychology, 23*(2), 103–107. https://doi.org/10.1016/S0272-4944(02)00108-1.

Harvey, D. (2003). The right to the city. *International Journal of Urban and Regional Research, 27*(4), 939–941.

Henshaw, V. (2013). *Urban smellscapes: Understanding and designing city smell environments*. New York: Routledge and Taylor & Francis Group.

Iveson, K. (2007). *Publics and the city*. Malden, MA: Blackwell.

Kellert, S. R., & Wilson, E. O. (Eds.). (1995). *The biophilia hypothesis*. Washington, DC: Island Press.

Kretzmann, J., & McKnight, J. P. (1996). Assets-based community development. *National Civic Review, 85*(4), 23–29.

Lerner, J. (2014). *Urban acupuncture*. Washington, DC: Island Press.

Lippard, L. R. (1997). *The lure of the local: Senses of place in a multicentered society*. New York: New Press.

Malpas, J. (2015). Place and singularity. In J. Malpas (Ed.), *The intelligence of place: Topographies and poetics* (pp. 65–92). London: Bloomsbury.

Norberg-Schulz, C. (1980). *Genius loci: Towards a phenomenology of architecture*. New York: Rizzoli International Publication.

Ogunseitan, O. A. (2004). Topophilia and the quality of life. *Environmental Health Perspectives, 113*(2), 143–148.

Potter, E. (2012). Introduction: Making Indigenous place in the Australian city. *Postcolonial Studies, 15*(2), 131–142.

Project for Public Spaces (PPS). (2007). *What is placemaking?* Retrieved from https://www.pps.org/article/what-is-placemaking.

Project for Public Spaces (PPS). (2008). *Placemaking for communities.* Retrieved from www.pps.org.

Relph, E. (1976). *Place and placelessness.* London: Pion.

Relph, E. (2008). A pragmatic sense of place. In F. M. Vanclay, M. Higgins, & A. Blackshaw (Eds.), *Making sense of place* (pp. 311–332). Canberra: National Museum of Australia Press.

Relph, E. (2017). *A pragmatic sense of place and the future of places.* Placeness, Place, Placelessness. Retrieved from http://www.placeness.com/a-pragmatic-sense-of-place-and-the-future-of-places/.

Richards, G. (2017). From place branding to placemaking: The role of events. *International Journal of Event and Festival Management, 8*(1), 8–23.

Talen, E. (2015). Do-it-yourself urbanism: A history. *Journal of Planning History, 14*(2), 135–148.

Tuan, Y. F. (1974). *Topophilia: A study of environmental perception, attitudes, and values.* Englewood Cliffs, NJ: Prentice Hall.

Tuan, Y. F. (2001). *Space and place: The perspective of experience.* 1977. Minneapolis: University of Minnesota.

United Nations Human Settlement Programme (UN Habitat). (2018). *New Urban Agenda.* Habitat3.Org. Retrieved from http://habitat3.org/wp-content/uploads/NUA-English.pdf.

United Nations (UN). (2017). About the sustainable development goals. In *United Nations Sustainable Development.* Retrieved from https://www.un.org/sustainabledevelopment/sustainable-development-goals/.

Village Well. (2019). *Introduction.* Retrieved from http://www.villagewell.org/.

3

Nature in Place: Placemaking in the Biosphere

Judy Bush, Cristina Hernandez-Santin and Dominique Hes

Introduction

This chapter provides placemaking practitioners with the background, knowledge and tools for embedding nature in their placemaking practices and approaches. We discuss the connections between individual and community values for nature, a sense of place created by nature in place, and ultimately how values and sense of place influence wider stewardship of the biosphere.

J. Bush (✉)
Clean Air and Urban Landscapes Hub, Faculty of Architecture, Building and Planning, University of Melbourne, Parkville, VIC, Australia
e-mail: judy.bush@unimelb.edu.au

J. Bush · C. Hernandez-Santin · D. Hes
Thrive Research Hub and Place Agency, Faculty of Architecture, Building and Planning, University of Melbourne, Parkville, VIC, Australia

D. Hes
e-mail: Dhes@unimelb.edu.au

Nature is fundamental to life and to health and well-being of humans and non-human biodiversity. Healthy ecosystems are essential for life, for liveability and thriveability. Nature contributes to our social cohesion and to thriving people, neighbourhoods and communities. These essential relationships, structures and functions can be understood as operating within an integrated social-ecological systems perspective.

Placemaking activities are inherently place-based, responding to and celebrating local context, and empowering people to have agency in their local place. Placemaking is a process that relies on community engagement and responding to the community's priorities and values that are articulated during engagement processes. When the community expresses values that are strongly embedded in nature, the resulting placemaking initiatives reflect this. However, there are challenges for embedding nature in placemaking if the community does not identify or highlight these during consultation. We argue that nature is always present in place, as part of its social-ecological make-up, and therefore placemaking practice must include nature.

Placemaking practice needs to engage with ecological thinking to re-embed nature and to expand beyond its current largely anthropocentric focus. This chapter discusses the <u>necessity</u> for embedding placemaking processes, outcomes and impacts into social-ecological systems, as well as the <u>potential</u> for expanding placemaking tools and outcomes through connecting with local ecological sense of place, and ultimately building people's stewardship of the biosphere.

Social-Ecological Systems, Sense of Place and Stewardship

In creating and sustaining *place*, nature can be considered both a passive element but also an active participant of place. In designing and building cities, green spaces are created within the urban fabric, as one of the elements of the built environment. Formalised urban planning approaches have long recognised the importance of urban green spaces for their aesthetic and recreational functions; more recently, green spaces are increasingly recognised as providing a wide range of benefits and 'ecosystem services' including regulating temperature, air pollution, storm water runoff and so on (Luederitz et al., 2015). As such, they are integrated into the built environment in the form of green–blue infrastructure for storm water, and as green roofs, walls and facades, as well as gardens, parks and street verges.

Nature is much more than the supporting cast for the buildings, more than simply the plants and landscaping elements introduced to green the edges of built form. Nature forms the biological building blocks for the landscape elements of place. Nature is also present in the undesigned spaces within cities, persisting in urban watercourses and wild spaces and continuing to flourish in parks, street verges and unbidden in the cracks in built form. And often we find that it is the elements of nature that connect us to place, and that make places special for us (National Trust (UK), 2017). This section explores the concepts of *social-ecological systems*, *sense of place* and *stewardship* and the connections between them. Together they provide the conceptual foundations for embedding nature in placemaking.

Social-Ecological Systems

Social systems and ecological systems do not operate in isolation from each other, being intrinsically interlinked across many facets (Folke, Hahn, Olsson, & Norberg, 2005). Humans are part of ecological systems both in their inherent biophysicality and also in their dependence on nature and its ecosystem services and functions. The basic requirements of life, including clean air, water and food, depend on healthy, productive ecosystems. At the same time, human (social) systems, with their global reach, affect and are affected by ecological systems (Collins et al., 2011). Bringing together ecological and social systems into a *social-ecological systems* perspective emphasises their interconnections (Masterson et al., 2017) and interdependencies (Elmqvist et al., 2013).

Social-ecological systems, as 'coupled human-natural systems' (Kibler et al., 2018), demonstrate complex dynamics and feedback loops that govern their functions. As such, social-ecological systems are 'complex adaptive systems': they are dynamic and non-linear, multi-sectoral, uncertain, interlinked and self-organising (Levin et al., 2013). Social-ecological systems are complex in that they are more than the sum of their parts, exhibiting properties created within and by the system itself (Hes & du Plessis, 2014). They are adaptive because they change over time, influenced by feedback loops within the system, and this change can be non-linear and uncertain or unpredictable. 'Complex adaptive systems are constantly unfolding and in transition … the dynamics within these systems are non-linear, which implies that small causes can have large results' (Hes & du Plessis, 2014, p. 32). Understanding that we exist within social-ecological systems emphasises the necessity to consider nature and ecology in all our planning, designing and decision-making, whether in urban areas or beyond the city boundaries.

To ensure that our social-ecological systems are healthy and resilient, as necessary for our surviving, thriving and well-being, requires a focus on maintaining and restoring ecosystems and their biodiversity (Biggs et al., 2012). Approaches such as 'biodiversity sensitive urban design' (Garrard, Williams, Mata, Thomas, & Bekessy, 2017) have identified the key principles and practices that can be applied to urban design, planning and decision-making. Biodiversity sensitive urban design (BSUD) involves learning about the ecology of the place, identifying objectives for 'renaturing', and then implementing actions that address the key BSUD principles. The principles include a focus on maintaining and creating habitat, minimising threats and disturbance, facilitating ecological processes and opportunities for human–nature interactions (Garrard et al., 2017). These BSUD principles and practices can be applied to embed nature in placemaking.

Placemaking practices are embedded within social-ecological systems; applying a social-ecological framing provides a 'useful concept for understanding interlinked dynamics of social and ecological change' (Fischer et al., 2015). The next section explores how our relationships with place can be encapsulated by the concept of 'sense of place'.

Sense of Place

A *social-ecological systems* framing underpins the understandings of the essential interlinkages between people and nature. But our relationship with nature is also often an 'emotional attachment to place' (Kibler et al., 2018) that extends beyond simply the biophysical interdependencies on the environment. 'Place' is the intersection of nature, social relations and meaning (Williams, 2014). 'Sense of place' includes the *meanings* and *attachment* that individuals or groups hold for a place (Tuan, 1977) and, like the social-ecological perspective, 'assumes an interconnected social and biophysical reality' (Masterson et al., 2017). Place *meanings* are the descriptive narratives and symbolic understandings, while place *attachment* is the evaluative emotional bond with the environment (Frantzeskaki, van Steenbergen, & Stedman, 2018; Masterson et al., 2017; Stedman, 2016). As such 'sense of place' provides a window into understanding how we connect with our local environments and the emotional meanings that we associate with places.

Nature often plays a central role in people's sense of place (National Trust (UK), 2017). Sense of place emerges through our interactions with our biophysical environment (Masterson et al., 2017). It is often the natural elements of place that provide the strongest building blocks for the stories and connections to place. The natural elements, the sounds and smells as well as the sights, can underpin our memories of favourite places and provide evocative links to memory and identity. The 'biophilia hypothesis', which proposes that humans have innate connections with nature (Kellert & Wilson, 1993; Ross, Witt, & Jones, 2018), emphasises the physical and psychological effects of connection with nature, and the resulting rejuvenation and sense of well-being and connectedness, both to environment and to community (Hes & du Plessis, 2014). Research has identified key areas within our brains that are activated by places that are special to us, reflecting a physiological basis for biophilia and a clear relationship with mental well-being (National Trust (UK), 2017). Our connections with place evoke feelings of calmness, joy and contentment, as well as feeling energised, and a sense of belonging, which in turn builds social connections and cohesion (Fink, 2016; National Trust (UK), 2017).

One of the objectives of placemaking is for people to play an active role in creating places that promote their happiness and well-being. Placemaking provides an opportunity for people to participate in creating and building a 'sense of place', by taking a direct role in building and deepening the meanings of and attachment to place. Furthermore, nature connectedness is strengthened through activities in nature that involve biophilic values of contact, emotion, meaning, compassion and beauty (Lumber, Richardson, & Sheffield, 2017). Lumber et al. (2017) found that integrating activities of contact, emotion, meaning, compassion and beauty significantly increased connection with nature, compared with knowledge and information-focused activities, or with more passive experiences of simply walking in nature. Active involvement in nature-based placemaking may, therefore, contribute to increased connection with nature and increased well-being.

Nature is integral to our well-being and connectedness and a key element in our sense of place and therefore should form an essential consideration in placemaking approaches. Furthermore, in developing connections with place and nature, people's care and protective norms, or *stewardship* for place, may be developed and strengthened (Chapin & Knapp, 2015; Masterson et al., 2017). The next section explores stewardship of the biosphere and social-ecological systems and links these with sense of place.

Stewardship

With increasing environmental issues and challenges, including urbanisation impacts, climate change and habitat destruction, that threaten our own well-being as well as the integrity and survival of biodiversity and ecological systems globally, there is an urgent need for a focus on stewardship of the biosphere (Bennett et al., 2018; Elmqvist et al., 2013). There are multiple definitions for 'stewardship', often focused on 'action in pursuit of sustainability' (West et al., 2018); key dimensions focus on care, knowledge and agency for the environment (Enqvist et al., 2018). West et al. (2018) highlighted the 'relational values'—reciprocal relationships between human and non-human life, as embedded in social-ecological systems—that lie at the heart of stewardship actions and linked 'sense of place' as a source of the care that emerges for place. As urban green spaces and nature in cities provide urban dwellers with opportunities to connect with nature, extending this connection may lead to broader concern and to active stewardship

(Andersson et al., 2014). By developing a strengthened and co-created sense of place through connections and relationships with local nature, the possibility for a broader environmental focus may unfold: 'scaling up a sense of place may influence pro-environmental behaviour' more broadly (Masterson et al., 2017).

For First Nations peoples, stewardship of the land is deepened to obligations for custodianship of Country, expressed as rights and responsibilities to land and social existence (Arabena, 2015). Custodianship of land and sea, articulated as *'caring for Country'*, is deeply embedded in Australian Aboriginal culture and has been handed down in stories, art, practices and spirituality across generations for tens of thousands of years (Atkinson, 2004, cited in CoM and MSI, 2016). 'Country' encompasses the land, peoples and non-human inhabitants; 'it is spoken about amongst Aboriginal Australians as if it were not only a person, but a blood relation such as a mother or a brother' (Neidjie, 2002, cited in CoM and MSI, 2016). Indigenous perspectives to stewardship of place, *caring for Country*, are based on fulfilling mutual responsibilities for the long-term survival, productivity and biodiversity of the land and knowledge of Country: 'Indigenous laws and customary practices have shaped the environments of Australia for thousands of years' (Arabena, 2015). 'To love country and to be loved by it is the basis of their survival, and ours' (Birch, 2018, p. 214) and indeed underpinned Aboriginal people's survival and thriving in Australia for tens of thousands of years (Arabena, 2015). Therefore, there is much we can learn from Aboriginal people's approaches; 'we must listen to those who have lived with country for thousands of years without killing it, and in order to live with a healthy planet we need to tell stories of our experience with it, and our love for it. Stories that speak of a love of place encourage us to act ethically towards it' (Birch, 2018, p. 208). Engagement with Aboriginal approaches to 'Caring for Country' that take a 'whole systems approach', a mutual responsibility to the other human and non-human parts of our complex social-ecological systems, through dialogue, not appropriation (CoM and MSI, 2016, p. 14), can underpin a deepened relationship to sustainable care of place. Indigenous perspectives of 'making place' and 'making space' are explored in more depth in Chapter 4 (this book).

As highlighted previously, the key dimensions of stewardship are care, knowledge and agency (Enqvist et al., 2018). Creating opportunities for people to actively engage in their local environment, including through placemaking activities, can enhance a strengthened commitment to landscape stewardship, particularly at a local scale (García-Martín, Plieninger, & Bieling, 2018). Placemaking that involves 'hands-on' urban nature activities such as habitat restoration provides tangible opportunities to reconnect with nature as well as develop stewardship to place (Church, 2018; Mumaw, 2017).

In the ongoing care and maintenance of placemaking interventions and installations, an *adaptive governance* approach can inform the development of management structures and processes that support the dynamic evolution of nature-based places and systems. Adaptive governance recognises that social-ecological systems change over time, and the changes may be uncertain and abrupt (Folke et al., 2005; Green et al., 2016). Therefore, flexible, integrated and responsive governance systems are required to be able to deal with the system's dynamism and uncertainty. To effectively manage and maintain social-ecological systems requires the involvement and coordination of a diversity of stakeholders, from different levels of government and from across the community. Adaptive governance also requires ongoing monitoring of the system and its parts so that health, functioning and changes are identified and can then be addressed.

With increasing sustainability challenges at both local and global scales, mechanisms for strengthening stewardship of our places, the landscapes and biodiversity, have increased importance. Likewise, the roles of values, meaning and perceptions in promoting action (West et al., 2018), highlight the potential for a developing 'sense of place' that is created through place meanings and place attachment, to reinforce stewardship.

A social-ecological systems perspective, that reinforces the links between the social and ecological, between people, place and nature, lies at the heart of a growing sense of stewardship for the biosphere. As the biosphere is understood as 'an assemblage that is constantly in the making through the active cohabitation of humans and nonhumans' (Cooke, West, & Boonstra, 2016), so too the actions of placemaking, the *making* of places, that build sense of place through developing place meanings and place attachments, can contribute to broader stewardship outcomes. Having outlined definitions of and the links between a *social-ecological systems, sense of place* and broader *stewardship* of nature and the biosphere, the following section details approaches to embedding nature in placemaking.

Reintegrating Nature into Placemaking

As placemakers, our intention is to work with people to create places that are meaningful to them, and trigger strong and positive reactions and responses. We want places to be important to people, to provide people with the services they need and to create living environments that are healthy and promote well-being. In the previous sections of this chapter, we have explored the interrelatedness between people and nature, our codependencies on nature and the necessity for nature to be part of our cities and towns to ensure healthy and resilient living environments for all of us. Furthermore, we discussed nature's role in our sense of place and in the connections that we feel with our local places. This section now considers how to integrate nature into our placemaking practice.

In Chapter 2, Mateo-Babiano and Lee (2019) introduced the five key elements that are consistently found in the 'best-practice' approaches to placemaking. These are:

1. *People*: identifying the values, needs, hopes and experiences of people in place, their activities and pastimes. Placemakers' roles are to *facilitate* the opportunities and mechanisms for community members to explore and discuss their perspectives of the place, and feed these into the placemaking process.
2. *Process*: designing place interventions that address the key values, needs and hopes identified in step one. Placemakers roles are to *design with* the community, or indeed to encourage design *by* the community, rather than designing *for* the community (Nguyen & Thanh Dang, 2018). Placemakers, therefore, aims to work with the

community in designing interventions rather than imposing design solutions onto places.
3. *Product*: implementing or installing the initiative or intervention in place that was designed in step two. The 'product' may be part of the built environment, a temporary installation or new materials or forms that strengthen people's connections to and use of place. Placemakers roles are to facilitate the *construction and installation* of designs in ways that are consistent with the community's design intent.
4. *Programme*: maintaining the 'product' that was created in step three. The 'program' may include the ongoing activities, management and governance strategies that continue to re-engage the community, connecting them to their site. Placemakers' roles include assisting the community to *plan and manage* the structures and processes to ensure continuity.
5. *Place evaluation*: monitoring and evaluating the intervention. Place evaluation focuses attention on what was achieved, the community efforts in this achievement, successes and failures, and opportunities for continued fine-tuning of the 'product' or 'program'.

While these five elements have been shown to effectively and creatively empower local communities to participate in placemaking (LeGates & Stout, 2016), they omit a clear and explicit recognition of the role of nature in spaces and in sense of place. There are some placemaking approaches emerging that seek to address this, for example, Village Well's inclusion of 'planet' in its '5Ps' approach (Village Well, 2018). Without an explicit reference to nature, opportunities may be overlooked or lost for embedding nature in placemaking projects, to ensure liveable thriving environments. Placemaking aims to represent the values of a community; we need to ask people to reflect on their values and thoughts towards nature.

We propose an approach to placemaking that embeds nature throughout the placemaking process (Table 3.1). With this framework, we aim to support nature-based placemaking that leads to resilient, healthy communities and an increased care for and stewardship of the biosphere. The following sections present the five placemaking

Table 3.1 Nature in place framework: guidelines for embedding nature in placemaking

Placemaking 5Ps	Nature in place
People: Map the values, patterns and uses of the place	Social-ecological systems: Identify the community's perspectives on the place's social-ecological values, its ecology and elements of nature
Process: Design (with) place interventions	Habitat and biodiversity: Apply biodiversity sensitive urban design principles (Garrard et al., 2017) to design and implement nature in place interventions
Product: Implement the place intervention	BSUD principles: Retain and restore habitat Facilitate species dispersal Minimise anthropogenic disturbance Recover ecological processes Promote positive human–nature interactions
Programme: Maintain and manage the place for the long term	Adaptive governance: Develop adaptive and participatory governance systems to maintain and manage the place for the long term
Place evaluation: Monitor and evaluate the intervention	Nature stewardship: Monitor and evaluate the *nature* in the place intervention; connect to the wider social-ecological context; build stewardship and maintain social-ecological relationships

elements, redirected towards an approach with nature at its core. Each element is discussed, and activities or exercises are presented to illustrate how nature can be embedded in placemaking.

From People to Social-Ecological Systems

From a socio-ecological perspective, we know that people, their social and cultural systems, institutions and built environments are interconnected and interdependent with the natural system that surrounds us. Not only is nature important for our health and mental well-being, but as discussed in the previous sections, it often plays a central role in people's sense of place. An emotional connection between *self* and *place*, or love of place, is predominantly developed through three pathways:

1. places belonging to or evoking childhood memories,
2. places that are significant to our loved ones through shared stories and experiences, and
3. places meaningful to our present life (National Trust (UK), 2017).

During engagement with the community, a placemaker is, in many ways, a researcher seeking to identify the different elements that make a community 'tick', including the individual, shared and collective values, experiences and memories. Through engagement activities and discussions, the placemaker acts as a facilitator, encouraging the local community to rediscover or reveal the elements of place that they collectively value the most. The engagement questions and activities can powerfully guide the conversation to open up ideas and help expand the thinking towards inclusion of nature and recognising the non-human elements of place.

The placemaker's facilitation skills are critical towards uncovering the holistic perspective of the social-ecological elements meaningful to the community. By incorporating nature-related questions and activities (Box 3.1) that elicit reminiscences of childhood, the shared experiences with loved ones and hobbies and recent discoveries, the placemaker helps the community reflect on their relationship with nature. As well as finding out about the place's potential for people, this step should explore the potential of the place for habitat and for biodiversity. As part of this step in the placemaking process, the patterns of nature, the site's ecology and biodiversity are also identified. Placemakers can work with community to find reference books and records that reveal the site's natural and cultural history, the area's flora and fauna.

Box 3.1 Connecting with nature in place: *facilitating* **reflections on nature in place**

Nature reflection prompts.
When you were a child, where did you like to spend your time?

> Tell me about your memories of when the sun was shining
> Tell me about your river (Birch, 2018)
> Who (or what) are your non-human neighbours?
>
> *Place ecology and nature identity discovery:*
> What are the plants and animals that thrive in this place?
> What lived here before it was part of the city (Ossola & Niemelä, 2018; Parris, 2016)?
>
> *Interrelatedness of systems:*
> Part 1: Get the group to stand up in a clear space, ask everyone to mentally choose two people within the group and start walking until they are standing at an equal distance from both individuals. The group will start moving to correct the distance. Keep exercise until the system stabilises.
> Reflection: Everyone represents a different part of a system, systems are in constant movement adapting to the changing situations.
> Part 2: Ask one participant to crouch, as soon as one-person crouches, those individuals who mentally linked themselves to that person should also crouch.
> Reflection: As everything is interrelated, when one element of the system collapses, those elements most closely related to it will also collapse. Ultimately it reaches a point where the whole system becomes unsustainable

From Process and Product to Habitat and Biodiversity

A best-practice placemaking process relies on inclusive, participatory approaches to design the placemaking initiative (Kyle, Graefe, Manning, & Bacon, 2004): the community is the 'expert' of the place, and the placemaker's role is to design *with* the community (Davies & Lafortezza, 2019), rather than imposing their own perspectives by designing *for* the community. Nguyen and Thanh Dang (2018) contrasted the different approaches to placemaking design. By designing *for* the community, community members are more passive participants and the designers are applying their expertise to analyse the context and make design decisions. A more active, participatory '*design with*' approach relies on a partnership or codesign process in which community and designers work together during different stages of the project.

Lastly, a '*design by*' the community involves the community being empowered to actively develop the design and make design decisions together.

For placemaking processes that embed nature, the challenge is to apply a *design with* participatory approach that includes the non-human participants of the place. In the previous section, we outlined some strategies to identify the place's ecology and nature as part of the first element of placemaking with nature. In this stage, we focus on principles and activities to embed *biodiversity sensitive urban design* principles (Garrard et al., 2017) into the place's design and implementation (Box 3.2).

Like humans, biodiversity's basic needs are focused on shelter, food and movement, which together create biodiversity habitat. Good biodiversity habitat includes features such as multiple layers of vegetation (trees, shrubs, grasses and groundcover), a diversity of species and plant forms (including tussocks, dense shrubs and so on) and leaf litter, logs and stones (Parris, 2016). In addition, connection between habitat patches is important to allow biodiversity to move across the urban landscape (Ossola & Niemelä, 2018). Applying the principles for *biodiversity sensitive urban design* to the placemaking design and implementation brings the focus to creating opportunities for nature and humans to flourish together, and minimising threats and disturbance (Garrard et al., 2017).

> **Box 3.2 Designing and implementing habitat and biodiversity: *co-designing* with nature in place**
>
> Ask community members to each act as spokesperson for a different element of nature—a plant, animal, insect, or bird. Explore how the principles for biodiversity sensitive urban design can be applied in the place's design using the following prompts
>
> | Principles for biodiversity sensitive urban design | Codesigning with nature: habitat and biodiversity |
> |---|---|
> | Retain habitat | Where do you live? What's the form of your habitat? |
> | | What landscape features do you need? |

Facilitate species dispersal	How do you move to find food, a partner?
	How far do you travel in a single day? How long does it take?
	How do you move through the landscape?
Minimise anthropogenic disturbance	How are you affected by noise, light and roads?
	How sensitive are you to the impacts of urbanisation – litter, water pollution, soil disturbance, removal of leaf litter, sealed and impervious surfaces?
Recover ecological processes	What do you eat?
	How do you reproduce?
	What other species or habitat elements do you rely on? What relies on you?
Promote positive human-nature interactions	What do people think of you? Are they afraid of you?

From Programme to Adaptive Governance

Following the design and implementation of a place intervention, the placemaker's role turns to supporting and empowering the community to be able to contribute to the ongoing maintenance and management of the place over the long term. Often the places created in placemaking projects are located in public spaces and there may be a range of public institutions, government bodies and stakeholders engaged in their ongoing management. Therefore, to ensure the ongoing success of the place intervention, it is necessary to coordinate with the range of stakeholders; to ensure the place's objectives, elements, structures and functions are managed and supported in sympathetic and appropriate ways that support the system to flourish.

When nature is an integral element of the place intervention, the complexity of ongoing management—and nurturing—of the place's biodiversity and habitat potentially increases the range of stakeholders involved, as well as the diversity of management actions. As discussed earlier, social-ecological systems are complex and dynamic, and therefore, *adaptive* governance is required to address complexity, uncertainty and change (Green et al., 2016). Adaptive governance treats management interventions as ongoing experiments that should be monitored and evaluated so that results can be used to alter or improve management (Green et al., 2016). Adaptive governance also recognises that a diverse range of stakeholders, with intersecting interests, responsibilities and knowledge bases, is involved in urban social-ecological systems management (Folke et al., 2005). Mumaw (2017) found that 'learning by doing, supported by rewarding results, validation, community involvement, and accessible resources' contributes to deepening participants' connections with place, and developing their knowledge and competencies. This stage of nature placemaking requires both maintaining and managing the place, as well as the relationships with key stakeholders who are also associated with the place. Therefore, a key role for placemakers is to support participants to build and maintain a range of skills that can *adaptively* contribute and respond to the place's management and governance.

The key elements of adaptive governance that should be integrated into placemaking's ongoing maintenance and management of place (Folke et al., 2005; Green et al., 2016) are presented in Box 3.3.

> **Box 3.3 Adaptive governance for placemaking:** *maintaining nature in place*
>
> In shifting from a design and implementation phase to an ongoing maintenance and management phase, placemakers' roles turn to building the communities' skills, agency and confidence:
> knowledge and understanding of the place's ecological processes and cycles;
> knowledge and skills in how and when to intervene to support the place's habitat and biodiversity;
> awareness of the place's range of stakeholders and governance participants who have responsibilities for different parts of the social-ecological system;
> maintaining communication, enthusiasm and active, collaborative relationships with the placemaking community participants and others; leading small groups, identifying and assigning key group roles, such as facilitating or chairing meetings, taking meeting notes, maintaining and communicating with group membership, organising activities, liaising with other stakeholders and government agencies.

From Place Evaluation to Nature Stewardship

The final stage of placemaking (though of course all the stages overlap and can be cyclic) involves monitoring and evaluating the nature placemaking intervention. Monitoring and evaluating the intervention over time allows issues and problems to be identified and addressed so that the potential of the place can be nurtured (Box 3.4). Monitoring and evaluation should include both the *social* and *ecological* elements of the place (Jordan, Sorensen, Biehler, Wilson, & LaDeau, 2019; McMillen, Campbell, Svendsen, & Reynolds, 2016). Building transdisciplinary teams of practitioners and researchers from across a range of disciplines (Buijs, Fischer, & Muhar, 2018; Silva & Krasny, 2016) can strengthen these efforts—placemaking thrives on bringing together a range of perspectives and knowledge.

Nature placemaking can contribute to developing a broader stewardship approach to nature. While adaptive governance (the previous stage) builds a sense of local stewardship, this final stage aims to widen stewardship, crossing spatial and temporal scales to expand the place's influences into the future and across a wider area (Krasny, Tidball, & Maddox, 2018). This includes finding opportunities to link to nearby nature placemaking interventions. This 'scaling-up', from building, park and street to neighbourhood, precinct and city scale, creates the potential to link individual nature patches into larger habitat corridors and networks. Nature stewardship focuses on the interrelationships between members of the community; between the place's humans and non-humans; between the place's past, present and future; and across the region to create an urban network of nature-places. Together, nature stewardship can contribute to creating biophilic cities that are sustainable and resilient (Beatley & Newman, 2013), promoting wider stewardship of the biosphere (Buijs et al., 2018; Elmqvist et al., 2013).

> **Box 3.4 Nature stewardship:** *monitoring, evaluating and caring for nature in place*
>
> Assess the health of the vegetation: look at the trees, shrubs and groundcover. Are they thriving; is there new growth? Are there patches of dead leaves or wilting plants? Start to connect with the indicators of healthy

> landscapes and the signs of stressed or struggling landscapes. Look at biophysical parameters (such as soil condition, water quality). Talk to ecologists and arborists to diagnose issues and potential responses.
>
> Choose some 'indicator' species on which to focus attention. Note when, where, in what numbers, which season they are observed.
>
> Keep records to be able to track the evolution and development of the place over time. Records can include notes and photographs of activities, plantings, germinations and plant deaths, birds and insects that visit or take up residence.
>
> Monitor the *social* as well as the *ecological* elements of the place: focus on relationships and communication (McMillen et al., 2016)
>
> Share your data collection and monitoring with others: local and state government officers and other stakeholders, citizen science groups, neighbouring communities.
>
> Learn from each other, and from other communities, experts and researchers, and others involved in nature placemaking and urban stewardship.
>
> Maintain a view on the longer term: How do your efforts fit in with patterns of change and evolution around you? What about seasonal patterns? What about longer-term cycles?

Conclusion

This chapter has explored how nature is integral to place and how to embed nature into placemaking approaches. Nature placemaking requires, as the first step, analysing the local context of the place (getting in touch with the 'beat' of the social-ecological system): the cultural, economic, social, ecological and biophysical elements of place. The placemaking codesign process acknowledges and incorporates the place's nature, and nature placemaking responses contribute to enhancing the potential of the place's nature.

One of the key features of placemaking is that its interventions can be inexpensive, quick and experimental. It provides the opportunity to trial multiple, different strategies in the process of finding long-term solutions. The benefits are that participants can feel involved, and they can see something is happening. As place interventions mature, the place's participants can build their knowledge and skills in management, monitoring and evaluation, leading to stewardship of place.

Placemakers' roles span facilitation, codesign, implementation, maintenance and monitoring and evaluation of both the social and ecological elements of place. Placemakers also have key roles in supporting the development of participants' knowledge and skills. Ongoing nature-place stewardship requires transdisciplinary teams that bring together a range of skills and perspectives from both practitioners and researchers. Placemaking spans communication, community engagement, ecology, underpinned throughout by a focus on building and maintaining relationships. Placemaking can contribute to building participants' 'ecological literacy' throughout the engagement, design, maintenance and monitoring processes, strengthening the relationship between sense of place and social-ecological systems (Davies & Lafortezza, 2019). By embedding nature in placemaking and providing opportunities for people to create connections with nature, placemaking can, in turn, contribute towards a wider stewardship of our biosphere.

Nature Placemaking in Essence

1. Connecting with nature in place: What are the memories, stories and sensual reminders of nature in place?
2. Co-designing with nature in place: What are the shelter, food and movement needs of the place's biodiversity?
3. Co-maintaining nature in place: How can the intervention's biodiversity habitat, as well as the community's interest, enthusiasm and engagement be maintained?
4. Caring for nature in place: As the intervention evolves and matures, how can connection with place deepen to stewardship for the biosphere?

References

Andersson, E., Barthel, S., Borgström, S., Colding, J., Elmqvist, T., Folke, C., & Gren, A. (2014). Reconnecting cities to the biosphere: Stewardship of green infrastructure and urban ecosystem services. *AMBIO, 43*(4), 445–453. https://doi.org/10.1007/s13280-014-0506-y.

Arabena, K. (2015). *Becoming Indigenous to the universe: Reflections on living systems, indigeneity and citizenship*. North Melbourne, VIC: Australian Scholarly Publishing.

Beatley, T., & Newman, P. (2013). Biophilic cities are sustainable, resilient cities. *Sustainability, 5*(8), 3328–3345. https://doi.org/10.3390/su5083328.

Bennett, N. J., Whitty, T. S., Finkbeiner, E., Pittman, J., Bassett, H., Gelcich, S., & Allison, E. H. (2018). Environmental stewardship: A conceptual review and analytical framework. *Environmental Management, 61*(4), 597–614. https://doi.org/10.1007/s00267-017-0993-2.

Biggs, R., Schlüter, M., Biggs, D., Bohensky, E. L., BurnSilver, S., Cundill, G., … West, P. C. (2012). Toward principles for enhancing the resilience of ecosystem services. *Annual Review of Environment and Resources, 37*(1), 421–448. https://doi.org/10.1146/annurev-environ-051211-123836.

Birch, T. (2018). Recovering a narrative of place: Stories in the time of climate change. *Griffith Review, 60*, 207–214.

Buijs, A., Fischer, A., & Muhar, A. (2018). From urban gardening to planetary stewardship: Human–nature relationships and their implications for environmental management. *Journal of Environmental Planning and Management, 61*(5–6), 747–755. https://doi.org/10.1080/09640568.2018.1429255.

Chapin, F. S., III, & Knapp, C. N. (2015). Sense of place: A process for identifying and negotiating potentially contested visions of sustainability. *Environmental Science & Policy, 53*, 38–46. https://doi.org/10.1016/j.envsci.2015.04.012.

Church, S. P. (2018). From street trees to natural areas: Retrofitting cities for human connectedness to nature. *Journal of Environmental Planning and Management, 61*(5–6), 878–903. https://doi.org/10.1080/09640568.2018.1428182.

Collins, S. L., Carpenter, S. R., Swinton, S. M., Orenstein, D. E., Childers, D. L., Gragson, T. L., … Whitmer, A. C. (2011). An integrated conceptual framework for long-term social-ecological research. *Frontiers in Ecology and the Environment, 9*(6), 351–357. https://doi.org/10.1890/100068.

CoM and MSI. (2016). *Caring for country: An urban application. The possibilities for Melbourne*. Melbourne: City of Melbourne and Monash Sustainability Institute.

Cooke, B., West, S., & Boonstra, W. J. (2016). Dwelling in the biosphere: Exploring an embodied human–environment connection in resilience thinking. *Sustainability Science, 11*(5), 831–843. https://doi.org/10.1007/s11625-016-0367-3.

Davies, C., & Lafortezza, R. (2019). Transitional path to the adoption of nature-based solutions. *Land Use Policy, 80,* 406–409. https://doi.org/10.1016/j.landusepol.2018.09.020.
Elmqvist, T., Fragkias, M., Goodness, J., Güneralp, B., Marcotullio, P. J., McDonald, R. I., ... Tidball, K. (2013). Stewardship of the biosphere in the urban era. In T. Elmqvist, M. Fragkias, J. Goodness, B. Güneralp, P. J. Marcotullio, R. I. McDonald, S. Parnell ... C. Wilkinson (Eds.), *Urbanization, biodiversity and ecosystem services: Challenges and opportunities. A global assessment* (pp. 719–746). Dordrecht: Springer.
Enqvist, J., West, S., Masterson, V. A., Haider, L. J., Svedin, U., & Tengö, M. (2018). Stewardship as a boundary object for sustainability research: Linking care, knowledge and agency. *Landscape and Urban Planning, 179,* 17–37. https://doi.org/10.1016/j.landurbplan.2018.07.005.
Fink, H. S. (2016). Human-nature for climate action: Nature-based solutions for urban sustainability. *Sustainability, 8*(3), 254. https://doi.org/10.3390/su8030254.
Fischer, J., Gardner, T. A., Bennett, E. M., Balvanera, P., Biggs, R., Carpenter, S., ... Tenhunen, J. (2015). Advancing sustainability through mainstreaming a social-ecological systems perspective. *Current Opinion in Environmental Sustainability, 14,* 144–149. https://doi.org/10.1016/j.cosust.2015.06.002.
Folke, C., Hahn, T., Olsson, P., & Norberg, J. (2005). Adaptive governance of social-ecological systems. *Annual Review of Environment and Resources, 30,* 441–473. https://doi.org/10.1146/annurev.energy.30.050504.144511.
Frantzeskaki, N., van Steenbergen, F., & Stedman, R. C. (2018). Sense of place and experimentation in urban sustainability transitions: The Resilience Lab in Carnisse, Rotterdam, The Netherlands. *Sustainability Science,* 1–15. https://doi.org/10.1007/s11625-018-0562-5.
García-Martín, M., Plieninger, T., & Bieling, C. (2018). Dimensions of landscape stewardship across Europe: Landscape values, place attachment, awareness, and personal responsibility. *Sustainability (Switzerland), 10*(1). https://doi.org/10.3390/su10010263.
Garrard, G. E., Williams, N. S. G., Mata, L., Thomas, J., & Bekessy, S. A. (2017). Biodiversity sensitive urban design. *Conservation Letters.* https://doi.org/10.1111/conl.12411.
Green, O. O., Garmestani, A. S., Albro, S., Ban, N. C., Berland, A., Burkman, C. E., ... Shuster, W. D. (2016). Adaptive governance to promote ecosystem services in urban green spaces. *Urban Ecosystems, 19*(1), 77–93. https://doi.org/10.1007/s11252-015-0476-2.

Hes, D., & du Plessis, C. (2014). *Designing for hope: Pathways to regenerative sustainability*. Abingdon: Routledge.

Jordan, R. C., Sorensen, A. E., Biehler, D., Wilson, S., & LaDeau, S. (2019). Citizen science and civic ecology: Merging paths to stewardship. *Journal of Environmental Studies and Sciences, 9*(1), 133–143. https://doi.org/10.1007/s13412-018-0521-6.

Kellert, S. R., & Wilson, E. O. (Eds.). (1993). *The biophilia hypothesis*. Washington, DC: Island Press.

Kibler, K. M., Cook, G. S., Chambers, L. G., Donnelly, M., Hawthorne, T. L., Rivera, F. I., & Walters, L. (2018). Integrating sense of place into ecosystem restoration: A novel approach to achieve synergistic social-ecological impact. *Ecology and Society, 23*(4). https://doi.org/10.5751/es-10542-230425.

Krasny, M. E., Tidball, K. G., & Maddox, D. (Eds.). (2018). *Grassroots to global: Broader impacts of civic ecology*. Ithaca: Cornell University Press.

Kyle, G., Graefe, A., Manning, R., & Bacon, J. (2004). Effect of activity involvement and place attachment on recreationists' perceptions of setting density. *Journal of Leisure Research, 36*(2), 209–231.

LeGates, R. T., & Stout, F. (2016). Part 7: Urban design and placemaking. In R. T. LeGates & F. Stout (Eds.), *The city reader* (6th ed., pp. 553–557). London: Routledge.

Levin, S., Xepapadeas, T., Crépin, A.-S., Norberg, J., de Zeeuw, A., Folke, C., ... Walker, B. (2013). Social-ecological systems as complex adaptive systems: Modeling and policy implications. *Environment and Development Economics, 18*, 111–132. https://doi.org/10.1017/s1355770x12000460.

Luederitz, C., Brink, E., Gralla, F., Hermelingmeier, V., Meyer, M., Niven, L., ... von Wehrden, H. (2015). A review of urban ecosystem services: Six key challenges for future research. *Ecosystem Services, 14*, 98–112. https://doi.org/10.1016/j.ecoser.2015.05.001.

Lumber, R., Richardson, M., & Sheffield, D. (2017). Beyond knowing nature: Contact, emotion, compassion, meaning, and beauty are pathways to nature connection. *PLoS One, 12*(5). https://doi.org/10.1371/journal.pone.0177186.

Masterson, V. A., Stedman, R. C., Enqvist, J., Tengö, M., Giusti, M., Wahl, D., & Svedin, U. (2017). The contribution of sense of place to social-ecological systems research: A review and research agenda. *Ecology and Society, 22*(1). https://doi.org/10.5751/es-08872-220149.

McMillen, H., Campbell, L. K., Svendsen, E. S., & Reynolds, R. (2016). Recognizing stewardship practices as indicators of social resilience: In living memorials and in a community garden. *Sustainability (Switzerland), 8*(8). https://doi.org/10.3390/su8080775.

Mumaw, L. (2017). Transforming urban gardeners into land stewards. *Journal of Environmental Psychology, 52,* 92–103. https://doi.org/10.1016/j.jenvp.2017.05.003.

National Trust (UK). (2017). *Places that make us.* Research report. Retrieved from Swindon, UK. https://www.nationaltrust.org.uk/stories/why-do-places-mean-so-much.

Nguyen, N. H., & Thanh Dang, H. (2018). *Adaptation of 'participatory method' in design 'for/with/by' the poor community in Tam Thanh, Quang Nam, Vietnam.* Paper presented at the Smart and Sustainable Built Environment Conference, Sydney, Australia.

Ossola, A., & Niemelä, J. (Eds.). (2018). *Urban biodiversity: From research to practice.* Abingdon: Routledge.

Parris, K. M. (2016). *Ecology of urban environments.* Hoboken, UK: Wiley.

Ross, H., Witt, K., & Jones, N. A. (2018). Stephen Kellert's development and contribution of relational values in social-ecological systems. *Current Opinion in Environmental Sustainability, 35,* 46–53. https://doi.org/10.1016/j.cosust.2018.10.007.

Silva, P., & Krasny, M. E. (2016). Parsing participation: Models of engagement for outcomes monitoring in urban stewardship. *Local Environment, 21*(2), 157–165. https://doi.org/10.1080/13549839.2014.929094.

Stedman, R. C. (2016). Subjectivity and social-ecological systems: A rigidity trap (and sense of place as a way out). *Sustainability Science, 11*(6), 891–901. https://doi.org/10.1007/s11625-016-0388-y.

Tuan, Y. (1977). *Space and place: The perspective of experience.* Minneapolis: University of Minnesota Press.

Village Well. (2018). *Placemaking projects: Our process.* Retrieved from Melbourne http://www.villagewell.org.

West, S., Haider, L. J., Masterson, V., Enqvist, J. P., Svedin, U., & Tengö, M. (2018). Stewardship, care and relational values. *Current Opinion in Environmental Sustainability, 35,* 30–38. https://doi.org/10.1016/j.cosust.2018.10.008.

Williams, D. R. (2014). Making sense of 'place': Reflections on pluralism and positionality in place research. *Landscape and Urban Planning, 131,* 74–82. https://doi.org/10.1016/j.landurbplan.2014.08.002.

4

There's No Place Like (Without) Country

Shannon Foster, Joanne Paterson Kinniburgh and Wann Country

This is not a site, it is a Songline. A connection to the memories of family that have been embedded in this Country and its earth, water, stars and sky since time began. Miluni is the mud that has squelched between the toes of feet that carry our stories and knowledges and miluni brings those memories, our knowledges through time and space to me here today. I do not see a "site". I *feel* Country and it welcomes me home. "Wedayeo" - Welcome I give my spirit to you. This Country's spirit holds all that has created me and brought me here. Its spirit is called Wann and I welcome you here onto my family's Country and ask that our Ancestors protect you and guide you

---

S. Foster (✉)
Centre for the Advancement of Indigenous Knowledges,
University of Technology Sydney, Sydney, NSW, Australia
e-mail: shannon.foster@uts.edu.au

J. Paterson Kinniburgh
School of Architecture, University of Technology Sydney,
Sydney, NSW, Australia

© The Author(s) 2020
D. Hes and C. Hernandez-Santin (eds.), *Placemaking Fundamentals for the Built Environment*, https://doi.org/10.1007/978-981-32-9624-4_4

while you are here. I also acknowledge the other custodians of Wann and pay my respects to their Ancestors both past and present. This work was also created with the assistance of my great grandmother's Country, Minimbah (Worimi Country in the Great Lakes Region of New South Wales) where the Ancestors guided me through the process of capturing these knowledges in a written form. Didjariguru guwanayio'miya (we thank you for remembering our Ancestors).

Shannon Foster
Sydney D'harawal Knowledge Keeper[1]

Introduction

In this chapter, we critique traditional placemaking approaches to site, through the Indigenous Australian concept of Country. We contest that a move away from the word 'placemaking' itself is overdue. We instead propose a practice of 'making place', and further, of 'making space' (i) that allows overlooked spatial (hi)stories to reclaim the sites that they have always occupied, and (ii) for the very occupants and stories that are ordinarily overlooked in urban and spatial design practice. To do so is to accept that we must look to those marginal occupants, practices and writings that challenge the gendered, heteronormative, white, neuro-typical and colonising discourses that dominate architecture. Placemaking practices employ community consultation, privileging local stories and quotidian ways-of-being in response. It is our position, that even these 'community-engaged' processes perpetuate erasure and marginalisation precisely through their conceptualisations of 'Site' and what constitutes community.

We present a model for an Indigenous/non-Indigenous collaboration that offers methods of spatially encountering site within a colonial context. We share our experiences of a project that we collaboratively

---

[1]This chapter is the collaborative work and shared voice of all authors. Through Australian Indigenous Women's Standpoint Theory (Moreton-Robinson, 2013), we have at times broken from our shared story, to offer Shannon's voice in the first-person reflections in bold text—as her solo contributions to the discourse.

produced in the Badu Mangroves at Sydney Olympic Park, to share the overlooked spatial histories and cultures of countless millennia. We have woven together Indigenous epistemologies, ontologies and axiologies, and design-as-research methodology.

Erasing Country (Site)

> We are told that we are extinct, that Sydney Aboriginal people didn't survive colonisation. Apparently, we're a race that disappeared. The only 'real' Aboriginal people that survived live in the Central Desert or Top End.

In Australia, the most glaring erasure in the urban fabric is consistently of Aboriginal stories, culture and knowledges (Potter, 2012). Colonial processes of city building in Australia in the past century deployed the neutralising *tabula rasa* of international modernism, but also prior to that the eradicating colonial practice of *terra nullius*. The anthropocentric concept of a utopian blank site continues to pervade city planning and design in Australia. It is upon this empty slate that the ideal of universal design is enacted.[2] It is an ongoing legacy of modernism that built environment disciplines typically presume site is a discrete space, marked out by 'boundaries' that connect it to other similar sites and infrastructural nodes.

Approaching site in these ways presupposes a deficit, a blank space needing to be filled—hence expressions such as 'space activation' and even 'placemaking', which are also vestiges of early modernist thought.

---

[2]This persists despite late twentieth-century developments to critique this notion. During the 1970s and 1980s terms like *genius loci* (Norberg-Schulz, 1979), critical regionalism (Frampton, 1983) and ideas of place identity emerged as a critique of modernist universalisation of site. Together with empirical approaches that placed ecological knowledge into readings of site (McHarg, 1992), these late twentieth-century developments ushered more phenomenological approaches and site-specificity. Largely today they remain in placemaking practices, landscape architecture and urban design as niche modes of practice. These new, increasingly discursive community-oriented practices reify the idea of unrepeatable instances of sited knowledge (Kwon, 2004), and therefore marginalise site-specificity in the globalised neoliberal property market.

Little respect has been given to local ecologies, as land clearance programs, parcelization and grid overlays amongst the existing Aboriginal pathways made way for rose gardens, lawns and suburban housing (Edmonds, 2010). Even less respect has been afforded the Aboriginal custodians of the land themselves who experience ongoing effects of 'spatially practised' colonisation. Emily Potter, literary scholar, claims this marginalisation and erasure enables colonial versions of site to be perpetuated. Through the false idea that Aboriginal people lived only in the outback or city fringes, non-Indigenous domination of city space could survive.

> With all [Aboriginal peoples] 'gone', Australian cities had no need to account for their presence, in spatial, cultural, or political terms. What was discursively constituted was consequently perpetuated in the material form cities took, in their design and construction, and in the laws that governed the use of their spaces. (Potter, 2012, p. 133)

The colonial response to Aboriginality in War'ran (Sydney) was relegation to physical and societal peripheries—to missions and reserves (Aboriginal Welfare, 1937). This practice imposed European spatiality as a means to overpower Indigenous connections to Country (Potter, 2012). For families with one Aboriginal and one European parent, they were relocated away from the missions, leaving behind family, language, culture and Country, to be forcefully assimilated into the white community (Goodall & Cadzow, 2009). These families have been overlooked in Sydney's history, which tells a binary narrative of Aboriginal people either being from missions or taken through the Stolen Generations (Foster, 2018a, 2018b).

> **But some of us found the in-between. Dudbaya'ora: The Hidden Ones (Bodkin, 2013, p. 2) Our Narinya (Living Dreaming) and Garuwanga (Ancestral Dreaming) stories have survived. But is anyone listening? So many decisions are made, projects developed and Country cleared that it appears to local Aboriginal people that, no, no-one is listening.**

In 2018, the New South Wales State government formally acknowledged this erasure: 'Currently, Aboriginal culture is largely missing from the planning process. It is considered when undertaking archaeological investigations and recording heritage but rarely in the design of spaces' (Government Architect NSW, 2018, p. 2). New planning policy has been introduced for the first time, outlining requirements for all State Significant Developments to address Indigenous knowledges.

The silencing and erasure of colonisation continues but we are still here. We exist.

Our cultures are not gone. Our stories are still being told. Our Connections to Country are strong and alive. Sovereignty was never ceded yet we are not consulted about the Country that owns us, the Country that we keep the stories and the knowledges for. Our Mother.

When creative spatial practitioners design, we imagine a future version of our built environment, but we also project an imminent version of ourselves into that place. It is a work of identity creation. The future we envisage is materialised to have an enduring effect in the world, and ongoing impacts on how we see ourselves within it.[3] The constraints we place on our design processes have deep consequences on who we become in that future.

Spatial disciplines start by researching site through drawings, writings and data, through which site analysis is performed. This process tends to produce a fixed understanding of site that is inherently bound up in the biases of the information used, translating them again into new design outcomes. Documents of little interest to the dominant narrative have been routinely overlooked, concealed or destroyed, meaning they are repeatedly neglected in our design methodologies. To extract other

---

[3]This premise is our extrapolation of a constructivist approach, in which site is construed and constructed by the designer who negotiates specific place-bound identities, while simultaneously negotiating identity as fluid (Kwon, 2004). For us this approach is helpful because it conflates manifold qualities of site and identity alongside the designer as co-creator. It remains problematic though, when it effaces the role of design in creating a future identity, and in neglecting effects of marginalisation and erasure within that future urban identity.

(hi)stories we must read between the lines of archives, look for what is omitted and listen for the whispers.

Placemaking practices draw on community consultation to surpass the normative analyses of traditional architecture praxes. Placemaking attempts to transcend the notion of a blank site through privileging local stories or everyday practices. More engaged placemaking practices continue to work through 'adaptive governance' (Folke, Hahn, Olssen, & Norberg, 2005) to maintain and sustain socio-ecological context. It is our position, that even these 'community-engaged' processes perpetuate an erasure and marginalisation within the formation of societal identity precisely through their conceptualisation of 'Site' and what it is that constitutes community. It is not a matter of what we include, but rather a matter of what we continue to overlook or neglect that is the problem.

Country

Instead of considering the colonial notion of 'site', we work with the Aboriginal concepts of Country and Countrys. Country is always capitalised to differentiate it from the English definition, and pluralised it retains its 'y'. In each Indigenous nation, there is a local language word for this concept of Country, each with their own lore, and subtleties of use and meaning.

Country is often misunderstood as being synonymous with land, but it goes far beyond that. It comprises ecologies of plants, animals, water, sky, air and every aspect of the 'natural' environment. Country is a spiritual entity: she is Mother. She is not separate to you: All things are connected, everything is interrelated. Everything you do will affect her and ultimately, come back to you. Kimberley law keeper, David Mowaljarlai explains 'Everything is represented in the ground and in the sky. You can't get away from it, because all is one, and we're in it' (Mowaljarlai & Malnic, 2001, p. 24). Mutijulu Elder Uncle Bob Randall describes his connection to Country: 'To care for my Country, care for my mother, you know to care for everything that is around me, the oneness' (2009). Uncle Bob's people call this 'Kanyini, caring with unconditional love, with a responsibility' (2009).

4 There's No Place Like (Without) Country

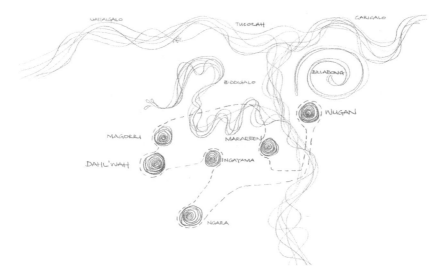

Fig. 4.1 Wann Country (Image by Shannon Foster and Joanne Kinniburgh)

Wann is the name of Country that is now known as Sydney Olympic Park. Bennelong belonged to Wann and there are trees in the mangrove forest old enough to have been there when his feet first squelched through the miluni (mud). The Wanngal[4] have lived there for millenia. Just ten days after the arrival of the British an expedition was sent up the Parramatta River in search of farmland. Elsewhere, the land was too rocky and sandy for growing European crops. Colonists arrived in Wann and renamed the Country 'The Flats' for its expansive mudflats. They found soil enriched by thousands of years of Wanngal nurturing and careful management of the mangrove ecology. Wann's mangroves emitted sulphurous fumes and bred pests like mosquitos. She was considered a wasteland to be 'reclaimed' by a people that had never owned her in the first place (Fig. 4.1).

Wann is still a contested space, not just between Aboriginal custodians and invading colonisers, but also amongst local Sydney Indigenous

---

[4]Wanngal (people of Wann Country).

peoples themselves. While the fact that the Country is known as Wann is not contested, the question remains, to which 'nation group' does she belong? Throughout Sydney there are many different overarching large nations including the D'harawal, Eora, Dharug, Gandangurra, Kur-rin-gai and Yuin. Under these Nations fall the smaller clan groups such as the Wanngal, Cadigal and Bidigal. There is a contemporary necessity to claim land under nation categories and push others out of their connections to that particular Country. We argue that this is based on a westernised, capitalist view that only one group of people can 'own' a place. In this way, it is clear that Country has been colonised alongside Aboriginal knowledges (Martin, 2008). It is widely accepted amongst Aboriginal peoples that an individual cannot own or claim a piece of Country in much the same way that you cannot 'own' your Mother. 'The land owns us. The land grows all of us up' (Randall, 2009). Instead, we belong *to* the Country and it is possible for many peoples to belong to the same Country. This understanding decolonises the notion of 'ownership' of Country and allows the idea that we all belong to Country. This not only reinforces Indigenous epistemologies but also reinstates them back into the practices of Country.

Practices of Country: Miluni

We were invited to design a placemaking intervention in Wann Country as part of a Myer Foundation Grant and a UTS Masters of Architecture design studio subject with 16 students, which we taught in collaboration with registered architect, Daniel Beasly and robotic fabrication specialist, Tran Dang. One option was to 'activate' a 100-year-old heritage-listed, industrial-military shed as a cultural centre and base for Indigenous education programs. On the reclaimed, concrete water's edge, lapped and periodically inundated by the king tide, the site on offer was a colonial armoury. It was a programmatic dead zone in a foreshore that welcomed ferries, heritage rail tours and churned out coffee in paper cups. On the first site visit there, the radio news filled the armoury with the story of thousands of Aboriginal artefacts that had been excavated in the construction of the new South East Light Rail at Moore Park in Sydney. Archaeological items thousands of years old were being destroyed, while a 100-hundred-year-old asbestos-ridden shed of questionable architectural value could not even be painted due to its heritage listing. It was a bewildering and yet familiar message: Aboriginal heritage is only of value when it doesn't interfere with progress or with construction deadlines.

The timing of the radio broadcast was as if the Ancestors were revealing the irony of refurbishing a colonial imposition on their own land for cultural space. Instead of working there, we chose to listen to the contemporary guardians of the Indigenous and environmental education programs nearby and to work with them in the natural environment of the mangroves.

We were powerfully drawn to the Biddigalo (sour or bitter water) of Wann Country. She exists here at Tucorah, where two waters meet. Garigalo (saltwater) and Nattaigalo (sweet water) meet to create the brackish waters of Biddigalo Country. She is the perfect example of overlooked spatial (hi)stories. When you visit her today you find grassy undulating hills, bike paths and picnic areas. Aside from contemporary recreation space, there is very little to encounter of her complex histories and knowledges. There is no evidence whatsoever that Aboriginal people have belonged here, connected to Country since the beginning of time. The remnants that exist are primarily industrial buildings from the early twentieth century. Today the park is an exemplar of western-centric urban development. The mangrove environment is preserved as a recreational 'break out' space for those living and working amongst the concrete, glass and steel of the commercial and residential towers.

The (hi)stories are still there, embedded in the miluni (mud) and this is the name we gave our project, the Miluni Songline. It is the miluni that triggers your sense of smell when you approach her concrete boundaries, leaving you hungry for fish, oysters and crabs. It is the miluni that you can see, brown and densely knotted with the hair roots of the mangroves. So dense that you can walk on it and not sink. You can even bounce if the tide is right and the miluni is floating on a bed of water. It is the sticky miluni that filters the tidal waters that return to the oceans cleaner than when they arrived. Unseen chemicals, oils, fertilisers and pesticides all stick to the miluni and are trapped in a time capsule of sediment layers and wait there to be decomposed by bacteriological processes.

It is also miluni, mud in the form of clay, that we chose as our material. To assist in telling the oldest of Garuwanga (Ancestral stories) we brought the miluni clay to the newest of technologies: a KUKA robotic arm. In the UTS Advanced Fabrication Lab, we negotiated a space of paradox between the predictable precision of robotic 3D-printing and the seemingly contradictory variability of natural clay.

Country as Method: 'Walking Up' and 'Talking Up' Country with Dahl'wah (the Casuarina Tree)

> When women moved through the country gathering food, we walked the trails that the Ancestors had walked and we sang the songs and told the stories of those ancestors, the stories of Country…. Our journeys – far from the random, nomadic wanderings of the European imagination – were ones of purpose, of teaching, of celebration, of caring for Country. Our "work" was a task that sustained and renewed ourselves, our connections to each other and the connections between women and Country. (Kwaymullina, 2017, p. 101)

The Miluni Songline is comprised of six works that each tell the stories of Wann: Dahl'wah (casuarina); Marareen (golden orb weaver spider); Ngara (listen); Magorri (to catch fish); Wugan (raven); and Ngayama (breathe). Each work reveals an important part of the Songline but we will focus on one, the Dahl'wah installation, to unpack the idea of Country as a method by exploring the concepts of 'walking up' and 'talking up' Country.

Performing Country and enacting Country triggers muscle memory: a memory of spirit and soul. To walk/talk her up is to open the connections to her knowledges and her presence. When we speak about her, sing about her and walk with intention on her (regardless of whether there is concrete on her) we are allowing her back to us. We are making space for her and her energies rise up to greet us. She is always there, it is us who get lost on the way. Our ability to connect to her, hear her, feel her and see her goes to sleep and we must wake that up by performing the rituals associated with her. Walking the Songlines, telling the stories and singing the songs all allow us to feel her and know her again. We engage with these principles of 'Country as method' through the stories of Dahl'wah (casuarina tree).

Within the context of 'site' Dahl'wah is a problem. Her tough roots destroy the concrete laid to keep her in her place. Her needle-like leaves incessantly fall, leaving the site 'unseemly'. Dahl'wah's seedlings are spindly and dry like gwibul (dead tree) not luscious and green like the foliage of introduced species. In the documents, our Dahl'wah is reduced to three words: 'natural buffer zone'. She stands like a sentinel between the aquatic and the terrestrial, the Biddigalo (sour, brackish water) and the Nattaigalo (sweet, freshwater), protecting them from each other. On Country, she protects from the damage of urbanisation. She filters the smog of the busy roads and drowns out the dust and noise of construction. She blocks out the sight of trucks barrelling past and the endless windows peering down.

Dahl'wah also protects the Diramu (tree, in this context, the Grey Mangrove) of Wann Country. Now a protected species the Diramu perches precariously inside a large rectangle created by a concrete bund wall and, with only one access point to tidal flow, most of the forest is barely reached by the tidal inundation. Diramu is now dehydrated, malnourished and tired. But Dahl'wah stands tall and tolerant, creating a community on the margins of the wetlands—a space that people may read as a place of deficit and loss but is actually a place of great value, a site of resistance (Hooks, 1990). It is here, within the grove, on the margins of a protected space, that we laid the work to tell Dahl'wah's story.

Talking Up Country

> The telling of stories is part of a process of understanding, of naming up and affirming what is important to Aboriginal life. (Watson 2017, 133)

Dahl'wah is the old women, the Biddi (grandmothers). They are our protectors and they will keep you safe. Stand amongst Dahl'wah and you can still hear the Biddi chatter as the breeze moves through her strange leaves; long, thin and stick-like, resembling pine-needles. As they fall to the ground, they lay here just like the fibres of Biddi's string that have fallen here since time began (Bodkin, 2013). Dahl'wah holds the spirit of our women, strong and proud.

The British eyed her greedily believing her wood to be like that of the oak used to repair their boats after long journeys. They didn't ask her name but gave her new ones: casuarina, swamp oak and 'she'-oak. They tried to use Dahl'wah, but she was too strong, and would not bend to their will. They found her difficult to work with and quite useless so they called her 'she' oak.

For us, Dahl'wah is the site of comfort and refuge—a space for weaving and stringing together, for talking and singing. Nothing grows around her, thanks to her thick carpet of fallen leaves. With no undergrowth, snakes and lizards have no place to find shelter and they will leave you alone. You are safe here, and comfortable, the leaves providing a soft seat. Dahl'wah is the safety tree and babysitter. Tell your children, 'Go to Dahl'wah if you are lost, we can see you there and she will keep you safe until we come back for you'. If you wake in the dark, afraid of the Night Spirits, Dahl'wah's seeds will help to bring you peace. Rub her seed pod in your hands and blow on it one, two, three times. The Bush Spirits will chase the Night Spirits away and your fears will get their feet stuck in the seed capsules. They will bother you no longer.

In the telling, these stories move out of the past and the mouths of those who told them to us, through our own bodies and emerge once more from within us onto Country—in our voices, our exhalations. Our storying becomes spatialised in the present moment, welcomed on the same Country where this practice has endured for countless millennia. The stories are absorbed through the ears and into the bodies of the listeners, who then share the embodiment with the ancestors. This is bringing ourselves into a spatial engagement with Country. This is 'talking up' Country, and why storying as a practice is about more than just conveying information, it is a recursive process of knowledge filtration, communication, connection and return.

D'harawal Storytellers Gawaian Bodkin-Andrews, Fran Bodkin, Gavin Andrews and Gomeroi scholar Alison Whittaker explain that '[t]o meaningfully unlock the varying lessons and layers of meaning requires a much deeper reciprocal interaction between the story, the storyteller, the story-listener, and Country for the story itself over time' (Bodkin-Andrews et al., 2016, p. 481). As we type these stories, we translate this practice from ears and body to one of eyes and mind, and the shared space of encounter becomes dispersed. We are aware that this shift affects the sense of engagement with Country and the shared spatiality. Without a bodily engagement with Country, there is no 'return' and the recursive nature of storying is lost. We share this to bring attention to the rupture in process when we rely simply on knowledge acquisition, on written documents and archives of 'otherness' to tell stories.

Walking Up Country

> The landscapes and the tracks we walk are ancient pathways that have been walked for thousands of years by our first nations people, connection to these tracks and the stories from land and people is a pathway we all should reflect upon as we walk and talk on this land. (Moroney, 2016, p. 5)

Walking up Country is a meditation. You are walking to bring the stories and knowledges of Country up out of the voids of colonisation and back into the sun. Country feels you and responds. This is more than just engaging with Country it is enacting Country, embodying Country, being with, and in, and of, Country, to acknowledge her and energise you both. This is an act of rematriation—returning to mother Country and understanding Country as mother (Muthien, 2018). You are feeling Country and experiencing her Naway (in the now). You are feeling and hearing what she has to say back to you.

For some, being 'on Country' means to be on the Country you belong to. It may also mean being out in the natural environment. But we would argue that Country is always there. We are always 'on Country' and should act accordingly. The layers of concrete, glass and metal have not changed the fact that Country is with us and can be interacted with at any time. To not consider yourself 'on Country' denies her presence: she is always there and we are always a part of her.

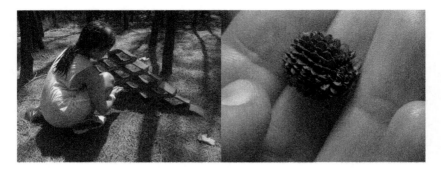

Fig. 4.2 Left: **Dahl'wah,** Yongliang Lio Chen, Luyiyang Louis Yuan and Rick Tian with Shannon Foster, Joanne Paterson Kinniburgh, Daniel Beasly and Tran Dang. Right: **Dahl'wah seed pod** (Photos by Joanne Kinniburgh, 2018)

The installation 'Dahl'wah' (Fig. 4.2) is made up of two low walls, each comprising fifteen 3D-printed, fired clay pieces. Each almond-shaped piece matches the outline of the tiny seed compartments in the casuarina seed pod (Fig. 4.2). Magnified to two hundred times actual size, the hollow pieces are approximately 400 mm long and 200 mm high, and lock together to create low walls that are welcoming and approachable for students as young as five years old.

Because of Dahl'wah's ability to inhibit the growth of other plants around her, the work is visible from beyond the trees but it must be approached to be examined and understood. To do so you must leave the designated walkway. The surface changes from crushed stone aggregate to fine brown leaves, and you feel a shift resonate in your body. You slow down and move more softly. As you make contact with the ground, you press into it ever so slightly, and it rises up reciprocally around your imprint, in a thickening of the connection to the earth. You are literally 'walking up' Country.

The lack of any undergrowth means you can see the clay pieces amongst the trees, but it also means there is no one path to the work, and no straight line will take you directly there. There are a multitude of possibilities and your eyes begin the work of scanning the trees to find a way through. Your ocular muscles must work to register the trunks of every tree, to note their verticality and where they have impediments to movement. You project yourself mentally through the trees, and in doing so, you begin to see one pathway more clearly and brightly through the forest. It isn't a matter of deciding on each step as you go, but a matter of knowing and seeing your entire path from the outset. Your eyes, your proprioceptors ... they are 'walking up' Country.

In the environmental and Indigenous education programs held on Wann Country, students can interact with the walls as they encounter Dahl'wah's story. The sounds are dampened in the forest, heightening the auditory senses to the voices of Biddi. As the students sit on the soft carpet of fallen leaves, their bodies press down, further thickening the connection to the earth underneath. They enact culture, as they use this place to reflect upon their worries, engaging haptically through the spiky seed pod in their hands, and literally leave their worries behind as they place it in the wall for Dahl'wah to heal. The wall then performs not just as an archive of the worries of each of the students but also as a guide for the re-enactment of cultural practices, as each student uses the seed pod to perform culture in the same ways that local D'harawal children[5] have done since the beginning of time here in Wann.

In each of these embodied ways, we bring ourselves into connection with Country. 'Walking up' doesn't refer to a resurrection of a Country that we fix with our preconceived ideas of what is required, but an awakening of ourselves to exist in connection with Country and then to understand. And as we walk, we also talk and sing ...

Talking up Country,
Walking up Country,
... is to awaken her and make your presence felt by Country.

Country as Method: Overlooked Spatial Histories with Wugan (Raven)

history/past (story and archives);
action/present (praxis and being);
futurity (becoming)

---

[5]Other nations with connection to Wann may have similar practices.

> Our Elders, grandfathers and uncles have come to Wann for generations to harvest mangrove wood for boomerangs and tools. They dreamed of a time when the world would want to hear their stories but they wondered, who would be here to tell them? Would anyone remain? They left footsteps deep enough to find, indelible marks on the Country that hold the memories, the footsteps, the stories of my family. They are embedded in the wood of their boomerangs and they fly through the air and return over time. I am here to catch them and throw them once more. This Country on the periphery: an abandoned billabong. Full of culture and story, footsteps and heartbeats.

We have articulated our position that when we design, we manifest the future, and that our disciplinary methods and the kinds of information we access have an impact on the futures we can imagine. We particularly critique both the disciplinary conventions and the sources we typically consult for their role in overlooking and marginalisation of any stories that do not fit the mould of neoliberal productive consumer who is white, heteronormative, male, neuro-typical, able-bodied and young. When designing public space, seldom is anything else designed for unless it is an explicit part of a brief.

We look now to another Miluni Songline work. We project ourselves towards an imagined, inclusive future in the Wugan installation, by effacing linear narratives of place, and spatially talking up Country. This work exposes the multi-layered overlooked histories of Wann Country. Wugan is located in a clearing on the banks of a man-made billabong, surrounded by a ring of Dahl'wah trees in the Badu Mangroves. It is comprised of four nested rings of tiles: the largest is 320 tiles lapped to form a circle 7200 mm in diameter; the smallest is 70 tiles, a diameter of 1500 mm. Each ring gently touches the adjacent rings, to create an asymmetrical pattern on the earth in the clearing (Fig. 4.3). The circular tiles are each 150 mm in diameter and 20 mm thick, most in fired terracotta, and some interspersed amongst the rings are unfired clay, which slowly melt back into the earth with each rain (Fig. 4.3). The tiles are robotically with objects that reflect the numerous overlooked stories the students encountered: the stories they did not find in the published histories. Wugan becomes a newly consolidated midden that draws attention to the middens and sacred sites that have been destroyed, built on

Fig. 4.3 Left: **Wugan**, by Tiffany Kuo, Jesse Del Valle and Kevin Chen with Shannon Foster, Joanne Paterson Kinniburgh, Daniel Beasly and Tran Dang. Right: **Wugan Detail**, showing the work of bull ants to move pieces, and unfired tiles melting back into the earth a month after installation (Photos by Joanne Kinniburgh, 2018)

top of or damaged in the processes of city building here. Some tiles are blank, leaving space for the stories yet to be discovered.

> We would eat oyster sandwiches, my father and I. Oysters from a jar of salty water. A jar that would land here when they made Country a rubbish dump. As we ate, Dad would tell stories of shell middens long gone not knowing that in the telling of these stories he was breathing life into culture. Despite the silence outside the walls of our house, on the fibro frontier of Kai-ee-magh (Georges River), inside the walls (and our hearts and minds) echoed a thousand voices singing our stories. The stories are there, walked into Country in a long forgotten time. They are now walked up out of the Country as I trace the tiles of Wugan, telling our stories in this peripheral, "insignificant" space. Each tile is the footstep of a story: a seed, a jar, a leaf, a shell. A story untold. Each circle is a walk enacted repeatedly for generations. And Wugan melts into the miluni and becomes a story too.

Conclusion

In this chapter and on the Miluni Songline we critique traditional architectural and placemaking approaches to site through Australian Indigenous 'Practices of Country', including Walking Up Country,

Talking up Country & prioritising the overlooked spatial (hi)stories of Indigenous Australians.

Key lessons on integrating Country into placemaking practice:

- Embedding knowledge of Country reduces the damaging effects of colonisation on Aboriginal cultures, while offering a learning opportunity that undoes the silencing and erasure of Aboriginal voices in the contemporary urban context.
- The constraints we place on our processes of design have deep consequences on who we become in the future. It is not a matter of what we include, but rather a matter of what it is that we overlook or neglect that is the problem.
- Integrating Country recognises the importance of Aboriginal people and cultures within placemaking practices throughout Australia, adding a richness to spatial experience and stories of place for all those who encounter it.
- Bodily engagement is a prerequisite for a recursive cultural process that involves story, storyteller, story-listener and Country. This cannot be achieved from books, online or in classrooms and offices.

Long after the installation is over, the podcasts, articles and interviews are done and the students have all gone their separate ways for the holidays we return to the Songline to see how Country has received our Miluni Songline. We find bull ants have colonised the concentric discs of Wugan, making a nest and tunnels through and under it, flipping and cracking some of the pieces, while spiders have built webs and created homes within the pieces of another work, the Marareen weaving wall. This reclaiming of the intervention by these overlooked occupants brings the project full circle. We have centred the needs of the overlooked. Every spider's web and channel of the bull ant's nest is testament to the enduring Narinya (living Dreaming) of this Country. This Country knows miluni and it welcomes the projects home with open arms.

> **I have worked on many cross-cultural collaborations that have appeared, from the outset at least, to be focussed on**

prioritising Indigenous knowledges and perspectives but I have often ended up feeling even more marginalised or erased in the process. Working on the Miluni Songline project was different.

Through Miluni we are heard, centred and valued
Miluni is evidence that we are still here
We are still rising up out of the earth generation after generation
Miluni tells us that we are not alone in this journey
That others have come along with us
Miluni is more than clay fired signposts directing you to stories of Country
It invites you to come with us
To walk up Country, and talk up Country.

References

Aboriginal welfare initial conference of commonwealth and state aboriginal authorities. (1937). Canberra, 21st–23rd April. Commonwealth of Australia. Digitalised by AIATSIS Library. Retrieved from https://aiatsis.gov.au/sites/default/files/catalogue_resources/20663.pdf Accessed 16 Feb 2019.

Bodkin, F. (2013). *D'harawal Climate and Natural Resources.* Sussex Inlet, NSW: Envirobook.

Bodkin-Andrews, G., Bodkin, F., Andrews, G., & Whittaker, A. (2016). Mudjil'dya'djurali Dabuwa'wurrata (how the white waratah became red): D'harawal storytelling and Welcome to Country "controversies" [online]. *AlterNative: An International Journal of Indigenous Peoples, 12*(5), 480–497.

Edmonds, P. (2010). *Urbanizing frontiers: Indigenous peoples and settlers in 19th century Pacific Rim cities* (p. 85). Vancouver: UBC Press.

Folke, C., Hahn, T., Olsson, P., & Norberg, J. (2005). Adaptive governance of social-ecological systems. *Annual Review of Environment and Resources, 30*, 441–473. https://doi.org/10.1146/annurev.energy.30.050504.144511.

Foster, S. (2018a). *Resisting assimilation* @IndigenousX. Retrieved from https://indigenousx.com.au/shannon-foster-resisting-assimilation/.

Foster, S. (2018b). White bread dreaming. In A. Heiss (Ed.), *Growing up aboriginal.* Carlton, VIC: Black Inc.

Frampton, K. (1983). Towards a critical regionalism: Six points for an architecture of resistance. In H. Foster (Ed.), *The anti-aesthetic: Essays on postmodern culture* (pp. 17–34). New York: New Press.

Goodall, H., & Cadzow, A. (2009). *Rivers and resilience: Aboriginal people on Sydney's Georges River*. Sydney, NSW: UNSW Press.

Government Architect New South Wales. (2018). *The Sydney Ochre Grid. Design Policy Document*. http://www.governmentarchitect.nsw.gov.au/projects/the-sydney-ochre-grid.

Hooks, B. (1990). *Yearning: Race, gender, and cultural politics*. Boston, MA: South End Press.

Kwaymullina, A. (2017). The creators of the future: Women, law and telling stories in country. In P. Dudgeon, J. Herbert, J. Milroy, & D. Oxenham (Eds.), *Us women, our ways, our world* (pp. 96–105). Broome, WA: Magabala Book.

Kwon, M. (2004). *One place after another: Site-specific art and locational identity*. Cambridge and London: MIT Press.

Martin, K. (2008). *Please knock before you enter: Aboriginal regulation of outsiders and the implications for researchers*. Brisbane, QLD: Post Pressed.

Moreton-Robinson, A. (2013). Towards an Australian Indigenous women's standpoint theory: A methodological tool. *Australian Feminist Studies, 28*(78), 331–347.

Moroney, K. (2016). *The language of country Australian Literacy Educators Association*. Retrieved from https://www.alea.edu.au/documents/item/1271.

Mowaljarlai, D., & Malnic, J. (2001). *Yorro Yorro everything standing up alive: Spirit of the Kimberley*. Broome, WA: Magabala Books.

McHarg, I. (1992 [1969]). *Design with nature*. New York: Wiley.

Muthien, B. (2018). *Rematriation of women-centred (feminist) Indigenous knowledge gift economy*. Retrieved from http://www.gift-economy.com/articlesAndEssays/rematriation.pdf.

Norberg-Schulz, C. (1979). *Genius Ioci: Towards a phenomenology of architecture*. New York: Rizzoli.

Potter, E. (2012). Introduction: Making Indigenous place in the Australian city. *Postcolonial Studies, 15*(2), 131–142. https://doi.org/10.1080/13688790.2012.708315.

Randall, B. (2009). *The land owns us*. YouTube, 6:14. Retrieved March 1, 2019, from https://www.youtube.com/watch?v=w0sWIVR1hXw.

Watson, I. (2017). Standing our ground and telling one true story. In P. Dudgeon, J. Herbert, J. Milroy, & D. Oxenham (Eds.), *Us women, our ways, our world* (pp. 128–143). Magabala Book: Broome, WA.

5

Community Engagement: What Is It?

Melissa Nursey-Bray

Introduction

Community engagement is a fundamental process used throughout the world to attract and involve stakeholders and communities' opinion and participation in various programmes. Engagement may occur in a reactive way, "after the horse has bolted", or it may be proactive engagement—the seeking of advice by a proponent or feedback on ideas about a development, a programme or an event. It can be superficial or "deep". Hence, community engagement as a practice can be as diverse as the tools used to implement it. In this chapter, the key tenets and process of doing community engagement are explored, and various case studies and examples used to highlight the points made.

M. Nursey-Bray (✉)
Geography, Environment and Population, University of Adelaide, North Terrace, SA, Australia
e-mail: melissa.nursey-bray@adelaide.edu.au

© The Author(s) 2020
D. Hes and C. Hernandez-Santin (eds.), *Placemaking Fundamentals for the Built Environment*, https://doi.org/10.1007/978-981-32-9624-4_5

What Is Community

The very first step in any form of engagement then is to understand what the community is. This will determine the modes of engagement that are used to progress it. Scholars have debated the nature of community for a long time—Hillery argues that there are 100 or so definitions of community. Benedict Andersen in his seminal work *Imagined Communities* reflects on the power of nationalism to define and prescribe a sense of community that transcends physical nature, but is located in the mind and heart. Social media affords an additional take on this idea with thousands of community networks online now guiding and influencing people's lives. The idea of communities of practice, pioneered by Etienne Wenger offers another window into how to interest "community". He argues that community is about working together as a practice. For example, people who are part of a Landcare group are mobilised around the practice of undertaking activities that protect the land. Or surf lifesavers are mobilised as a community of practice around lifesaving. For some, community is defined by culture—in Australia, many people identify as being part of a local to international Indigenous community.

The key questions in engagement will be who are the people most affected by and most likely to be interested in the project? Their interests may vary from being affected by a decision, to wanting to make a difference to a project, a community or a region, and to having specific information or having the experience or knowledge to contribute to outcomes.

The idea of community has been defined as a place, as in a territory or place-based community where people have something in common, or there is a shared geography. Communities of interest are another way of understanding what a community is, where people share a common characteristic other than place. They are linked together by factors such as religious belief, sexual orientation, occupation or ethnic origin. Communities are also formed via attachment, and they are communities of meaning (Cohen, 1985). Tonnie famously relates the notion of community to the idea of gemeinschaft, which is basically a group of people that share common bonds around traditions, beliefs or objectives, while Bartle (n.d.) states that community is essentially a collection of human individuals organised as a sociocultural system within six dimensions relevant to community and culture. These dimensions include: (i) technological, (ii) economic, (iii) political, (iv) institutional (social), (v) aesthetic-value and (vi) belief-conceptual.

Others define community as "a set of interrelationships among social institutions in a locality" (Lee & Newby, 1983, p. 19) while Kaufman notes that "Community is, first, a place, and second, a configuration as a way of life, both as to how people do things and what they want, to say, their institutions and goals" (Kaufman in Lee & Newby, 1983, p. 30). Johnson (1986, p. 692) argues that community "is a collection of people who share a common territory and meet their basic physical and social needs through daily interaction with one another". The idea of connection, networks, geographical co-location and common interests are all themes in definitions of community.

Today, virtual communities are another type of community that form a central part of contemporary society. Social media platforms such as Facebook, Instagram and Twitter are obvious examples, but many others exist allowing individuals to be part of diverse activities and communities, from religious, gaming, social/dating and professional communities such as LinkedIn.

Community Engagement

While communities exist in multiple forms and cultures, the question remains—why engage with them and to what purpose? Who is to be engaged, when is the right time to do it and how/what techniques will be applied? For those doing the engaging, asking the community for their opinion may just be a rubber stamp needed to secure programme legitimacy or to obtain feedback that can be used to value add to the project and its evolution per se. As Koehler and Koontz (2008, p. 143) note of citizen participation in environmental management, "Local citizens are seen as essential participants in collaborative environmental management because they can provide vital information about the area's natural and socio-political systems as well as support for measures to address non-point source pollution". The need for engagement has also been partly driven by the fact that as societies and communities we face problems of great complexity ('wickedness') that will require multiple solutions driven by multiple agents—community, industry and government together (Head, 2007). For placemakers, the idea of engagement offers an opportunity to articulate a dialogue between the place itself and the public and to enable them to support regions and communities to develop their own social and economic capacities and build social capital (Reddel & Woolcock, 2004) thus enabling placemaking in practice by mobilising attachment.

However, there is no commonly agreed definition of community engagement. Other terms such as consultation, empowerment, participation, collaboration and stakeholder engagement all signify similar intent. This has not stopped people trying to capture the essence of what it is—it can be "mutual communication and deliberation that occurs between government and citizens that allows citizens and government to participate mutually in the formulation of policy and the provision of government services" (Cavaye, 2004, p. 3). Dare, Schirmer, and Vanclay (2008, p. 2) describe community engagement as: "A wide range of activities in which stakeholders exchange information and/or negotiate mutually acceptable actions". These actions range from providing simple information signs on plantation boundaries to establishing multi-stakeholder dialogues that lead to joint action on issues such as game management or road funding. For placemaking, engagement occurs in the context of the planning, design, management and programming of shared use spaces. These are just a few of hundreds of definitions; however, almost all include the idea of an interaction between community and an external body(ies).

Overall the defining features of community engagement strategies are that they start from the articulation of a community's own needs and priorities rather than being externally directed that they invest in local autonomy and leadership, are flexible and serve local needs and provide balanced partnerships between all parties based on mutual trust and respect. Those working on placemaking projects need to commit to working with the community rather than doing it for them and ensure that activities at all stages of the placemaking process activate deep and enduring connection and engagement with the place. However, the process of engagement is not a simple one, and many challenges accrue in implementing engagement projects, such as placemaking. The Australian Centre for Excellence (Morris, 2012) in a study based on a national survey of Australian local governments synthesised these challenges as a series of issues around (i) developing a supportive culture, (ii) the translation of policies into practice, (iii) ensuring there are adequate support structures and that they are resourced properly, (iv) being clear about the boundaries and (v) understanding the limits of community consultation. They also found there are extra challenges when trying to effectively meet the needs of rural, remote and Indigenous communities and in being able to build staff capacity and to give them the skills to actually do community engagement.

A major challenge for placemakers is the decision of what level of engagement should occur; community engagement often occurs on a continuum, from the not very engaged to the very engaged. Arnstein's Ladder of Citizen Participation (1965) argues that there are degrees of participation and therefore empowerment for communities. She starts with what she calls forms of non-participation (manipulation, therapy) to forms of tokenism which imply some bounded engagement (inform, consult and placate), finishing with higher forms of empowerment and power (partnership, delegated power and control).

Arnstein's work laid the foundations for multiple discussions and reflection on the nature and business of community engagement. One organisation, in particular, the International Association for Public Participation (IAP2) has taken her ideas to new levels, developing an international set of principles and their own continuum that provides the basis for engagement practitioners worldwide (see http://www.iap2.org/). The IAP2 presents operating principles that should be adhered to in undertaking community engagement. This includes ensuring that you are flexible, open and transparent, accessible, that relationships are consolidated and connected at multiple scales, open to all views and cultures and committed to continuous feedback and due diligence to name a few. Ultimately, their idea of public participation is based on the belief that those who are affected by a decision have a right to be involved in the decision-making process and the promise that the public's contribution will influence the decision.

Their continuum starts with an inform stage, through to empower as shown in the summary below:

Inform: To provide the public with balanced and objective information to assist them in understanding the problem, alternatives, opportunities and/or solutions.
Consult: To obtain public feedback on analysis, alternatives and/or decisions.
Involve: To work directly with the public throughout the process to ensure that public concerns and aspirations are consistently understood and considered.
Collaborate: To partner with the public in each aspect of the decision including the development of alternatives and the identification of the preferred solution.
Empower: To place final decision-making in the hands of the public (https://www.iap2.org.au/Tenant/C0000004/00000001/files/IAP2_Public_Participation_Spectrum.pdf).

There are many successful examples of the application of this continuum, one being the application of the IAP2 in Kapunda South Australia, on a local archaeology project. In this case, De Leiuen and Arthure (2016) found that the implementation of the collaboration via stages of the continuum provided clear guidance on how to engage with stakeholders in Kapunda, but also enabled them to build genuine relationships between themselves, community members and their descendants. They used it as a mechanism to build place identity in Kapunda around its history. In Adelaide, the South Australian government has established the "Your Say" programme which is a one-stop portal for community engagement. It specifically aligns with the IAP2 spectrum and is based on six engagement principles/ideas which aim to provide a consistent approach across government and to guide best practice. The government adheres to the following principles: (i) we know why we are engaging, (ii) we know who to engage, (iii) we know the history, (iv) we start together, (v) we are genuine and (vi) we are relevant and engaging. For examples of the wide-ranging types of engagements, the government undertakes they have created a website which offers an online portal for engagement: https://yoursay.sa.gov.au/initiatives/yoursay-engagements.

Doing Community Engagement

Community engagement remains a concept that is utilised as a continuous by industry, government and community groups and aligned very often with the IAP2 Spectrum. In making decisions however around what tools to use and who to engage, stakeholder analyses need to be undertaken. This process will assist placemakers to establish what the community is going to get out of it and to ensure that deeper engagement can occur—important given, it is usually logistically impossible to engage ALL of the community.

A stakeholder is an individual or collective group that is likely to be affected directly or indirectly, positively or negatively by the programme/project. Many stakeholders also are likely to have enough access to or influence of the use of resources and power, to create some impact on or affect the outcome of the decision.

Stakeholder analysis requires two things: (i) identification of the key stakeholders and (ii) assessment of their relative influence and power. Placemakers need to ask themselves, (a) are there any stakeholders likely to have a predetermined position about the project/proposal?, (b) what are their likely underlying interests and concerns, (c) what level of interest is each stakeholder group likely to have and (d) what impact could they have on the project/process at hand. This process will help identify who is of highest priority for engagement and what are the best modes of engagement to employ to build a strong and rigorous placemaking process.

This point echoes those made and discussed in Chapter 4 that considers how to engage the marginalised, the disempowered, the hidden, the shy, the "other" and, in Chapter 3, the non-human.

Tools and Techniques

While engagement itself needs to establish its baselines and parameters as discussed above, once these frameworks have been decided the next step is to consider what forms and types of engagement may be useful. Unsurprisingly, there are a multiplicity of techniques for community engagement available, and this is the point at which it is crucial to map the type of community you need to engage with and what would be the most appropriate forms of engagement. For example, if your demographic shows you that you are dealing with a community that has low levels of literacy, then written forms of engagement would not work. If you are working in a remote region where time is of the essence and getting to and from places a matter of driving for long time periods, then a public meeting would probably not be the best investment of resources.

It is important at this point to differentiate between short-term and long-term engagement. For example, a short-term engagement may be galvanised around a specific issue (like a road proposal or a mine establishment) while others will be long-term campaigns catalysed around a specific goal (e.g. reduction of breast cancer, getting people to recycle, building more cycle paths in a city or getting people to do tests for breast, bowel or prostate cancer).

Fortunately, today, there exist a very diverse suite of tools and techniques which can be harnessed to engage the community at multiple scales. In this next section, a snapshot of a range of these is presented. The application of a range of tools (within budgetary constraints) will enable the practitioner to accommodate different levels of interest, time availability and preferred styles of receiving or giving information.

The Usual Suspects—Common Engagement Approaches

While there are many new techniques that have helped revitalise community engagement, especially in a world where attention is in scarce supply the "old faithfuls" still work. There are a range of conventional and still relevant techniques which can be used, both written and face to face, that enable in-depth interaction with the community via public meetings, focus groups, interviews and other face-to-face interactions. Table 5.1 summarises a range of these techniques, with an example of where they have been used in practice in Australia.

Beyond these well-known techniques, a few other approaches merit discussion as they are particularly useful for placemaking engagement practice. One of these is digital engagement: today, there is also a wide and diverse range of digital engagement tools that are used to gauge community concern, get their feedback or develop genuine engagement on an ongoing issue (Barr, 2011; McDonald, Hickey, & Reynolds, 2016; The Digital Engagement Guide [https://www.digitalengagement.info/section/techniques/]) that offers a wide range of helpful information, tips and case studies on how to implement digital engagement strategies, including advice on blogging, Twitter, YouTube and interactive websites. As a mode of ensuring place centredness, digital applications are crucial as most Australians are regular users of digital technologies (Bakke, 2010; Tomitsch & Haeusler, 2015). The embeddedness and ubiquity of digital technologies mean they are crucial to future and current engagement practice (Deuze, Blank, & Speers, 2012). A creative digital storytelling initiative in Toronto shows the power of digital engagement tools, building leadership and placemaking for women (Brushwood-Rose, 2016). Another example of digital engagement for placemaking includes situated voting technologies which have been used as a means of collecting feedback from citizens around local contexts, for example energy by the installation of an urban screen in a public square (Hespanhol, Parker, Zhou, & Tomitsch, 2018). Further discussion of digital placemaking can be found in Chapter 13.

While face-to-face engagement remains important (Scruby, Canales, Ferguson, & Gregory, 2017), digital placemaking initiatives such as these provide opportunities not only to value add to other engagement mechanisms but also to create inclusive city making within local areas.

Citizen science is another engagement mechanism particularly suited to building placemaking strategies as it literally and often physically engages the local community on key issues. They offer the opportunities for sustained engagement that facilitates a deep connection to place, but also the type of dynamism that assists in activating place

Table 5.1 Summary of engagement approaches

Engagement approach	Benefits	Disadvantages	Useful tools or case studies
Paper-based approaches such as flyers, newsletters, fact sheets	Can access people in remote areas Can be accessed in public sites such as libraries, council offices	Many people miss seeing these outputs and hence miss the opportunity to comment Literacy and access issues may prevent dissemination	City of Newcastle, NSW has a PlaceMakers Toolkit, which provides a series of paper-based techniques to undertake engagement around placemaking
Art and digital storytelling	Interactive Engaging Encouraging development of a common vision	Challenging if participants lack confidence in their creative skills Sometimes difficult to interpret their intent or message from their outputs	Vox Pop Sharing Stories: via focussing on attachment to place, the Sharing Stories Foundation, Australia uses digital storytelling techniques and art to build community engagement around Indigenous children school education and assists in building digital literacy acquisition, self-representational storytelling, cultural maintenance, capacity building and fulfilment of standard curriculum requirements

(continued)

Table 5.1 (continued)

Engagement approach	Benefits	Disadvantages	Useful tools or case studies
Mapping	Can help structure complex ideas Assist in disseminating ideas of giving feedback to the community. Help people see and understand their community in different ways Stimulates discussion	Maybe hard to understand or interpret some of the ways the mapping evolves Sometimes ideas, which cannot be actioned, will emerge, and lift community expectations	Dakota County, USA—place-making project designed to assist in updating the East Lake Byllesby Regional Park Master Plan, used social pin-point a digital platform to get community feedback by utilisation of two interactive maps (https://www.socialpinpoint.com/case-study-place-making/)
Focus groups/workshops/public meetings	A useful way of bringing together a few specific individuals or many who have a common concern can support short or long-term engagement programmes Offer opportunities for deeper engagement Resource effective and timely	Can get dominated by a few individuals Requires tight facilitation Can result in conflict	Focus groups in rural Australia about how young people engage with place Public meetings in Kangaroo island around a port development that affects attachment to place

(continued)

Table 5.1 (continued)

Engagement approach	Benefits	Disadvantages	Useful tools or case studies
Websites	Have facility to present a lot of information all together Can provide portals to map community feedback	Not everyone has equal access to the Internet Not everyone has digital skills/literacy Can be quite resource-intensive	Landsborough Draft PlaceMaking Master Plan, in the Sunshine Coast Council, used a website to advertise and get feedback on its place-making plan (https://haveyoursay.sunshinecoast.qld.gov.au/landsborough-place-making-master-plan)
Surveys	Surveys are useful when quantitative data or "evidence" is needed Theoretical breadth or wide scope can be achieved	Often there is a small—a 10–20% response rate so not always as representative as wished for Designing and implementation is very time consuming Often expensive	2500 residents of the Wabash Heartland Region in Indiana, USA, responded to a place-making survey. This survey provides the Wabash Heartland Innovation Network (WHIN) a solid foundation to begin its work in convening and catalysing the region through the Regional Cultivation Initiative
Committees	Enables broad representation of stakeholders Provides ongoing access to community Helps disseminate key messages/get feedback into placemaking processes	Committee members do not always feedback to their constituents People can't always attend Not always culturally appropriate	Citizen committee in Australian local government, and include: advisory committees, delegated committees, not-for-profit incorporated committees of management and grassroots committees such as "friends" groups

attachment over the long term. They are also a rich source of information and possibilities for increased awareness and participation (Follett & Strezov, 2015; Silvertown, 2009; Thiel et al., 2014). They are very diverse and can take multiple forms, from species counts and biological sampling and monitoring, training and education programmes, workshops and focus groups to name a few. Many citizen science programmes also use digital technologies such as the Internet to promote their programmes, encourage participation and showcase information collected (Aristeidou, Scanlon, & Sharples, 2017; Mullen, Newman, & Thompson, 2013; Verhagen, Swen, Feldberg, & Merikivi, 2015). These technologies utilise applications to promote projects, improve scientific endeavour and make participation easier and more accessible across wide geographical locations (Jennett, Eveleigh, Mathieu, Ajani, & Cox, 2013, p. 2).

Citizen science offers specific advantages in building placemaking by engaging citizens in an active way and giving them ownership of the issue at hand. In many cases, this has encouraged the development and maintenance of green spaces in cities and/or raised awareness about key issues. Phadke, Manning, and Burlager (2015) highlight the utility of a citizen science programme to build adaptation capacity for under-represented and socio-economically disadvantaged groups in Saint Paul Minnesota. They engaged under-represented communities in climate change adaptation decision-making using a neighbourhood consensus conference model. This enabled them to build trust and social capital as well as inviting new community members to voice their concerns and have conversations about their climate change adaptation concerns and priorities. A citizen science project on intergenerational knowledge sharing along the Pacific Northwest coast of Canada used storytelling workshops, mapping sessions, species counts, monitoring and participant-driven photo-elicitation to place community at the centre of the project—actors rather than observers. As knowledge producers, these forms of engagement ensured that stakeholders felt their knowledge was valued, represented in decision-making and community voices heard. In such ways, citizen science can play a transformative role in engagement practice but also democratises the forms of enquiry (McAteer, 2018).

Additional Skills

Mapping an engagement strategy with the appropriate tools is crucial, but in practice, being able to manage community members and expectations necessitates the deployment of two other more specific skills: cultural engagement and conflict management. In most cases, the community is unlikely to be homogeneous and ensuring differentiation of techniques and that they are culturally appropriate, or a good fit will amplify the success of the engagement. Similarly, especially in navigating engagement on contentious issues, being able to manage stakeholder conflict or upset/outrage is another core skill. The next section provides some starting points around how to approach these two key elements.

Engaging Different Cultures

Given the influence of globalisation and the multi-cultural nature of most cities and regions, effective engagement must consider the cultural context within which it is to occur. For example, in Australia, a key cultural group that must be considered is Australia's Aboriginal and Torres Straits Islanders. In any consultation, local Indigenous groups need to be consulted, yet there are very specific means by which this engagement can occur and what would be considered appropriate in each circumstance.

Basic principles of engagement would include acknowledgement of the original traditional owners of that region at every meeting and/or inviting the local group to welcome everyone to country. Country for Indigenous peoples represents the boundary of the original nation that existed prior to colonisation and to which those groups will have maintained an ongoing affiliation. Country represents not just the physical boundary of the territory but also the emotional, social and cultural knowledge that pertains to that region, including traditional lore. Under the *Native Title Act 1993*, which is a Commonwealth Act, all proponents are legally required to seek advice from the native title owners as part of any engagement process and see if it will affect or compromise native title interests. Engagement with Indigenous communities must go beyond the superficial; thus, management mechanisms must build levels of cross-cultural literacy to ensure effective engagement occurs (see Chapter 4 for a longer discussion and case study on engagement with First Nations).

There also exist a wide range of Indigenous engagement protocols across Australia, but there are some key principles which will always be useful. These include:

- Acknowledge the diversity of Indigenous groups in the region and identify who they are, do not assume or apply the same techniques to every group. Seek in the first instance to identify the particular circumstances/needs of the particular Indigenous group/s in that region.
- Ensure the meeting is held in places that Indigenous people can get to.
- Make sure/identify the appropriate person to be part of the engagement process.
- Where possible, involve Indigenous mentors/advisors to assist in giving guidance on how best to discuss the issues at hand.
- Be aware that there are cultural sensitivities around who holds and keeps knowledge and the different roles men and women play. Develop interest and trust in one another's forms of knowledge. Consider protocols for the appropriate use of knowledge.
- Face-to-face engagement will obtain the best results.
- Build, work through and maintain relationships. Process is as important as the outcome, and since relationships are highly important to Indigenous people, outcomes are difficult without good relationships.
- Try to understand each Indigenous group's context: culture, values, histories, geography, community composition, leadership and poverty can all affect aspirations, issues and relationships. Further, be aware that internal community structures and politics play a role, just as they do within agencies.
- Compare "interests" and seek common interest. What are each party's aspirations and what underlying needs do these represent?
- Recognise that governance systems and associated issues differ for each party and that this can create logistical challenges. The parties have different spokespeople (with different systems of authorisation

and accountability) and different decision-making structures, processes and protocols. They are responsible for different topics and at different scales. While Indigenous organisations can play a valuable coordinating and advisory role at large geographical scales, traditional owners can speak only for their own country and feel compromised by expectations that they work through representatives. The processes of engagement and decision-making adopted must suit Indigenous decision-making structures and timeframes, not be forced into those of agencies.
- Start modestly and do research on what protocols and engagement guides are available to help frame what type and kind of engagement can be undertaken.

Conflict Management

Any engagement process has the potential to cause or face conflict. Stakeholders may hold passionate views on the subject or object to the way in which the engagement is being navigated. Stakeholders may have long-standing feuds or differences with each other. Part and parcel then of undertaking effective engagement are developing confidence in dealing with conflict. A moderator or facilitator who can deal with conflict will be able to get the most out of the engagement and sometimes can use the conflict to build deeper outcomes, once grievances have been aired—and heard. A conflict per se can be understood at one level as an incompatible interaction between at least two actors, whereby one of the actors' experiences damage, and the other actor causes this damage intentionally or ignores it. In engagement practice, the conflict can also be in between perspectives on different world views or about the perception of the impacts the suggested issue will have. Key to understanding and resolving conflict is to understand its causes which can be located within the information provided or over resources, relationships, interests, structure and values. The conflict may be intrapersonal, interpersonal, groups, culture, regional or international. In Australia, conflict may occur in major infrastructure projects such as the construction of a road, a marina or an entertainment/sports centre. It may occur over the removal of trees for development or the establishment of bike paths. Conflict may occur in response to proposals to develop marine parks or establish wind farms; the possibilities are endless.

However, conflict is not to be feared and conflict and change are natural parts of life and embedded in every agency, organisation and nation. As Knope notes, "These people are members of the community that care about where they live. So what I hear when I'm being yelled at is people caring loudly at me". Conflict resolution provides fora by which to find a solution or an agreed compromise between two or more parties over an issue. In engagement practice, this may mean navigating broad strategic outputs to confront an outraged member of the community in a public meeting. Conflict resolution seeks to produce a solution that all parties can agree to, in as timely way as possible and with minimum harm/upset to all concerned. Other benefits of undertaking conflict resolution are that it usually enables all participants to learn more about the ideas, beliefs and backgrounds of each other and hence obtain insights into each other's motivations. Conflict is seen as a normal part of life. Exploring alternatives as part of the conflict resolution process is also helpful as is setting up channels of communication that are open and transparent, hence building mutual trust.

There are many tools available to manage conflict. One of these is to undertake a conflict analysis which can assist in developing the boundaries and parameters of the conflict. These analyses help placemakers to analyse conflict by working out community needs (what we must have), community interests (what we really want) and positions (what we say we want). In so doing, the gaps between perception and reality become more articulated and stakeholders can "see" each other more clearly. Conflict trees enable practitioners to visualise causes and impacts so that the key actors can identify the core problem of the conflict and find out ways to resolve it. The Harvard approach emphasises the difference between positions (what people say they want) and interests (why people want what they say they want) and is based on the presumption that conflicts can be resolved when actors focus on interests instead of positions and develop jointly accepted criteria to deal with these differences.

Alternatively, the conflict transformation approach sees conflicts as destructive or constructive interactions, an interaction of positive and negative energies. Emphasis is given on understanding different perceptions, and the social and cultural contexts in which reality is constructed by the actors involved in the conflict. Constructive conflict transformation seeks to empower actors and support recognition between them. Finally, conflict mapping or needs-fears mapping allows for a clear mapping of the concerns, issues, needs and fears of stakeholders, which as part of the process also facilitates identification of similarities.

These are just a few of the types of tools, among many that are available to assist practitioners to manage and hopefully resolve conflicts, but key to any conflict resolution is the need to let go of the fear it often provokes and to seek commonalities and mutually agreements where possible and work up from that. As Laws, Hogendorn, and Karl (2014, p. 39) note, "Management practices must find a way to cope with the diverse reasonable views that are anchored in the divergent framings and cope with the differences to which the diversity give rise". The energy inherent in conflict, likened by Olsson, Folke, and Berkes (2004) to "shooting the rapids", can capture the "hot forms" of interaction (Laws et al., 2014, p. 42), where participants who have detailed historical knowledge of the issues and a direct stake in the outcome "can enhance the quality of practical deliberation and decision making". Conflict thus becomes a mechanism that actively contributes to learning within engagement practice and by its very nature challenges the embedded assumptions that are part of any developed threat or other frame across both expert and professional realms (Nursey-Bray, 2017). Conflicts or disagreements that are created by introducing new knowledge and alternative values and worldview can, in fact, stimulate learning, creativity and change (Cundill, Fabricius, & Marti, 2005).

A related advantage to confronting and using conflict head-on is that it usually has the effect of binding groups together and creating mini-publics who provide feasible alternatives around controversial issues (Nursey-Bray, 2017). People often exhibit a high degree of agency when faced with conflict and adaptively learn from each other about how to solve problems: "The heat of conflict can contribute to the active engagement of stakeholders who are willing to challenge habits of thought and action and whose emotion and commitment can inform and sustain a process of moral and practical learning" (Laws et al., 2014, p. 45). This also has the effect of enabling more equitable entry points for groups who may traditionally feel intimidated or unable to assert themselves into the discussion. Conflict in placemaking then can be used as a process rather than a subject or object to be managed and can yield productive results.

Does It Work?

Once the engagement process is implemented a key question is of course, did it work? In many cases, engagement programmes are so fast and furious that it is hard to know or have the time and resources to seriously evaluate if it worked. Often the efficacy of the programme is obvious—stakeholders will have contributed to discussion or action on an issue, development or programme and that will be documented (de Weger, Van Vooren, Luijkx, Baan, & Drewes, 2018). In other cases, reports, websites and social media responses can be tracked, monitored, logged and then analysed for their effectiveness (Burton, Goodlad, & Croft, 2006). In ongoing, long-standing engagement programmes, targets can be used to assess the success of a campaign but more often the principle of continuous improvement is applied to assess and then build on lessons learned.

However, if a formal evaluation is to be undertaken, it should be a structured and planned process that reflects the purpose, audience and the scale and significance of the community engagement activities (Burton et al., 2006). Evaluation should, whenever possible, be a participatory activity. Evaluation also contributes to setting best-practice standards and benchmarks, in turn, helping to build an evidence base for innovative approaches to community engagement. Ultimately, the aim of any evaluation is to improve engagement practice by the identification and articulation of lessons and achievements (see Chapter 13 for further discussion on place evaluation).

Conclusion

We live in an age where social media demands our daily attention, and our cities and regions face multiple challenges; placemaking is more important than ever. Anchoring people to place, and successfully engaging them, is a dynamic challenge. There remain multiple issues and programmes which require community participation. Participative democracy indeed is de rigour. This chapter has summed up some of the key elements and steps that are required to undertake a competent engagement process. A later chapter focusses specifically on placemaking via public art as a process of community engagement that is gaining increasing currency. Ultimately, though, true engagement is a real skill and requires diligence, good faith and investment from both people and agencies. When done well, it creates transformative possibilities for placemaking that is owned by all people and the multiple communities they represent in any given region.

Key Learnings:

As placemakers who wish to support communities to express their voice and values related to place, here are the key take-home ideas from this chapter:

- Engaging communities in placemaking will require knowledge of the community.
- Effective engagement for placemaking will benefit from application of a wide range of tools and techniques.
- Digital engagement tools and citizen science programmes have particular merit for placemaking.
- Building skills in cultural engagement and conflict management will help build stronger and more enduring placemaking engagements.

References

Aristeidou, A., Scanlon, E., & Sharples, M. (2017). Profiles of engagement in online communities of citizen science participation. *Computers Human Behaviour, 74,* 246–256.

Arnstein, S. R. (1965). A ladder of citizen participation. *Journal of the American Institute of Planners, 35*(4), 216–224. https://doi.org/10.1080/01944366908977225.

Bakke, E. (2010). A model and measure of mobile communication competence. *Human Communication Research, 36,* 348–371. © 2010 International Communication Association.

Barr, S. (2011). Climate forums: Virtual discourses on climate change and the sustainable lifestyle (Report). *Area, 43*(1), 14–22.

Bartle, P. (n.d.). *What is community? A sociological perspective.* Retrieved from https://edadm821.files.wordpress.com/2010/11/what-is-community.pdf.

Brushwood-Rose, C. (2016). The subjective spaces of social engagement: Cultivating creative living through community-based digital storytelling. *Psychoanalysis, Culture & Society, 21,* 386–402. https://doi.org/10.1057/pcs.2015.56. Published online 29 October 2015.

Burton, P., Goodlad, R., & Croft, J. (2006). How would we know what works? Context and complexity in the evaluation of community involvement. *Evaluation, 12*(3), 294–312.

Cavaye, J. M. (2004). Governance and community engagement—The Australian experience. In W. R. Lovan, M. Murray, & R. Shaffer (Eds.), *Participatory governance: Planning, conflict mediation and public decision making in civil society* (pp. 85–102). Hants, UK: Ashgate.

Cohen, A. P. (1985). *Symbolic construction of community.* London: Routledge.

Cundill, G. N. R., Fabricius, C., & Marti, N. (2005). Foghorns to the future: Using knowledge and transdisciplinarity to navigate complex systems. *Ecology and Society, 10*(2), 8.

Dare, M., Schirmer, J., & Vanclay, F. (2008). *A brief guide to effective community engagement in the Australian plantation sector.* Hobart: Cooperative Research Centre for Forestry. Retrieved from http://www.crcforestry.com.au/publications/downloads/TR181-Dare-community-engagement.pdf.

De Leiuen, C., & Arthure, S. (2016). Collaboration on whose terms? Using the IAP2 community engagement model for archaeology in Kapunda, South Australia. *Journal of Community Archaeology & Heritage, 3*(2), 81–98.

Deuze, M., Bank, P., & Speers, L. (2012). A life lived in media. *Digital Humanities Quarterly, 6*(1). Retrieved from http://www.digitalhumanities.org/dhq/vol/6/1/000110/000110.html.

de Weger, E. J., Van Vooren, N., Luijkx, K. G., Baan, C. A., & Drewes, H. W. (2018). Achieving successful community engagement: A rapid realist review. *BMC Health Services Research, 18*(1), 285. https://doi.org/10.1186/s12913-018-3090-1.

Follett, R., & Strezov, V. (2015). An analysis of citizen science based research: Usage and publication patterns. *PLoS One, 10*(11), 1–14.

Head, B. (2007). Community engagement: Participation on whose terms? *Australian Journal of Political Science, 42*(3), 441–454.

Hespanhol, L., Parker, C., Zhou, D., & Tomitsch, M. (2018). Blending pop-up urbanism and participatory technologies: Challenges and opportunities for inclusive city making. *City, Culture and Society, 12,* 44–53.

Jennett, C., Eveleigh, A., Mathieu, K., Ajani, Z., & Cox, A. (2013, May 2–4). *Creativity in citizen cyber-science: All for one and one for all.* WebSci'13, Paris, France.

Johnson, A. G. (1986). *Human arrangements.* Orlando: Harcourt Brace Jovanovich Publishers.

Koehler, B., & Koontz, T. M. (2008). Citizen participation in collaborative watershed partnerships. *Environmental Management, 41,* 143–154.

Laws, D., Hogendorn, D., & Karl, H. (2014). Hot adaptation: What conflict can contribute to collaborative natural resource management. *Ecology and Society, 19*(2), 39.

Lee, D., & Newby, H. (1983). *The problem of sociology: An introduction to the discipline.* London: Hutchinson Education.

McAteer, B. (2018). *Citizen science as a means of democratizing urban environments.* Retrieved from http://theprotocity.com/citizen-science/. Accessed 25 Feb 2019.

McDonald, L., Hickey, A., & Reynolds, P. (2016). Discerning the air: Locating local government community engagement practice—Reflections on selected Australian experience. *Asia Pacific Journal of Public Administration, 38*(3), 154–167. https://doi.org/10.1080/23276665.2016.1213034.

Morris, R. (2012). *Community engagement in rural-remote and Indigenous local government in Australia.* Australian Centre of Excellence for Local Government, University of Technology, Sydney.

Mullen, K. C., Newman, G., & Thompson, J. L. (2013). Facilitating the development and evaluation of a citizen science website: A case study of repeat photography and climate change in southwest Alaska's national parks. *Applied Environmental Education & Communication, 12*(4), 261–271.

Nursey-Bray, M. (2017). Towards socially just adaptive climate governance: The transformative potential of conflict. *Local Environment, 22*(2), 156–171. https://doi.org/10.1080/13549839.2016.1181618.

Olsson, P., Folke, C., & Berkes, F. (2004). Adaptive co-management for building social-ecological resilience. *Environmental Management, 34*, 75–90. https://doi.org/10.1007/s00267-003-0101-7.

Phadke, R., Manning, C., & Burlager, S. (2015). Making it personal: Diversity and deliberation in climate adaptation planning. *Climate Risk Management, 9*(C), 62–76.

Reddel, T., & Woolcock, G. (2004). From consultation to participatory governance? A critical review of citizen engagement strategies in Queensland. *Australian Journal of Public Administration, 63*(3), 75–87.

Scruby, L., Canales, M., Ferguson, E., & Gregory, D. (2017). Promoting face-to-face dialogue for community engagement in a digital age. *Canadian Journal of Nursing Research, 49*(4), 170–177.

Silvertown, J. (2009). A new dawn for citizen science. *Trends in Ecology & Evolution, 24*(9), 467–471.

Thiel, M., Penna-Díaz, M. A., Luna-Jorquera, G., Salas, S., Sellanes, J., & Stotz, W. (2014). Citizen scientists and marine research: Volunteer participants, their contributions, and projection for the future. *Oceanography and Marine Biology: An Annual Review, 52*, 257–314.

Tomitsch, M., & Haeusler, M. (2015). Infostructures: Towards a complementary approach for solving urban challenges through digital technologies. *Journal of Urban Technology, 22*(3), 37–53.

Verhagen, T., Swen, E., Feldberg, F., & Merikivi, J. (2015). Benefiting from virtual customer environments: An empirical study of customer engagement. *Computers Human Behavior, 48*, 340–357. http://dx.doi.org/10.1016/j.chb.2015.01.061.

6

Local Governments and Developers in Placemaking: Defining Their Responsibilities and Capacities to Shape Place

Robyn Creagh, Courtney Babb and Holly Farley

Introduction

Local government and developers are key stakeholders in placemaking projects and initiatives. Local government and developers often engage in and support placemaking activities when these projects help them to achieve their various responsibilities in creating, enhancing and managing good quality places and when the activity works within, or extends, their capacity to address their responsibilities. In this chapter, we focus on these responsibilities and capacities of local governments and developers, as a way to understand why they value placemaking.

R. Creagh (✉) · H. Farley
School of Arts and Sciences, The University of Notre Dame Australia, Fremantle, WA, Australia
e-mail: robyn.creagh@ND.edu.au

C. Babb
School of Design and the Built Environment,
Curtin University, Perth, WA, Australia

Building on Place Governance (see Chapter 11), we begin by identifying local governments and developers as two of many potential stakeholders within the networked governance of place (Pierce, Martin, & Murphy, 2011). We outline the expectations on local government to deliver an expanded field of responsibilities in regard to place, and the responsibility of developers to meet a social contract, as well as provide a return to their shareholders. We then examine the capacity of local government and developers to deliver against these responsibilities, considering resource allocation; accountability; organisational culture and knowledge; risk and regulation.

Throughout the chapter, we draw on interviews with placemakers who work within government, private and community sectors to illustrate the value that local government and developers find in placemaking projects. In 2018, we conducted interviews with seven key placemakers and place leaders in Western Australia.[1] The interviewees included placemakers from within local governments, private companies, state government developers and local community groups who work closely with local governments and developers. From these interviews, we have drawn first-person accounts of placemaking in partnership with local government and developers.

From these interviews, we identified a nested case study that illustrates the value of placemaking to developers and local governments at various scales. The first case study introduces the Town Team Movement, a not-for-profit organisation based in Perth, Australia, serving a growing network of placemaking groups nationally and internationally. The second case study looks in more detail at the relationships and activity of Inglewood on Beaufort, one of the town teams.

---

[1] The interviews ranged from 30 minutes to 1 hour in duration. Using a semi-structured approach, the same set of [eight] questions were asked of each of the interviewees with follow-up questions typically focusing on Western Australian examples of placemaking. The questions for the first half of the interview focused on the value of placemaking and the second half on leadership within placemaking. Chapter 10 draws on the leadership themes of the interview. Interviewees were selected to compose a cross section of placemaking activity in Western Australia including local community organisations, local government urban planning and placemaking (in both inner suburban and outer suburban contexts), major private investor developments and major state government developments.

These two cases studies illustrate the value of placemaking to local government and developers in helping them to meet extended place responsibilities with limited capacities.

As placemakers this chapter will support you in how to engage effectively with government and developers. If you are not familiar with the activities and motivations of local governments and developers, this chapter will introduce these stakeholders' engagement with placemaking, what motivates their involvement, and what constraints they are managing as part of their everyday activities. This information is likely to be useful to community groups or individuals who are looking to get more involved with placemaking and seeking collaboration with local government or developers for their influence as place-shapers. This chapter may also be of use as a prompt for reflection for those working within local governments or land development organisations—the Town Team Movement case study is particularly relevant. Finally, this chapter will be of interest to students of placemaking and built environment development as an outline of some of the networks of influence that shape places. Other chapters in this volume pick up some of the themes that are touched upon in this chapter. Further exploration of the idea of governance can be found in Chapter 11 'The Systems of Place Agency: Adaptive Governance for Public Benefit', and although this chapter asserts the value of placemaking to local governments and developers, Chapter 8 'Economics of Place' goes into some details of the costing and economic evaluation of placemaking initiatives.

Case Study One: Recognising the Value of Placemaking Through the Town Team Movement

The growing value placemaking has to local governments and developers is reflected in the emergence of the Town Team Movement in Perth, Western Australia, in 2017. The Town Team Movement is a non-government organisation that aims to foster and support community-specific, place-focused collectives, known as town teams. Town teams are place-based, non-politically aligned organisations, often representing a mix of local residents, businesses and landowners who are striving to improve the quality of places, such as main streets and neighbourhoods.

The Town Team Movement emerged from the activities of the Beaufort Street Network (www.beaufortstreet.com.au), which formed in 2010 in the inner Perth suburbs of Mount Lawley and Highgate, and the other town teams, which formed soon after in the City of Vincent: Leederville Connect, Mount Hawthorn Hub and North Perth Local. The Beaufort Street Network comprised a group of place-focused and pro-active residents and business owners, all concerned that opportunities were not being realised in the Beaufort Street precinct. Initially, it was a group of people who 'wanted to see more cool stuff happening in the area'.[2] However, the role of the Beaufort Street Network expanded when local governments began to see the value in the Beaufort Street Network's placemaking work as an initiative that (1) invites community into place-shaping processes, (2) enables accurate understanding of the community values and vision, and (3) builds positive relationships between community and local government. The Beaufort Street Network was soon providing support and advice about the process of establishing community-driven, collective organisations focused on placemaking to local governments and community groups across the Perth metropolitan area. The Town Team Movement emerged as an under-arching, supportive organisation, endeavouring to change the way people think about space and placemaking through supporting communities in forming their own town teams. The Town Team Movement support new town teams and local governments to effectively communicate with each other.

> ...this is a conscious way of working, with the organisation being more interested in developing community groups who have governance over their own space and supporting the development of resilient town teams. (Dean Cracknell, CEO Town Team Movement)

---

[2]Unless otherwise cited, quotations and background information for this section were provided by Dean Cracknell, CEO of the Town Team Movement, through interview and conversation with the authors.

Fig. 6.1 Inaugural Town teams conference (*Source* Town Team Movement (2018b) Engagement summary report)

The Town Team Movement is based on a vision and philosophy of placemaking grounded within the practicalities of running a place-focused collective—running meetings and working with other stakeholders like local government. To achieve this vision, the Town Team Movement has developed an inclusive organisational model for town teams (Town Team Movement, 2018a). The model responds to place and situation, with the intent of developing resilient communities, networks and citizen stewardship. The founding objective was to develop an organisation that could support town teams Australia wide.

In Western Australia, local government acknowledgement of the value of community-led placemaking in helping local governments meet their place responsibilities is evident in the support shown to the Town Team Movement. The inaugural Town Team Movement conference was held in 2018 (Fig. 6.1). The conference had the support of thirty-two local governments (Town Team Movement, 2018a), with the City of Vincent and the Town of Victoria Park being the two primary presentation partners. Nationally, the Australian Capital Territory (ACT) government engaged the Town Team Movement to work with local community groups to formally establish town teams. In such, they are acknowledging the Town Team Movement's ability to bridge the gap between aspirational visioning, on-ground action and local government partnerships—effectively extending the capacity of local governments to achieve place quality objectives.

The property industry is also starting to understand the role of placemaking and is seeing the market value in investing in place and community. The Town Team Movement is partly resourced by philanthropic donations made by members of the property industry. This support is reflective of developers responsibilities to meet social contract expectations to enhance places in town centres, main streets and precincts, and the value some are seeing in partnering with community and place-based groups to achieve this.

Places, Placemaking and the Responsibilities of the Local Government and Developers

Local governments and developers have an interest and investment in the quality of places for a number of reasons. One key reason is that placemaking allows them to meet their various responsibilities. The range and types of responsibilities of stakeholders involved in placemaking have undergone a significant transformation over recent decades with a shift from a top-down approach led by central governments to one of networked governance. The outcome of place-based governance approaches, as distinct from government-led approaches, is that responsibilities for placemaking and shaping are decentralised, and that a space is opened for a network of state and non-state 'voices' in the planning, management and decision-making regarding places (Coaffee & Healey, 2003). Although governance structures vary from place to place, in this new arena of placemaking, local government and developers are key players governed by complex arrangements of actor partnerships, procedures, rules and responsibilities. To understand how local governments and developers shape places, it is important to understand the basis for their responsibilities in delivering, managing and providing opportunities to enhance the function and quality of places.

Local government in Australia is referred to as the third tier of government, after the Federal and State tiers of government. Local government is considered the tier of government that is closest to the people as it is concerned with aspects that impact everyday lives of people and communities. However, state governments are arguably more powerful than local governments, as they set out the legislative powers, organisation structures and processes for local governments. There has been a shift away from the state and federal governments to the local government level in various responsibilities for service delivery and regulation (Dollery, Wallis, & Allan, 2006). These shifting responsibilities have exacerbated the demands placed on local government with regard to their responsibilities. A report into local government sector in Australia (LGSA, 2006) found that the public perceives that the local governments have a larger responsibility and more resources at hand to fulfil that responsibility than they actually do.

The traditional focus of local government on public works and property services, encapsulated in the often-stated mantra of 'roads, rates and rubbish', has broadened to encompass a more extensive set of responsibilities. Drawing on a term popularised by Sir Michael Lyons in his 2007 review of the local government sector in the UK, local governments are increasingly becoming 'place-shapers', involved in community capacity building, economic development and opening their processes up to the communities they represent (Lyons, 2007). The requirement for accountability opens possibilities for the public to participate in local government activities.

Local governments are responsible and accountable to their electors—property owners, business owners and residents with their jurisdictions. Local governments have revenue raising and regulatory powers that correspond with their responsibilities, as set by elected officials (LGSA, 2006). Placemaking projects provide the apparatus for councillors to engage with, learn from and potentially represent their constituents in decision-making, thus fulfilling one of their key responsibilities. A local government placemaker described it in this way:

> We have the opportunity to give them [Local Councillors] a call, and say, 'Do you want to come out in the street, we'll have a sit-down, introduce you to people, talk about the story?' You're building their understanding of the process as well. You're introducing them to positive, excited people on the street where often they're only receiving complaints, and that was really great. That's a very simple communication tool that we used that flipped the elected members around from being a bit suspicious to being champions of placemaking.

Placemaking helps local governments meet the expectation to open up processes and decision-making to community participation, but often does so in creative ways. Interviewees variously highlighted that placemaking activities and projects offered a direct, fun and inclusive approach to governance, noting that placemaking processes can enable a longer, place-focused and therefore richer conversation with the community. These longer conversations were seen as valuable around instances of urban change, where the prolonged time frames of engagement increased the ability for more nuanced conversation, and built support for positive change informed by opinions within local communities. An example provided by one local government place-maker emphasises how an element of fun or silliness can help address power-differentials between community and experts within local government:

> For Project Robin Hood, we set up this group called the 'Ombeardsmen'… we made them wear these knitted woollen dwarf beards we bought off the internet. And these are professionals in their organisation: our directors and people with specific technical expertise we wanted to bring to some placemaking projects… It was a town hall meeting… but because we slapped these beards on the authorities, it changes the power in the relationship. It humanises them and makes them vulnerable, and it shows that we're thinking about doing things a little bit differently, and that was fun to do as well.

Longer collective conversations have potential for building trust and collaboration between local government and communities. Interviewees noted positive experiences with projects on the ground built goodwill on both sides, and place-based projects enabled continued collaborative working relationships that cut across power structures embedded in various governance arrangements. The focus on place and placemaking also provided a focal point of reference for when navigating the often contested arena of community engagement. One local government placemaker gave an illustrative example where a reminder of a commitment to a shared vision for place was sufficient to shift the proposed use for a vacant space from car parking for an organisation to an outdoor cafe.

> We didn't use a policy lever or a financial lever or legal lever or anything like that. We had a conversation with them saying, 'Actually… this is your vision as well. This doesn't match up with what you told us you wanted for the street.'

Placemaking is an activity that provides opportunities for local governments to engage in more meaningful conversations with the individuals, organisations and communities who they represent. However, it is important to note that the underlying philosophies of local governments can differ, which has implications for the way they meet their various responsibilities. The Independent Inquiry into the Financial Sustainability of NSW Local Government (LGSA, 2006, p. 12) identified three approaches. Local governments can take a *minimalist approach* where they regulate private property and manage common property similar to the role of a body corporate. A *maximalist approach* fully addresses the needs of the community to the extent that there is duplication of the functions of other tiers of government. The third approach is the *optimalist approach*, where local governments achieve 'maximum leverage' from minimal resources by taking a leadership role and harnessing the capacity of organisation and individuals in their community to deliver services and functions. Reflecting on this typology in the Australian context, Dollery, Grant, and O'Keefe (2008) considered, given their precarious financial status and the withdrawal of state and federal sectors from traditional service and infrastructure responsibilities, the optimalist approach was likely to be the most ideal for Australian local governments. We return to the topic of capacity in the third section of this chapter.

Responsibilities also vary internally within local government organisations. Local governments serve a variety of functions ranging from decision-making by council to more administrative functions. The administrative function of local government is diverse, spanning infrastructure delivery, environmental management, land use planning, service delivery, assessment management and enforcement of local laws. Although guided by overarching principles and strategic goals, these administrative responsibilities and objectives may sometimes be contradictory.

Placemaking was seen by our interviewees as a means to address different though aligned objectives through the delivery of good quality places for people—places that are comfortable to be in, nice to walk through, for people to 'take their families to', and buy a coffee in. Interviewees from local government and community placemaking contexts emphasised the value of placemaking in supporting community, building layers of meaning, supporting 'an increase in someone's love of place' and catalysing not just a 'people friendly place that people want to be in and spend money in, a place where everyone gets involved'. As another interviewee from a state government developer perspective noted: 'We've got a series of objectives for the organisation which really do drive how we approach things, and one of those is sense of place, so that's a big part of what it's about, connectivity and inclusion, urban efficiency, economic well-being and environmental responsibility'.

Land developers are also a diverse and important group of actors in the production of urban places, with a broad range of responsibilities (Adams, Croudace, & Tiesdell, 2012). Developers' responsibilities are different from local governments in that they are largely accountable to more contained ranged actors that have a stake in particular developments. As developers range from large, to medium and small private corporations, the people they are responsible to may range from shareholders in a company to individuals and families. In the case of government-based land development and redevelopment agencies, responsibilities are to the state and its people and these agencies are required to act in response to various pieces of legislation that govern the public sector. Government or quasi-government land development agencies can operate to achieve various goals in the public interest, such as wealth redistribution, subsidising of social housing and infrastructure funding, although Land Development Agencies have increasingly taken on a corporate agenda and profit-seeking activities (Davison & Legacy, 2014).

Return on investment is one key responsibility developers have to their stakeholders. One of our interviewees reflected on her placemaking work with developer clients:

> Ultimately it comes back to return on investment on their asset. For commercial, it's attracting the types of tenants that they want. It's about tenant satisfaction… For the retail team, it will be about 'Well, we've got a great retail mix… and those guys are performing well.' For the community team, it will be 'We've got some really well established embedded partnerships that are making this place stand on its own two feet, and soon we'll be able to draw back.' From a residential perspective, it will be, 'How much are we selling and how quickly?' But also, 'How much are people upgrading within our place?' …I think that from a process point of view, it [place] is successful when it doesn't become an extra process anymore, it's just embedded. It's really just embedded.

Though financial return to their stakeholders is a key responsibility, developers are also bound by a broader social contract. This means they are responsible also to the public, particularly others who may be impacted by their developments such as nearby property owners or users of a place. For developers, placemaking can be an approach to demonstrating community benefit, which in turn can help to build support and a compelling narrative of benefit to brief design processes and negotiate approvals. A local place consultant discussed a project for a recent large-scale development:

> [It was about] having a very compelling conversation with regulatory authorities and stakeholders around what you're delivering and why… [and] what's the community benefit going to be, not only for the people that live there, but what's the experience at the ground floor for the local community?

Planning regulations are key instruments that define the responsibilities of developers to act. Developers are required to address various planning regulations which include limiting the impact of development on surrounding places, addressing various issues such as overshadowing, access and egress from a site, privacy, aesthetics or amenity. Placemaking can, therefore, play an important role in mitigating the impacts and leveraging benefits of developer activity and its influence on the quality of places and the public realm. As one of our interviewees commented:

> For government it [placemaking] is really a tool that enables them to get the best out of the private sector. Because they're very much setting a vision, they're setting their expectation around what's required from a place perspective.

The Capacity of Local Government and Developers to Shape Place

Although local governments and developers both have responsibilities for making, shaping and managing places, this does not necessarily mean that they do so to the full extent. Their various responsibilities are only partly what determines the role of local governments and developers in placemaking. Local government and developers operate within various institutional contexts that define their capacity to influence the quality and function of places in different ways. These capacities are defined both by external factors, such as market conditions and community expectations, as well as internal factors, such as organisational structures and cultures. An understanding of the set of enabling and constraining factors that define the capacity of local governments and developers to shape places is important to understanding the role of agents in the governance of places and placemaking. This section identifies some key capacities: resource allocation; accountability to key interest groups; organisational culture and knowledge; and risk.

The capacity to shape place is often largely determined by the resources allocated to place enhancing activities. Engaging in activities to make better places can be very resource intensive—in time, money and skills. Local governments are accountable to the communities they represent, and their distribution of resources must reflect communities' interests when making decisions and administering functions. In fiscally constrained local governments, scarce resources are required to be distributed equitably across the range of the communities they represent and act in the interest of. For developers, boards and executives are key actors in determining the overall commitment to placemaking and place enhancing activities, accountable to the interests of their shareholders and various groups they represent.

Interviewees highlighted that placemaking activities were valuable in both allowing limited resources to be better allocated, and enabling the responsibilities of local governments and developers to be met. By empowering community groups to take responsibility for places, local governments and developers could 'tap' into the energy of locally based community groups to effect and enact change to enhance places. Interviewees from state government developers, local councils and community groups valued the ability to move quickly with low-cost placemaking projects as part of a learning and relationship building process. Low-capital short time frame projects were valued as opportunities to build working relationships between groups and individuals who did not have a track record of collaboration. It was also noted that seeing projects completed builds up goodwill with local stakeholders such as local businesses and residents.

The capacity to support placemaking objectives and to create great places within a local government or as part of a development largely rests on whether there is the organisational structure or culture to support placemaking activities. When we asked placemakers and place leaders in WA how to begin to partner with local government or developers, their key advice was to understand the organisation's needs and capacities in order to identify synergies through which a placemaking idea helped achieve objectives and meet responsibilities.

Some local governments and developers have discrete departments and personnel whose job is to develop placemaking strategies or support placemaking activities. In these cases, placemaking is considered a normal part of the duties and activities of the organisation. The formalisation of this role reflects the value that local governments are placing on community placemaking groups as significant partners that are helpful in achieving the local government's place-shaping responsibilities—we see this in the conclusion of the second case study, Inglewood on Beaufort. For organisations without dedicated place-focused roles, often leaders or change agents within the organisation were an important catalyst for a change in organisational culture. A second piece of advice provided by our interviewees was related to situations where placemaking was a new approach. In this situation, their advice was to keep talking to people within the organisation to find a champion, someone who 'gets it'. Chapter 10 further unpacks leadership in the context of placemaking.

The way that placemaking projects challenged established disciplinary and organisational silos and culture was identified as highly valuable to local government and developer interviewees. Across the board, the interviewees identified that placemaking both fosters and demands a diversity of perspectives and interdisciplinary approaches. Improved integration between groups was identified as valuable by all the interviewees—whether between state government bodies, between disciplinary teams within developer organisations or within local governments. For example, describing an experience as a place consultant for a large-scale suburban developer one interviewee emphasised the challenge to typical development approaches of a placemaking framework and the potential value of this approach in bringing together disparate parts and re-focusing the business:

> So, that will be about bringing together all the people in the room that are needed at the front end of a process to define its positioning, its vision and the framework in which the rest of the project will respond. That's as much a stakeholder management exercise around breaking down silos and building common knowledge amongst inter-disciplinary teams as it is about a lesson on placemaking. And about us basically re-orienting their development cycle.

According to the interviewees, placemaking processes also acted as catalysts for culture change within local government. These culture changes internal to the organisation were typified in two ways: firstly in the increased communication and integration between different groups and secondly in the shift in priorities from regulation to facilitation of community projects. Placemakers within local government particularly valued the opportunity to develop new understandings of their organisations as a facilitator and a supporter of community, as we see below.

> For us, as an organisation, it also helped change the culture. Council's saying 'No' a lot because we're based on regulation but our vision says we want these amazing places and we want these amazing streets. Our mechanisms say, 'Don't do anything in your streets because it's unsafe,' and there's a real imbalance there. So it's an opportunity for us to shift those core policies and procedures and all the mechanical stuff in the organisation, and change that culture around as well so that it's easy to do [things] as a person in the community or a developer or whoever you might be.

As we see in the quote above, risk to public health and safety is a key consideration when it comes to the capacity of local governments to engage in placemaking. The management of risk can be an important consideration for decision-making about changes of use in public places. The responsibilities to manage risks for local government are evident in a number of forms. Local governments often have, for example, laws relating to restrictions on consumption of alcohol in certain places; signage, advertising and promotion of events; the conduct of recreation activities and hobbies; the use and development of spaces of co-ownership, such as verges; and the use of spaces for street entertainment, temporary business, alfresco dining or food trucks. Many of these activities are important to placemaking initiatives, whether it be activating a street, putting on an event, or building a community space. Local governments can use these by-laws to effectively manage risks and ensure a quality of experience for various users of space and private property owners or they can over-regulate spaces so that temporary activities that attract people to places are outlawed.

Case Study Two: A Town Team in Action. Inglewood on Beaufort Captures Community Energy and Builds Agency

The story of the town team, Inglewood on Beaufort, illustrates an evolving relationship between a place-based community group and local government. Inglewood on Beaufort is a town team located within the

City of Stirling, an inner-northern region of the Perth metropolitan area. Like many other town teams, the group formed in response to the needs and desires of residents and business owners to bring new life and activity to their main street. To do this Inglewood on Beaufort engages in a range of placemaking and place improvement activities and projects. Three projects illustrate the development of this relationship: the renaming and improving the Inglewood Civic Centre, the weekly Night Markets, and local traffic and parking changes.

A significant catalyst for the ongoing relationship between Inglewood on Beaufort and the City of Stirling was the repositioning of the City's Civic Centre and its subsequent activation. An Inglewood on Beaufort town team member described the Civic Centre as 'a beautiful little space in Inglewood, which is where our library is and there's a little restaurant off to one side, and then there's a community centre and a nice little bit of lawn and trees in the middle', but, it's also 'really dark and scary at night'.[3] As a space, the Civic Centre was underused and lacked a sense of community ownership. Inglewood on Beaufort had a vision to turn the space into a community town square.

Inglewood on Beaufort was able to facilitate an increased use of the space by different groups, which subsequently built a sense of ownership over the space. Inglewood on Beaufort are '…starting to see mothers' groups hang out there. We're starting to see people more naturally want to go and hang there as friends and the library staff are seeing themselves as champions of the space'. As a result of the work of Inglewood on Beaufort, the City of Stirling agreed to change the name from the Inglewood Civic Centre to the Inglewood Town Square (Fig. 6.2).

> So now every time we have a media release or there's anything in the paper [it says] 'Meet at the town square.' We feel like that's really important in identifying the actual heart of our main street.

---

[3]Unless otherwise cited, background information and direct quotations within this section were provided by a member of Inglewood on Beaufort through interview and conversations with the authors.

Fig. 6.2 The Town Square during an Inglewood on Beaufort Night Market event (Photo by Rebecca Stone)

Another important project to the ongoing relationship of Inglewood on Beaufort with the City of Stirling was the creation of the Night Markets, held on Monday evenings during the warmer months of the year. The ambitious idea to establish markets on a busy arterial road has been wildly successful and considered one of the most successful continuing street markets in Australia (Dean Cracknell, CEO, Town Team Movement, 10/1/2019). The Night Markets bring together local businesses, food trucks, a pop-up bar, local musicians and thousands of people in reclaiming the street and creating a buzzing atmosphere. The Night Markets have turned around some perception of the area as being under-utilised.

During the process of setting up the Night Markets, Inglewood on Beaufort worked closely with a champion within the City of Stirling, who supported the town team in navigate the formal government process of establishing the large-scale community event. In turn, Inglewood on Beaufort called upon Local Councillors to support the initiative and worked with the City executive to find creative solutions that seemed insurmountable at an administrative level.

> ...we had a really good champion in there, who saw it upon herself to really help to try to make things happen. With the markets, the first season, there were so many roadblocks in place. She did a really good job of trying to break all of those down and having the difficult meetings internally and being our champion.

This local government staff member negotiated internal silos, worked to address the organisational culture and used seed-funding to resource Inglewood on Beaufort's initial steps as both a trust-building process between local government and community and a way to extend the place-shaping capacity of the local government.

Beaufort Street is the major northern arterial road into the Perth CBD and traffic has a major impact on the quality of the street as a place, particularly for pedestrians. Together with the City of Stirling, Inglewood on Beaufort identified the fast-paced traffic as a major barrier to repositioning Beaufort Street from a road to a community gathering place.

> ...we've been working really closely with the City, and they've been encouraging us to keep advocating for ways that we can slow down traffic. So we've worked with them to convert a traffic lane into on-street parking outside of peak times, and getting more things happening along the street.

In tackling the identified traffic issue, Inglewood on Beaufort has been 'advocating to the state government to look at reducing the speed along Beaufort Street'. Again, with the intent to change the dominant perceptions of the area and shift the focus from Beaufort Street as an arterial road, to a focus on people, pedestrians and place. And, like the Night Markets, in this initiative, Inglewood on Beaufort's efforts are working in line with the local government's objectives for place quality.

As a result of the successful placemaking partnership with Inglewood on Beaufort, the City of Stirling is seeing ongoing value in developing strong and positive relationships with town teams. To facilitate positive place outcomes, the City of Stirling has employed a number of place managers to facilitate and work with local community groups and town teams, evidencing a shift in organisational culture and capacity.

Conclusion

Through interviews with placemakers across government, private and community sectors, as well as the case study of the Town Team Movement and Inglewood on Beaufort, this chapter has demonstrated how the value of placemaking plays out at different scales for local governments and developers. Local governments' responsibilities have expanded but their resources have not. As we see in the Inglewood on Beaufort case study above, local governments are seeking ways to meet these growing expectations to deliver place outcomes and have identified partnering with local community as one way to help achieve this. Developers are required to make a profit, but are also bound by social contract. These two drivers may be met through investment in place quality which both services users and attracts investment. Because of this tension between responsibilities and capacities, local governments and developers see value in placemaking whether through partnering with local community placemaking groups, or undertaking placemaking activity themselves. This recognition of value is evident in the enthusiastic buy-in by local government and developers into the emerging Town Team Movement. This value can be said to be 'triple bottom line'. It includes social, economic and, more rarely in our interviews, environmental qualities. These topics are further unpacked in Chapters 2, 3 and 8, respectively.

Local government and developers valued the dialogue with external groups that placemaking could catalyse. Placemaking was seen as a novel approach that invited community into decision-making and delivery. The opportunity for enhancing communication and positive media coverage was valued by both local government and developers. A shared vision and the externally perceived authenticity of that vision were also considered valuable. For developers, the shared vision and improved relationships with the community can help achieve community and regulatory support for a proposal. For state government developers, this 'credible' position was also helpful in having 'honest' conversations about what outcomes were possible in place. For local government, a shared vision with stakeholders could enable a collaborative, rather than regulatory approach to place improvements.

For local government, this shared vision for place is valued as part of a larger shift in operational culture and moves to re-build trust between community and local government. Rich understandings of a place were seen to enable placemaking activity to build on existing investment and what is already working and in a place; to understand common 'threads' between stakeholders to establish shared visions; and to deliver on community and commercial needs—a valuable approach when capacity to act is constrained. For local government, placemaking was valued because it helped tap community capacity and develop community agency to shape places, helping to deliver on local government's expanded place responsibility.

For developers, placemaking made 'commercial sense'. 'Making place' was presented as a focus to achieve good experiences for stakeholders—be they commercial lessors, tenants or users. Placemaking was valued by developers as one way through which to achieve their dual responsibilities of delivering profit to shareholders and fulfilling social contracts.

In addition, placemakers reported that for both local government and developer organisations placemaking has value for the new approach to operations that it offers. The quick and inexpensive testing often embedded in placemaking processes were valued not only for the quick wins to stakeholders, but also the way in which this rapid prototyping enabled organisational learning. Thinking about place experience was understood to demand a stepping out of disciplinary specialities, and for both local government and developers, placemaking was valued as a catalyst for working across specialisations within organisations. The value attributed to working across silos to address common goals is reflective of broader societal moves to holistically address complex situations and is increasingly understood as good business management (see Chapter 10).

The following five points outline key things for placemakers to consider when wanting to partner with local government and developers:

1. With the distribution of responsibility and the scarcity of resources, local governments are looking to tap the energy of community groups and partner in placemaking.

2. Commercial and state developers are increasingly seeing the business sense of placemaking as part of delivering quality place outcomes and satisfaction to clients, tenants and local community.
3. Understand the different place-related responsibilities and capacities of the organisation you want to work with.
4. Identify the potential benefit of your placemaking project to the place, community and partnering local government or developer.
5. If your first approach does not land well, try talking to someone else within the organisation. Local governments and developers are made up of individuals, themselves with different capacities and responsibilities.

References

Adams, D., Croudace, R., & Tiesdell, S. (2012). Exploring the 'notional property developer' as a policy construct. *Urban Studies, 49*(12), 2577–2596.

Coaffee, J., & Healey, P. (2003). "My voice: My place": Tracking transformations in urban governance. *Urban Studies, 40*(10), 1979–1999.

Davison, G., & Legacy, C. (2014). Positive planning and sustainable brownfield regeneration: The role and potential of government land development agencies. *International Planning Studies, 19*(2), 154–172.

Dollery, B., Grant, B., & O'Keefe, S. (2008). Local councils as 'place-shapers': The implications of the Lyons report for Australian local government. *Australian Journal of Political Science, 43*(3), 481–494. https://doi.org/10.1080/10361140802267266.

Dollery, B., Wallis, J., & Allan, P. (2006). The debate that had to happen but never did: The changing role of Australian local government. *Australian Journal of Political Science, 41*(4), 553–567. https://doi.org/10.1080/10361140600959775.

Local Government and Shires Associations of NSW (LGSA). (2006). *Are councils sustainable: Final report*. NSW. Allan Report 2006. https://www.lgnsw.org.au/files/imce-uploads/35/final-report-findings-and-recommendations.pdf.

Lyons, M. (2007). *Place-shaping: A shared ambition for the future of local government*. London: The Stationery Office. Retrieved from https://www.gov.

uk/government/publications/place-shaping-a-shared-ambition-for-the-future-of-local-government-final-report.

Pierce, J., Martin, D. G., & Murphy, J. (2011). Relational place-making: The networked politics of place. *Transactions of the Institute of British Geographers, 36*(1), 54–70. https://doi.org/10.1111/j.1475-5661.2010.00411.x.

Town Team Movement. (2018a). *Town Team Movement Brochure*. Retrieved from https://www.townteams.com.au/wp-content/uploads/2018/11/TOWN-TEAM-MOVEMENT_4pp-BROCHURE_EMAIL.pdf.

The Town Teams Movement. (2018b). *Engagement Summary Report*. Retrieved from https://www.townteams.com.au/wp-content/uploads/2018/11/TTM-ENGAGEMENT-SUMMARY-REPORT_FINAL-incl-MEDIA.pdf.

7

Design for Change: An Adaptive Approach to Urban Places in Transformation

Elisa Palazzo

How much can a city change before becoming a different city?
Brian Walker

Cities as Places in Transformation

Cities are dynamic socio-ecological systems (see Chapter 3), shaped by the combined work of people and nature. Thriving and healthy urban places are the result of communities' collective efforts in long-term adaptation to existing geophysical and climatic conditions. These slow incremental processes have determined place identity, resilience and liveability. Besides the physical space, they have generated the social cohesion that determines the sense of a community and attachment to place (Friedmann, 2010).

In recent decades, planners have rediscovered the combined role of people and nature in the development, physical and metaphysical,

E. Palazzo (✉)
Faculty of Built Environment, University of New South Wales,
Sydney, NSW, Australia
e-mail: Elisa.Palazzo@unsw.edu.au

of our contemporary urban environment. It is now commonly acknowledged that planning practices and governance strategies are more successful in achieving environmental, social and economic goals if they include all urban actors (Legacy & van den Nouwelant, 2015). Widespread interest in participatory planning has led to the definition of novel approaches, including placemaking, with successful outcomes all around the world, as shown in the case studies described in the present book. Co-management and co-design initiatives have provided a plurality of new perspectives across planning and project implementation. These approaches seem to be more appropriate for achieving urban sustainability because they maintain the sense of place, include complex thinking, and generate physical, psychological, social, health, spiritual and aesthetic benefits (Frumkin, 2003). Applications of collaborative approaches to urban design can also address issues of social justice by supporting local populations to face change and guaranteeing equal rights and shared access to resources (Anguelovski et al., 2016), while driving design innovation and novel spatial solutions (Palazzo, 2019). However, the relationship between placemaking and rapid urban change has been relatively underrepresented in urban studies.

This chapter focuses on the application of adaptive design thinking in the context of rapid urban change. It examines which strategies can be put in place, and how placemaking initiatives can assume a substantial role in urban design, to respond to the complex challenges posed by urban transformations.

Change and Urban Resilience

Urban environments are now changing more rapidly, and local communities are struggling to cope with high-pace environmental, economic and socio-demographic changes. Transformations affect planning practice in all its aspects, from governance to spatial dimensions. Traditional approaches to place management are no longer suitable to deal with these unpredictable forces. More research is needed to understand the multifaceted relationships of people and places in transformation.

Rapid urban transformations require the introduction of novel strategies and skills able to embrace change in a different way.

A significant reassessment of the urban system is also needed to accommodate uncertainty and increase urban resilience with practices able to respond to and leverage environmental change, sustain urban liveability, create equitable development and build adaptive capacity. However, operationalising the concept of resilience in urban design and placemaking practice requires a significant mindset change. A truly innovative approach is required to upgrade traditional design principles to respond to current urban dynamics.

It is possible to design for rapidly changing urban socio-ecological systems and generate resilience within people, places and the urban environment. Placemaking is a promising approach to deal with urban transformation.

Who Makes Places?

As highlighted in Chapters 1 and 2, the definition of placemaking describes a series of techniques and approaches to current planning practices that aim to engage local communities in the self-determination of their living environment (Whyte, 1980). Placemaking goes beyond endorsing better urban design, but it 'capitalizes on a local community's assets, inspiration, and potential, and it results in the creation of quality public spaces that contribute to people's health, happiness, and well-being' (PPS, 2018). If 'place' is the focus of community interactions as well as a liveable space (Mant, 2000), then the term 'making' implies the practical process to imagine, design, modify and manage spaces in urban areas. This approach includes both the dimension of the built environment and the dimension of the 'emplaced' communities that inhabit it (Friedmann, 2010).

Placemaking is a promising conceptual tool for inclusive governance in space management. However, most deliberative and participatory processes with a truly active role of the community still only occur in the strategic phases of the planning process and are significantly underrepresented in the design and implementation phases (Friedmann, 2010). A truly inclusive process, from planning to project delivery, has yet to be achieved. The integration of placemaking practices in urban design to achieve more than simple retrofit operations for place branding and beautification needs further research in order to provide responses to broader governance, programmatic and environmental concerns generated by change (Gertner, 2011).

At a governance level, change in leadership and new planning agendas determined by political change often require re-prioritising planning outputs and may hinder the completion of projects (Legacy & van den Nouwelant, 2015). On the contrary, including the community in the implementation phases of shared planning objectives provides a greater chance of continuity and coherence in achieving project outcomes. Urban projects consistently supported by the local community have a higher possibility of success and generate transformative and shared knowledge and expertise appropriate to achieve urban sustainability (Legacy & van den Nouwelant, 2015; Palazzo, 2019).

At a programmatic level, contested places and conflicting uses are increasingly common in the contemporary urban environment. Urban redevelopment and population growth affect the availability of public space. For instance, densification of low-density neighbourhoods in many Australian capital cities means more users sharing the same open spaces. Moreover, large-scale land use transformations may conflict with residents' expectations. The involvement of the local community, as the repository of multiple and complex interests, can be an opportunity to guarantee equal shares, understand the values generated by a negotiated project and meet different needs.

There are also challenges unique to the urban design process. Urban design is a highly institutionalised process aimed at generating pre-defined spatial outputs that allow few modifications. This approach reduces the possibility of innovating and harnessing the potential of rapid change in urban areas while dealing with high degrees of uncertainty (Palazzo, 2019). Urban design is often a closed process led by experts only and excludes non-disciplinary knowledge in the planning process (Iskander, 2018). This also represents a limitation to community participation in the implementation phases of the planning process.

Finally, conflicting urban agendas are hindering the possibility of achieving a holistic and inclusive approach to change in cities. Environmental objectives are not always aligned with socio-economic objectives and the pursuit of urban resilience often conflicts with urban sustainability goals (see Chapter 3). For instance, research on urban climate adaptation suggests that land use planning for environmental management is intensifying socio-spatial inequalities (Anguelovski et al., 2016; Shi et al., 2016). Effective solutions at an ecological level are usually unable to embrace the social dimensions of cities. In the case of flood risk reduction measures, post-disaster recovery programmes such as those in New Orleans have been opportunities for central governments to reshape urban areas with top-down decisions that do not engage with the needs expressed by local communities and do not include local participation in the redevelopment process (Neville & Coats, 2009).

This chapter explores the applications of adaptive design thinking by examining the relationship between placemaking and rapid urban change through the governance, programmatic and environmental dimensions of planning. Using a green corridor case study in inner Sydney, the research examines which strategies can be put in place and how placemaking initiatives can have a substantial role in urban design to address the complex challenges posed by urban transformations.

Questions, Objectives and Methods

Placemaking is a well-known approach to community planning and urban design and is often associated with the regeneration of degraded spaces in disadvantaged communities. Nevertheless, few studies focus on the relationships between placemaking and current urban transformations and placemaking's capacity to address transitions and leverage urban change. It is not yet clear whether and how placemaking can support the creation of new urban places as well as sustain existing 'emplaced' communities.

The case study in this chapter is showing how an adaptive approach to urban design could support communities affected by rapidly changing conditions and maintain the emphasis on 'place' as the centre of community interaction.

Examining the existing scientific literature, the research has identified four adaptive design strategies to deal with urban change:

the governance, programme, method and performance of the urban design process. The theoretical framework outlined is tested against a case study to gain a better understanding of how these dimensions are applied to current placemaking practices (see also Chapter 9).

The research applies a 'most likely' case study analysis method (Flyvbjerg, 2006). A strategic sampling identified a case study able to reveal a better level of insight than representative samples. The case study has been chosen for its validity and capacity to exemplify the four adaptive design strategies in the theoretical framework. This method is suitable to falsification of propositions. For instance, by isolating potential weaknesses in the 'most likely' case study we will presumably inform other 'weaker' cases (Flyvbjerg, 2006).

The GreenWay project in inner Sydney is an outstanding example of over two decades of collaboration between the local community, councils and other agencies around a shared proposal of an ecological corridor connecting two water catchments in the Sydney metropolitan region (Fig. 7.1).

Green corridors within urban areas are complex projects involving the scale of a whole water catchment that needs the integration of a plurality of planning dimensions. In this context, the GreenWay project represents an opportunity to explore long-term environmental management processes led by the local community. This project exemplifies how initial environmental initiatives led by a small group of citizens were able to embrace increasing complexity over time by incorporating more views and competing interests. Progressive adjustments to changing conditions allowed the project to remain relevant while building the adaptive capacity of places and communities.

Four Strategies for Adaptive Design

In urban design and placemaking, adaptability relies on a range of intersecting themes including sociopolitical, functional-technical, temporal and environmental dimensions of urban systems and places. Four adaptive approaches indicating responses to environmental change have been identified in the literature (Table 7.1) relating to the transdisciplinary, multifunctional, incremental and resilience dimensions of urban design.

7 Design for Change: An Adaptive Approach to Urban Places ...

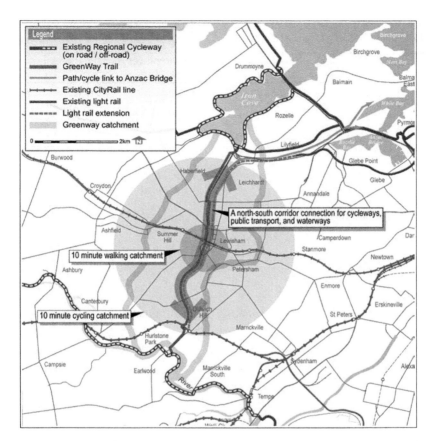

Fig. 7.1 Cooks River to Iron Cove GreenWay masterplan and coordination strategy (*Source* GCSWG, 2009, p. 20)

Each dimension is explored with examples to illustrate their contributions. These include issues of community inclusion, design thinking, resources co-management and equitable approaches (Palazzo, 2019).

Transdisciplinarity

The conceptualisation of cities as the result of a plurality of human decisions over time highlights the role of communities in the process of collective construction of the urban environment. However, modern

Table 7.1 A theoretical framework for adaptive design of changing urban places

	Adaptive design strategies	Planning dimensions	Urban places dimensions	Practices
A	Transdisciplinarity	Governance	Sociopolitical	Inclusiveness/engagement/co-design/traditional knowledge/open process
B	Multifunctionality	Programme	Functional/technical	Uses/users/integration/coexistence
C	Incremental change	Method	Temporal/economic	Maintenance/re-use/progressive implementation/process vs. output/iterative learning/adaptive cycles
D	Resilience	Performance	Environmental	Nature-based/biodiversity/biophilic/regenerative approaches

urban planning and design have often excluded local communities from determining their environment. Spatial transformation of contemporary cities is often driven by large-scale top-down urban design schemes that overlook space collaborative management and design approaches (Boone, 2013).

Increasing public awareness around sustainable and equitable management of the commons requires the establishment of new partnerships between government, the design professions and local communities. This suggests that, in order to achieve an equitable management of public space, a plurality of perspectives is required, not just experts and local inhabitants must be included.

Co-management and transdisciplinary practices have been identified as the main approaches to achieve urban sustainability (Anguelovski et al., 2016) because they address complexity and support local populations in facing social and environmental challenges (Armitage, Berkes, & Doubleday, 2007). Open collaborative approaches and co-generated solutions, including non-expert knowledge, define spatial outcomes that are based on people's needs and perceptions of their own environment. User-centred approaches can be a driver of social justice, adaptive capacity and sustainable places (Anguelovski et al., 2016). These practices require strategies of 'interpretive engagement' (Iskander, 2018) based on understanding the deep connections of places and people and inclusive governance practices. The integration of specific disciplinary knowledge with the local knowledge of a place by the people who inhabit it needs to be developed.

Moreover, methods that facilitate the interactions, discussions and creative expression of all the stakeholders involved can trigger design innovation and novel spatial solutions (Sanders & Stappers, 2014).

An example of transdisciplinary management of a green urban corridor is the urban renewal project for the Cheonggyecheon canal in Seoul, South Korea where local committees were established to oversee the project's implementation.

Multifunctionality

Growing urbanisation implies greater complexity and congestion of cities. Less open space is available per capita, as many different and sometimes competing functions need to be considered. Diverse practices and uses need to be accommodated in the same area.

Higher densities and the imperative of sustainability call for optimisation of land development in urban areas, introducing the idea of multifunctional spaces. In landscape planning, the concept of 'multifunctional land use' or 'multifunctionality' defines the combination of multiple functions in the same space by clustering natural, social and economic processes. Multifunctionality extends beyond the concept of mixed-use zoning, including the dynamic integration and synergy of different functional aspects.

Ecological infrastructure has been identified as a key strategy to achieve multifunctional land use in public urban space (Ahern, Cilliers,

& Niemelä, 2014) and directly contribute to placemaking (Vernon & Tiwari, 2009). Multifunctional practices based on the provision of green networks provide significant cultural ecosystem services that bring multiple socio-ecological benefits. They operate at various levels of implementation, providing urban amenity and health benefits, enhancing place identity, spiritual and recreational values, and sustaining urban liveability, resilience and economic development (Yu, 2011).

In placemaking, this approach suggests a plurality of programmes and sociocultural targets such as user-friendly design, children and gender-friendly design, and design for all. The design of adaptive and flexible places requires active engagement of the community to support the coexistence of diverse uses and to address the unexpected, creative and changing social attitudes to space by users and the idea of place as a living system.

An example of multifunctional land use planning is the composite ecosystem services, including amenity, public health and ecological functions, provided by the Red Ribbon Park in Qinhuangdao, China, designed by Turenscape.

Incremental Transformations

Historically, urban spaces were generated by the reiteration of social practices (Cresswell, 2004) that included the interaction of inhabitants with the surrounding environment. These slow incremental processes have taken place in small imperceptible steps, as transformations were triggered by low-impact alterations and daily maintenance of the urban space.

Only in recent times has urban development started to be regulated comprehensively by institutionalised procedures through unitary 'designed' interventions in an effort to control cities' growth centrally. However, today's rapid global changes do not guarantee the viability of conventional master-planning practices triggered by top-down approaches. Shifting economic, social and environmental contexts require a constant revision of scopes, and new objectives have to be accommodated along the way (Palazzo, 2019). In addition, large-scale urban transformations often generate resident opposition and are unlikely to be accepted by local communities.

The slow and composite, layered processes that generated cities in the past could be reconsidered in contemporary planning discussions on how to manage and develop places gradually (Qviström, 2018). Especially within contested urban spaces, long-time frames are essential for the local population to take ownership of transformations. Gradual changes driven by incremental projects can facilitate this process. Slow and small transformations can be progressively negotiated and lead to expected results over a longer perspective (Esposito De Vita, Trillo, & Martinez-Perez, 2016). Moreover, long-time frames offer the possibility of gradually settling new spatial configurations in the collective imagination of local residents, especially when they are directly invested in processes of placemaking (Benson & Jackson, 2013).

Projects that do not comprehensively alter the existing context can integrate and retrofit available resources and infrastructure with new localised, low-cost interventions. The synergy between old and new may generate novel spatial outcomes and significantly improve the performance of pre-existing contexts.

The process of incremental transformation has a background in urban economics where it is often referred to as 'macroprudential policy' or 'layering' (Baker, 2013). A lack of resources may trigger operations diluted over time, to take advantage of deferred funding when available. Small-scale interventions with low economic impact can be implemented as independent projects or aggregated according to location and available resources (Palazzo, 2008; Palazzo & Pelucca, 2014).

An example of incremental change providing an implementation strategy 'by-points' is the Urban Acupuncture project by Studiostudio in Florence, Italy.

Resilience

The need to define new conceptual frameworks to face global change and, in particular, the variability of environmental conditions in urban areas, has provided the ground to adapt some primary concepts from landscape ecology to the urban environment (Pickett, Cadenasso, & McGrath, 2013). The understanding of cities as an interdependent system of people, places and nature, or socio-ecological systems (see Chapter 3), has changed the way we conceptualise urban space design and the objectives of 'placemaking'.

Ecological sciences have described natural and anthropogenic processes as interdependent systems whose interrelations are unpredictable and non-linear. Resilience theories have provided a means of understanding how to generate adaptive capacity in the frame of challenging rapid transformations, in particular climate change, in both ecological and social systems (Folke et al., 2002). Resilience has been defined as 'the capacity of a system to absorb disturbance and reorganise while undergoing change so as to retain essentially the same functions, structures and feedback and therefore identity' (Walker & Salt, 2012). In order to build cities' resilience, scientific research proposes to translate the tools defined for the natural environment to the urban context. This means applying adaptive management and multi-level governance approaches to involve the local community and allow adaptive learning (Folke et al., 2002).

Adaptive design refers to the capacity of an urban project to respond to the effects of climate change with different measures while driving spatial regeneration (Palazzo & Wan, 2017). Green, soft and flexible strategies can be deployed in urban public space to respond to extreme weather events. For instance, flooding can be controlled through the implementation of 'nature-based solutions' or 'designed ecologies' (Saunders, 2013). These approaches respond to weather hazards in a way that the system itself is able to self-reorganise and recover from disturbance without modifying its intrinsic state (Ahern et al., 2014). They also provide significant cultural ecosystem services to the local community including health, spiritual and aesthetic benefits (Frumkin, 2003).

In landscape architecture, adaptive design applied to climate change has led to new spatial aesthetics, based on the variability of seasons, recurrent flooding, water level transitions, etc. (Palazzo, 2019).

An example of the resilience approach in urban design is the green strategy for Singapore's Bishan Park wetlands, by Atelier Ramboll-Dreiseitl.

The GreenWay Project, Inner Sydney

The GreenWay is a proposal for a linear green corridor in the inner west of the Sydney metropolitan region stretching for about 5.8 km between Cooks River in the south and Iron Cove in the north. The corridor is an ambitious project initiated in the 1990s by grass-roots community initiatives, primarily aiming to achieve a continuous bicycle path and biodiversity restoration sites along the water catchment of the Hawthorne Canal and the Rozelle freight rail line (Crawshaw, 2009; George, 2018; George, Ottignon, & Goldstein, 2015). Hawthorne Canal is a waterway, in part natural and in part humanmade, resulting from the dredging of the shallow waters of the Iron Cove on the Paramatta River in the 1890s (McLoughlin, 2000; Sabolch, 2006). Its catchment is state heritage listed with important local cultural values for the surrounding neighbourhoods. An historical freight line, the Rozelle 'goods line', also runs in part along the same waterway. Decommissioned in 2009, the freight line was repurposed as a light rail passenger line which opened in 2014.

The project was started by a group of volunteers living in the area. Initially concerned about the degraded environment of the water catchment, they became aware of the wider potential of the initiative and its metropolitan impact only later. The initial objectives had two major aspects: an active transport corridor with a new cycleway surrounded by native vegetation. The popularity of the first initiatives, including the establishment of bushland restoration areas managed by the community, further reinforced an emerging vision of a new green corridor, free of cars, in a strategic area of Sydney's inner west (Crawshaw, 2009). In the following years, a broader group of stakeholders joined the project and new strategic directions emerged. Complex governance arrangements among the councils of Ashfield, Canterbury, Leichhardt and Marrickville were established, also involving several state agencies, such as the railways and river authorities, as well as community and environmental groups located in the area.

The initial aims shared by a small number of community groups—to take advantage of the green corridor along the canal to regenerate the surrounding natural and cultural environment—were gradually integrated by new objectives. New priorities emerged with substantial shifts of focus for the area planning objectives (George et al., 2015). In particular, the light rail line generated new opportunities for the development of medium density transit-oriented neighbourhoods along the corridor. The shift from an active transport corridor towards more articulated objectives of public transport and urban densification substantially altered the scale and scope of the initial proposals.

Today, different sustainability agendas, socio-demographic change, gentrification processes and urbanisation pressures are competing with the ongoing implementation of the GreenWay which is more and more characterised as a contested space (George, 2018; George et al., 2015). In spite of the challenges encountered in the development of the project, a new GreenWay masterplan has recently been adopted by councils and funding made available by the NSW state government to complete the missing links of the corridor (McGregor/Coxall, 2018).

GreenWay and Urban Change

The GreenWay is an evolving project which has not yet reached a conclusion. Many early objectives (i.e. the spatial continuity of the green corridor) have been partially achieved and only recently funded. However, the capacity of the project to maintain a clear focus around defined objectives shared by all urban actors and to include community inputs has attracted considerable attention in research and the media as a case study of good governance and best practices.

The other significant aspect that emerged from this research is the capacity of the GreenWay project to adapt to changing external conditions for over 20 years. A better understanding on how it was possible to maintain the project's traction and the focus around the community's ownership still needs to be developed.

There are three aspects of urban change that may need to be examined. First, the role of governance and political volatility within a complex jurisdiction of land ownership has consistently made it difficult to get funding. Second, in Sydney's transport and development planning strategy, urban densification programmes for the catchment will significantly increase the population living in the area. Finally, the effects of environmental and climatic change experienced in recent years have provided a robust justification for a comprehensive environmental strategy to increase urban resilience (Fig. 7.2).

Fostering a Shared Vision: Transdisciplinarity

Despite significant changes in the original planning scope and objectives for the GreenWay, the initial vision for a green linear corridor shared by a group of motivated citizens has endured for over two decades.

The community was able to capitalise on divergent values of the early programme. Conflicting interests in the first stages of the GreenWay—on the one side the environmental objectives and on the other the public transport objectives—became strengths. This was in part possible because collaborative forms of governance and initiatives based on adaptive arrangements were supported by local governments (George et al., 2015). In the early stages, small state government grants supported a first formalisation of the governance process, facilitating community advocacy, enhancing stakeholders' coordination and establishing community education programmes to foster a shared vision within councils and residents. However, the unstable political environment in 2010–2012 which threatened the project's momentum represented a real turning point for the project. In order to sustain traction around the GreenWay vision, a 'shared place management approach' was initiated (George, 2018) with the establishment of a 'place manager'. This new role was essential in maintaining a clear vision with shared objectives and served as a catalyst of community and government activities and events to leverage change in the following years.

More recently, in 2017, in the frame of an inclusive governance approach, a series of community consultations was organised with the specific aim to inform the GreenWay masterplan including the outcomes of the collaboration of a team of experts and non-experts. A series of recommendations were included in the official document for

Fig. 7.2 The GreenWay timeline and incremental process (Image by Elisa Palazzo based on McGregor/Coxall [2018], Legacy and van den Nouwelant [2015], Jennifer George [2018])

the implementation of the GreenWay missing links (McGregor/Coxall, 2018). The strategic plan, adopted by councils in 2018, was still able to capture the four strategies reflecting the GreenWay early vision: ecology, active transport, recreation and culture. However, despite previous successful experiences of community direct involvement in co-management initiatives, the masterplan does not include or support any suggestion or strategy to engage residents in the realisation and maintenance phases of the GreenWay once the masterplan is implemented.

Coexisting: Multifunctionality

Since the very early phases of the GreenWay, the awareness which developed around the idea of possible shared benefits deriving from a multifunctional approach was at the core of the success of the project. The multifunctional project initially included environmental, recreation and public health issues: an urban ecology protection programme with biodiversity conservation areas and bushcare activities; active transport with walking and cycling routes and sports grounds; and a recreation project with playgrounds, cafes, dog exercise areas, art installations and community events (Crawshaw, 2009).

Later, the conversion of the freight line to a passenger light rail line was proposed. With public transport gaining traction, residents expressed some resistance, concerned about the risk of conflicting objectives and a shift in the focus of the project (George et al., 2015). When the light rail did become an integral part of the project in 2011, increased interest in new transit-oriented developments emerged. Since then, several new developments proposals have been put forward, with the population living in the GreenWay catchment forecasted to increase in the next years (George, 2018).

This shift of focus has required a reconsideration of urban density and population growth, with new challenges deriving from increasing cultural diversity of the social structure, and possible conflicts in the coexistence of new uses and users, in addition to the multiple uses already existing.

To some extent, the new 2018 masterplan does acknowledge the need to integrate old and new uses of the corridor including spatial, natural and cultural dimensions. The plan reinforces the vision for a multifunctional programme, envisioning a 'green grid' infrastructure able to weave together different spatial uses and space users. Besides re-proposing the four objective from the early GreenWay shared vision of ecology, active transport, recreation and culture, the plan adds 'integration' as strategy to create synergies between new old and new objectives: active and public transport; recreation and culture; public health and sports; environmental, ecological and biodiversity protection; climate change resilience and water management (McGregor/Coxall, 2018).

A Project 'By-Points': Incremental Change

The GreenWay is located in a dense urban area of Sydney's inner west. Besides a complex jurisdiction of multiple authorities and land ownership, the corridor is characterised by the spatial encroachment of different urban infrastructure. The physical interruption created by roads and rail tracks crossing the linear park has so far prevented the achievement of a continuous linear corridor without a substantial financial investment.

In the initial phases of the grass-roots project, the difficulty in ensuring a substantial investment by the state government dictated an alternative road map towards non-conventional implementation schemes. The implementation had to be organised in small steps, relying on intermittent sources of funding and based on strategic spending, to target low-cost and high-effectiveness projects and guarantee multiple benefits and high returns from investment.

The Lords Road mural and the Hawthorne Canal community mosaic projects in 2011 are an example of this strategy (Fig. 7.3). Security and lighting issues initially triggered the need for an intervention under the tunnel that connects Leichhardt, on the east of the light rail tracks, to the GreenWay linear park. The tunnel is a strategic access to the green corridor and one of the few connections between the two sides of the GreenWay. The installation consists of murals and a mosaic realised by

Fig. 7.3 The Lords Road mural and the Hawthorne Canal community mosaic projects in August 2018 (Photo by Elisa Palazzo)

local schools and community artists in a joint initiative of Leichhardt Council and the NSW government rail agency. The art installation, representing the aspirations and history of the place, has been the catalyst for collaborative efforts and co-design by several volunteering organisations and the engagement of students (IWC).

The tunnel project is just one of the elements of a network of significant cultural sites along the GreenWay (Inner West Council, 2019). An art and cultural strategy involve the community in the direct implementation of small projects that respond to the programmatic levels of low-cost, effective, engaging and incremental. Bushcare conservation activities by volunteer groups also sustain the focus and build community ownership around shared objectives.

The recent masterplan seems to have, in part, retained the early approach. Subdividing the plan into smaller localised and easily manageable projects, and organising them in seven precincts, the plan seeks to strategically prioritise future implementations that work in synergy in an interconnected network (McGregor/Coxall, 2018). However, there is no mention of the possible involvement of the community in implementation activities, and how the original 'incremental' tactic will be included in the GreenWay in the future (Fig. 7.4).

148 E. Palazzo

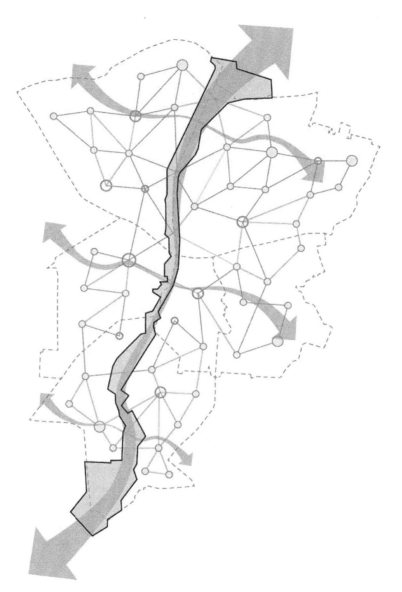

Fig. 7.4 Long-term objectives and evolving project (*Source* GreenWay Masterplan 2018 [McGregor/Coxall, 2018])

Building Adaptive Capacity: Resilience

The natural system of the GreenWay catchment has been significantly altered since the first Europeans arrived in Sydney. Water and vegetation systems were compromised by progressive soil sealing and native vegetation clearing. However, the linear structure of the freight corridor, only partially accessible by the community and unmaintained, preserved a certain level of biodiversity (Crawshaw, 2009). These factors, in addition to recent decades of deliberate bush site conservation, have gradually recovered native species and wildlife habitat, including a rare species of microbat uncommon in other metropolitan region parks.

In terms of environmental sustainability, the 2009 GreenWay sustainability project has been acknowledged for its positive outcomes, including a vast tree-planting programme and the introduction of new bushcare sites along the corridor. Among the 50 actions identified by the plan for implementation, several addressed primary ecological and environmental concerns, seeking the direct engagement of the community in bush care, weed control, environmental education and water management issues, among others (George, 2018).

The GreenWay is now, even before the completion of the 'missing links' (McGregor/Coxall, 2018), prime urban green infrastructure that responds to both metropolitan and local scales with different ecosystem services: the supporting and regulating ecological benefits of a biodiversity corridor connecting two urban water catchments within the high-density fabric of inner Sydney; the positive impacts on human health of an active transport strategy; and spiritual and recreational benefits deriving from the community's direct engagement in bushcare site management and public gardens.

More recently, water management issues have been considered with Water Sensitive Urban Design initiatives addressing water quality and pollution control. In response to climate change and in order to recognise the more frequent flash floods affecting the area, open public space resilience has been explicitly addressed in the most recent 2018 GreenWay masterplan. A detailed project on water edges proposes solutions for rising tide levels including new naturalised edges with mangroves, submersible surfaces and a bioretention rain garden (McGregor/Coxall, 2018).

Lessons Learned from the GreenWay

In August 2018, a new comprehensive masterplan for the GreenWay corridor was adopted by the newly amalgamated Inner West Council. This policy document can be considered the culmination of a process lasting over two decades, establishing formal obligations between the urban actors involved and investing $25.6 million for implementation.

In the early stages, the GreenWay project was driven by community efforts and managed through an open governance structure and collaborative leadership allowing a high degree of flexibility to achieve the project's objectives. This informal structure gradually developed into a more sophisticated mechanism as the project gained traction and moved towards institutionalised processes, with the need to manage substantial funding and more complex jurisdictions (George et al., 2015). In its most recent phases, the project has also been in part informed by formal processes of community consultations, through focus groups in November 2017. These inputs are reflected in the 2018 masterplan that well represents the vision developed over many years of community support and active engagement. In this sense, this latest masterplan has to be given credit for its capacity to capture the community's perspectives, work as a 'catalyst' for different interests and maintain the vision of the early GreenWay project.

However, the plan's main objective is to define the detailed description of missing links to be implemented along the corridor, the resources required and a comprehensive set of design guidelines (McGregor/Coxall, 2018). In the process of translating the GreenWay experience into a normative document, a conventional understanding of urban design and placemaking is emerging and the informal knowledge and governance experience generated by years of trial and error that could accommodate ongoing environmental change or evolving contexts is not represented. Likewise, no further input of the local community is considered besides the initial consultations, which could be essential to inform the implementation phase of the project with the first-hand experience of the community.

Once the spatial objectives of transformation have been achieved there is a risk that community-led collaborative projects will be perceived as no longer a benefit (George, 2018). The question is then how to maintain the GreenWay at the centre of community interaction, environmental education and participation within the process of implementation.

There are several opportunities that could be explored to engage the community in the implementation and post-implementation phases of the project. First, there is an opportunity to involve the community in the actual phases of design and construction, through co-design workshops and experimental construction sites, in collaboration with the professions, schools and volunteer groups.

The community and the groups involved in bushcare management could support environmental research in collaboration with local universities in post-implementation and environmental monitoring projects.

Finally, an important opportunity for urban research is the governance-building process that led to the implementation of the corridor, as a continuing and evolving experimental project in adaptive urban design.

Conclusions

This chapter explored an application of adaptive design in the context of rapid urban changes in the Sydney metropolitan area. It examined which placemaking strategies and urban design approaches have been deployed in order to respond to the complex challenges of urban transformation (Table 7.2).

The GreenWay project in inner west Sydney is a unique case study in the Australian context. As an outstanding example of adaptive urban design deployed over a long-time frame, significant lessons can be learnt by unravelling the processes of urbanisation that determined its development. More research is needed to disentangle the overlaying

Table 7.2 Summary of placemaking strategies and urban design approaches deployed to respond to urban transformation in the GreenWay project

	Placemaking activities supporting adaptive outcomes
Transdisciplinarity	Fostering a shared vision: a place management approach
Multifunctionality	Coexisting: inclusive strategy of programmes, users and uses
Incremental change	A project 'by points': progressive transformations including community-led collaborative projects
Resilience	Building adaptive capacity: continuity of ecological corridor maintained by residents

mechanisms and opportunities of an existing context to process transformations and adapt to changing urban conditions.

Facing socio-environmental change in urban areas requires the active involvement of local communities across all phases of the design and placemaking process. However, there is a risk that institutionalising the process of public participation will discourage and dilute the traction of grass-roots initiatives, especially in the implementation phases.

Placemaking and place management approaches can support a more just and effective making of urban environments. However, these processes are time and resource consuming and require long-time frames. An incremental 'layering' approach requires accurate planning and understanding of the context. A detailed knowledge of social, spatial and ecological drivers is also required to recognise where change can be negotiated with the community to guide environmental dynamics.

More nuanced forms of 'design skills' are needed to set up effective collaboration between experts and non-expert urban actors. Urban designers are required to be 'catalysts' in the expression of community demands but also serve as facilitators of collaborative processes including co-design with the active participation of the community.

More transdisciplinary design experiments are needed to seek the collaboration of researchers, community, local governments and all the other actors involved to inform policy and guidelines to be able to effectively address the challenges of urban transformation.

Key Learnings

- Fostering a shared vision inclusive of all the possible dimensions of a place can help address the challenges emerging from rapid urban change.
- An inclusive strategy helps to synchronise diverse conflicting programmes, users and uses in order to achieve a harmonious coexistence in increasing urban densities.
- Spatial transformations can be implemented gradually with incremental steps also including small-scale community-led collaborative projects.
- The environmental and ecological objectives of an ecological corridor support the process of building adaptive capacity and defining community identity in providing opportunities for active engagement.

References

Ahern, J., Cilliers, S., & Niemelä, J. (2014). The concept of ecosystem services in adaptive urban planning and design: A framework for supporting innovation. *Landscape and Urban Planning, 125,* 254–259. https://doi.org/10.1016/j.landurbplan.2014.01.020.

Anguelovski, I., Shi, L., Chu, E., Gallagher, D., Goh, K., Lamb, Z., & Teicher, H. (2016). Equity impacts of urban land use planning for climate adaptation. *Journal of Planning Education and Research, 36*(3), 333–348. https://doi.org/10.1177/0739456x16645166.

Armitage, D. R., Berkes, F., & Doubleday, N. (2007). *Adaptive co-management collaboration, learning, and multi-level governance.* Vancouver, BC: UBC Press.

Baker, A. (2013). The gradual transformation? The incremental dynamics of macroprudential regulation. *Regulation & Governance, 7*(4), 417–434. https://doi.org/10.1111/rego.12022.

Benson, M., & Jackson, E. (2013). Place-making and place maintenance: Performativity, place and belonging among the middle classes. *Sociology, 47*(4), 793–809. https://doi.org/10.1177/0038038512454350.

Boone, C. G. (2013). Social dynamics and sustainable urban design. In S. T. A. Pickett, M. L. Cadenasso, & B. McGrath (Eds.), *Resilience in ecology and urban design: Linking theory and practice for sustainable cities*. New York: Springer.

Crawshaw, P. (2009). *The future of Greenways in Sydney*. Sydney: UNSW.

Cresswell, T. (2004). *Place: A short introduction*. Oxford: Wiley-Blackwell.

Esposito De Vita, G., Trillo, C., & Martinez-Perez, A. (2016). Community planning and urban design in contested places. Some insights from Belfast. *Journal of Urban Design, 21*(3), 320–334. https://doi.org/10.1080/13574809.2016.1167586.

Flyvbjerg, B. (2006). Five misunderstandings about case-study research. *Qualitative Inquiry, 12*(2), 219–245. https://doi.org/10.1177/1077800405284363.

Folke, C., Carpenter, S., Elmqvist, T., Gunderson, L., Holling, C. S., & Walker, B. (2002). Resilience and sustainable development: Building adaptive capacity in a world of transformations. *AMBIO: A Journal of the Human Environment, 31*(5), 437–440. https://doi.org/10.1579/0044-7447-31.5.437.

Friedmann, J. (2010). Place and place-making in cities: A global perspective. *Planning Theory & Practice, 11*(2), 149–165. https://doi.org/10.1080/14649351003759573.

Frumkin, H. (2003). Healthy places: Exploring the evidence. *American Journal of Public Health, 93*(9), 1451–1456.

George, J. (2018). *The contribution of community governance towards the sustainable planning and management of urban and regional green infrastructure*. Doctoral dissertation. Retrieved from https://espace.curtin.edu.au/bitstream/handle/20.500.11937/70520/George%20J%202018.pdf?sequence=1&isAllowed=y.

George, J., Ottignon, E., & Goldstein, W. (2015). Managing expectations for sustainability in a changing context—In Sydney's—Inner west—A GreenWay governance case study. *Australian Planner, 52*(3), 187–198. https://doi.org/10.1080/07293682.2015.1034736.

Gertner, D. (2011). Unfolding and configuring two decades of research and publications on place marketing and place branding. *Place Branding and Public Diplomacy, 7*(2): 91–106. https://doi.org/10.1057/pb.2011.7. IWC, G. GreenWay—Arts.

GreenWay Coordination Strategy Working Group. (2009). *Cooks River to Iron Cove GreenWay masterplan & coordination strategy*.

Inner West Council. (2019). *GreenWay—Arts*. Retrieved from https://www.greenway.org.au/community/arts. Accessed 25 Feb 2019.

Iskander, N. (2018). Design thinking is fundamentally conservative and preserves the Status Quo. *Harvard Business Review*. Retrieved from https://hbr.org/2018/09/design-thinking-is-fundamentally-conservative-and-preserves-the-status-quo.

Legacy, C., & van den Nouwelant, R. (2015). Negotiating strategic planning's transitional spaces: The case of 'guerrilla governance' in *infrastructure planning*. *Environment and Planning A: Economy and Space, 47*(1), 209–226. https://doi.org/10.1068/a140124p.

Mant, J. (2000). Putting place outcomes at the centre of planning law and administration. *Australian Planner, 37*(2), 59–64. https://doi.org/10.1080/07293682.2000.9657878.

McGregor/Coxall. (2018). *GreenWay masterplan—Cooks to cove GreenWay*. NSW.

McLoughlin, L. C. (2000). Shaping Sydney Harbour: Sedimentation, dredging and reclamation 1788–1990s. *Australian Geographer, 31*(2), 183–208. https://doi.org/10.1080/713612246.

Neville, J., & Coats, G. (2009). Urban design and civil society in New Orleans: Challenges, opportunities and strategies in the post-flood design moment. *Journal of Urban Design, 14*(3), 309–324. https://doi.org/10.1080/13574800903087940.

Palazzo, E. (2008). Il progetto del Pedibus a Firenze. In M. Morandi, E. Palazzo, & B. Pelucca (Eds.), *I materiali del progetto urbano*. Padova: Il Prato.

Palazzo, E. (2019). From water sensitive to floodable: Defining adaptive urban design for water resilient cities. *Journal of Urban Design, 24*(1), 137–157.

Palazzo, E., & Pelucca, B. (2014). Agopuntura urbana. *OPERE—Premio Architettura Territorio Fiorentino, 38*, 68–73.

Palazzo, E., & Wan, N. M. W. M. R. (2017). Regenerating urban areas through climate sensitive urban design. *Advanced Science Letters, 23*(7), 6394–6398.

Pickett, S. T., Cadenasso, M. L., & McGrath, B. (Eds.). (2013). *Resilience in ecology and urban design: Linking theory and practice for sustainable cities* (Vol. 3). New York: Springer.

Project for Public Space. (2018). *What is placemaking*. Retrieved from https://www.pps.org/article/what-is-placemaking.

Qviström, M. (2018). Farming ruins: A landscape study of incremental urbanisation. *Landscape Research, 43*(5), 575–586. https://doi.org/10.1080/01426397.2017.1353959.

Sabolch, M. (2006). *Hawthorn Canal: A history of long Cove Creek*. Ashfield, NSW: Ashfield and District Historical Society in association with Inner West Environmental Group.

Sanders, E. B. N., & Stappers, P. J. (2014). Probes, toolkits and prototypes: Three approaches to making in codesigning. *CoDesign, 10*(1), 5–14. https://doi.org/10.1080/15710882.2014.888183.

Saunders, W. S. (2013). *Designed ecologies the landscape architecture of Kongjian Yu*. Basel: De Gruyter.

Shi, L., Chu, E., Anguelovski, I., Aylett, A., Debats, J., Goh, K., ... Van Deveer, S. D. (2016). Roadmap towards justice in urban climate adaptation research. *Nature Climate Change, 6*(2), 131–137. https://doi.org/10.1038/nclimate2841.

Vernon, B., & Tiwari, R. (2009). Place-making through water sensitive urban design. *Sustainability, 1*(4), 789.

Walker, B., & Salt, D. (2012). *Resilience thinking: Sustaining ecosystems and people in a changing world*. Washington, DC: Island Press.

Whyte, W. H. (1980). *The social life of small urban spaces*. Washington, DC: The Conservation Foundation.

Yu, K. (2011). Ecological infrastructure leads the way: The negative approach and landscape urbanism for smart preservation and smart growth. In *Applied urban ecology* (pp. 152–169). West Sussex: Wiley-Blackwell.

8

Economics of Place

Neil Sipe

> ....*doing a cost benefit analysis for a placemaking project requires both quantitative skills and creative thinking.*
> Neil Sipe

Introduction

In doing the research for this chapter, we began with a web search on the economic impacts and/or benefits of placemaking. Interestingly, the results provided many reports and websites focused on how placemaking can be used as an economic development tool. Many of these results were based in the United States and were not really what we were looking for; however, it does imply that placemaking can be an effective way to improve the local economy.

N. Sipe (✉)
School of Earth & Environmental Sciences,
University of Queensland, Brisbane, QLD, Australia
e-mail: n.sipe@uq.edu.au

© The Author(s) 2020
D. Hes and C. Hernandez-Santin (eds.), *Placemaking Fundamentals for the Built Environment*, https://doi.org/10.1007/978-981-32-9624-4_8

There is a general belief that walkable connected places that can result from placemaking initiatives are more desirable and thus command higher commercial leases, retails rents and sales and residential rents and sales. While there have been a couple of recently completed reviews of the literature on valuing placemaking (e.g. Carmona, 2019; Cohen et al., 2018), there is not much available that provides guidance on how to do an economic analysis of placemaking in a way that is understandable to non-technically trained professionals. That is the goal of this chapter.

For anyone contemplating evaluating placemaking from an economic perspective, the following literature should be examined. While Carmona (2019) identified almost 90 papers on this topic, we have provided a summary of the most relevant and important ones.

The most complete and current analysis is that of Carmona (2019). He provides an extensive review (49 pages) of the literature related to evaluating place across the health, social, economic and environmental sectors. For the economic sector, he identified 21 studies related to property values and greenspace, 24 studies on residential property values and urban design; 15 studies on commercial property values and urban design; ten studies on streets, public realm and economic value; 12 studies on economic development and regeneration; and 16 studies on public spending and savings. Based on his review of these studies, he concludes that placemaking can deliver: property value uplift in the residential, retail and office sectors; enhance competitiveness; reduced public expenditures; increased tax revenues; and lower costs of living.

Another current review is that of Cohen et al. (2018) who provide a detailed review of the literature on valuing creative placemaking. The 58-page report is the first stage of a project initiated by LandComm (the public land development arm of the New South Wales government) to develop a toolkit for valuing placemaking. The report is valuable because it not only describes the relevant and current research on the topic, but it also provides a number of useful tables that list the range of indicators used to value placemaking as well a list of frameworks, methodologies and toolkits currently being used to value placemaking.

Flanagan and Mitchell (2016) are included in our summary because it provides one of the few detailed economic analyses we could find of the Renew Newcastle project. This study examined the Renew Newcastle discusses details on how the cost–benefit analysis was done. Because of its detail, we have used it to illustrate some of the challenges involved in what benefits to include and how to quantify those benefits (60 pages).

Robinson et al. (2017) produced a short report (14 pages) examining placemaking and its impact on value. They focus on placemaking indicators and provide a summary of eleven global placemaking case studies. For each case, they provide: What happened; what was the outcome; property value change; and the Gehl (2017) score based on criteria for protection, comfort and enjoyment.

Millard, Nellthorp, and Ojeda Cabral (2018) are included because it is one of the few papers we could find that discusses the methodology developed by Transport for London for valuing the urban realm (VURT). In addition, the article is useful because of its description of how to value the urban realm using hedonic regression analysis for the Greater London area.

Similarly, Boffa Miskell Limited and Auckland Design Office City Centre (2017) are included for its discussion of Transport for London's VURT. The report examines the feasibility of using the VURT methodology to value placemaking in Auckland, New Zealand.

Savills (2016) was included because it provides a private sector perspective of placemaking. The report provides a summary of the economic value of placemaking for three case studies—Alconbury Weald, Heyford Park and Poundbury in England.

Finally, Stern (2014) provides a useful academic perspective on measuring the outcomes of creative placemaking. He provides a useful discussion of possible benefit categories, indicators and sources of data.

The remainder of the chapter focuses primarily on approaches that can be used value including: cost–benefit analysis; economic modelling; willingness to pay; and financial analysis. The last section briefly examines the role of business cases which links the economic and financial analysis with project implementation.

Cost–Benefit Analysis

There are several ways to evaluate a placemaking project from an economic perspective, but the most common one is cost–benefit analysis (CBA) or alternatively benefit–cost analysis (BCA). It provides a systematic method of examining a project's costs and benefits. The results of a CBA are typically shown as a single number: either as the project's overall benefits minus the costs; or as the ratio of the benefits to costs.

Like any analytical tool, CBA has a number of advantages and disadvantages. The advantages include: the ability to evaluate a range of similar projects using a common and widely accepted framework that is often required for when making a business case for funding. Another advantage is that it helps to align a project's costs and benefits. While a placemaking project might have many benefits, its costs might be great as well. One of the keys for successful implementation of any placemaking project is for the benefits and costs to be in balance—or at a minimum make that the benefits outweigh the costs. The key disadvantage of CBA is the requirement that all benefits and costs need to be expressed in monetary terms.

The level of effort required to do an economic evaluation should not be under-estimated as it often requires careful thinking about: (1) When to conduct the CBA; (2) what are the most appropriate things to measure; (3) how to best quantify them and sourcing the appropriate data; what timeframe; (4) what time period to use; and (5) what spatial area to use in measuring the impacts. The following discussion about CBA is organised around these five questions.

When to Conduct the CBA?

A CBA can be done for both proposed and completed placemaking projects. For a proposed project, baseline data on property values, rents and retails sales need to be collected before the project begins. This is the approach used for the Centre Improvement Program projects discussed briefly below and in more detail in Chapter 9. The Renew Newcastle analysis, also discussed below, is an example of a CBA that was several years after the project was completed. This is a rare case because few projects get evaluated after they are completed due to lack of funding, time and interest. The lack of interest is due to the fact that once the decision is made to fund a project (particularly those that are funded by government), decision makers are not interested in evaluations as they assume that the project will work as planned.

What to Measure and How to Measure It?

The types of economic benefits that may result from placemaking activities include increases in property values; lease rates/rents; and retail sales. There are also a range of other placemaking benefits, not typically presented in monetary terms, including improved: aesthetics; environmental quality; well-being; and sense of place. Incorporating these non-monetary benefits into a CBA can be done, but is difficult and time-consuming. As noted above, this is the main disadvantage of doing this type of analysis, but it should not be a reason not to do the CBA.

To illustrate what is involved in deciding what to measure and how to measure it, we use the Renew Newcastle project. The goals of this project were to: create vibrancy in the CBD by using empty buildings; and make the CBD more appealing by cleaning up streets and buildings (Flanagan & Mitchell, 2016). The results of the CBA are provided in Table 8.1. The table has been extracted from a report by Flanagan and

Table 8.1 Estimated costs and benefits of the Renew Newcastle project. Estimations based on data from Flanagan and Mitchell (2016, p. 42)

Benefits	Estimate ($)
Creation of jobs and skills development	2,358,436
Conversion to commercial leases	191,828
Volunteer engagement	62,763
Mitigation of blight	100,698
Improved business and community confidence	55,183
Improved regional brand value	234,069
Total benefits	3,002,977
Total costs	208,000
Net benefit	2,794,977
Benefit–cost ratio	14.4

Mitchell (2016) which summarised, in part, the results of a consultancy report done by SGS (2011). The project was evaluated three years after the project was completed.

A short summary of what was measured and how the monetary benefits for each category were calculated is provided below. This example provides a good demonstration that doing a CBA for a placemaking project requires both quantitative skills and creative thinking.

Creating jobs and skills development estimates the value of increased employment and income attributable to the project. The benefit calculation was based on surveys of Renew project participants. This was based on data from 2015/16. This calculation was based on only those directly involved in the project, so the benefit area is at the project level.

Conversion to commercial leases accounts for "graduates" of the Renew project that are now paying commercial rents rather than lower rates for those tenants part of the Renew project. These estimates were based on surveys of Renew graduates. This was based on data from 2015/16. This analysis was based on only graduates of the project. Thus, the benefit area was the same as the project area.

Volunteer engagement was the value attributable to volunteer involvement in the project. This was measured by using an estimate of the opportunity cost per hour based on Hensher and Wang (2016) and multiplying it by the total number of volunteer hours. This was based on the number of volunteers in 2015/16. This calculation was done for only those volunteers directly involved in the project. Similar to the previous three categories, the benefit area was the same as the project area.

Mitigation of blight was measured by examining the decrease in the crime rates for: criminal damage; break and enter; robbery; and assaults. It was assumed that the project was responsible for half of the decrease in the number of crimes in these four categories. These decreases were then multiplied by the average cost of each type of crime as established Smith et al. (2014). This was based on the decrease in crime between 2007/8 and 2014/15. This benefit calculation was done for the 2300 postcode as that is how the data are made available to researchers.

Improved business and community confidence was estimated by attributing a portion of the increase in median property values to

Renew Newcastle. Five per cent of the increase in property values was assumed to be a result of the project. Given the lack of research to justify this assumption, it is a conservation estimate. This was based on the increase in median property values between 2014 and 2015. This analysis was done for three suburbs that surrounded the project.

Improved regional brand value was estimated by assuming that five per cent of the growth in domestic and international visitors came to Newcastle as a result of the project. The five per cent value was a conservative estimate and was based, in part, on surveys of cruise ship passengers visiting Newcastle. Then the Renew Newcastle visitor numbers were multiplied by the average daily visitor expenditure. This was based on the increase in tourism between 2007/8 and 2015/16. The benefited area for this category was the Newcastle area.

What Timeframe to Use?

Time is a critical factor to consider when assessing the economic impact of a placemaking project. This is due to the fact that most project costs are incurred at the start of the project, while the benefits accrue over many years particularly because many projects need time to develop and mature.

There is no fixed timeframe for a CBA—it should be based on project type (temporary or permanent), scale (small or large) and context (e.g. where the project is located, data available data). There is also a strategic consideration as extending the timeframe should also increase the dollar value of the benefits. Thus, more expensive projects need to consider longer timeframes in order to justify the project costs.

Regardless of the timeframe used, it should be consistent across the cost and benefit categories. The Renew Newcastle analysis shown above in Table 8.1 contains a mixture of single year evaluations combined with ranges between 2007/8 and 2015/16. A more accurate way to do this is to show the project's impacts on an annual basis.

Using the three projects that are discussed in Chapter 9 as examples, we consider how project scale might impact on the project timeframe decision. For a small-scale project involving public art, the timeframe

Table 8.2 Example placemaking project characteristics

Initial project cost	$1,250,000
Net cash flow	
Yr 1	$100,000
Yr 2	$250,000
Yr 3	$400,000
Yr 4	$450,000
Yr 5	$470,000

might only involve a few years and in many cases might not even need a CBA. The medium-scale project, Gold Coast's Centre Improvement Program, has a ten-year timeframe that is built into the programme guidelines. For large projects, such as Brolga Lakes, the timeframe decision needs to consider how long it will take for the project to be completed. For many projects of this scale, it might take five to ten years to complete the project, so the timeframe for examining benefits might not even begin for a decade. However, it might be appropriate to begin the CBA once the first homeowners move into the project and continually updating the CBA until the project is completed. While this would be the optimal way to approach a large project, it is probably not feasible given the costs of doing one CBA, let along doing it on an annual basis.

Once the timeframe decision is made, it is important to consider how to calculate the project benefits and costs over time. To illustrate the considerations involved in how time can be dealt with in CBA, we use a hypothetical project with the characteristics as shown in Table 8.2.

The easiest way of calculating the net profits and the benefit–cost ratio for this project is to use Microsoft Excel© as shown in Table 8.3. The format for "Net profit" in cell B7 is: =SUM(B2:B6)−B1 and for "Benefit/cost ratio" is: =SUM(B2:B6)/B1.

This simple analysis shows that the proposed project results in a net profit of $420,000 over the first five years and has a benefit–cost ratio of 1.34. However, this analysis does not account for the time value of money. It assumes that receiving one dollar today is the same as getting one dollar at some future time, but this is not accurate because receiving one dollar in five years does not have the same value as one dollar

Table 8.3 Simple cost–benefit analysis

	A	B
	Initial project cost	$1,250,000
1	Yr 1 cash flow	$100,000
2	Yr 2 cash flow	$250,000
3	Yr 3 cash flow	$400,000
4	Yr 4 cash flow	$450,000
5	Yr 5 cash flow	$470,000
6	Net profit	$420,000
7	Benefit/cost ratio	1.34

does today. To factor in the future value of money, a cost–benefit analysis should present the results as the net present value (NPV) or as an internal rate of return (IRR).

Net present value analysis compares the annual cash flow (benefit–costs) over a fixed time period while incorporating the time value of money. Determining the time value of money requires the use of a discount rate which is the current market rate or cost of capital. The results are particularly sensitive to the discount rate and predicting an average discount rate over a five- to ten-year period can be challenging. A NPV analysis provides a single monetary value that allows a comparison of different projects with different timeframes. Typically, if the NPV for a project is negative the project is rejected, but if positive, then the project would be accepted.

The easiest way of calculating the NPV for a project is to use the NPV function in Microsoft Excel© as shown in Table 8.4. The format for the NPV formula in cell B8 is: =NPV(B1,B2:B7) which instructs Excel to use the discount rate shown in cell B1 to calculate the NPV for the cash flows shown in cells B2 through B7.

This means that the return on the investment of $1,250,000 with a ten per cent discount rate is a loss of $47,968 over five years with a 0.96 ($1,202,032/$1,250,000) benefit–cost ratio. This is far less than the $420,000 profit (or the benefit–cost ratio of 1.34) determined using the initial analysis that did not account the time value of money.

To show how sensitive the NPV calculation is to the discount rate, the same analysis is shown in Table 8.5 using a five per cent discount rate.

Table 8.4 Cost–benefit analysis using net present value with a 10% discount rate

	A	B
1	Discount rate	10%
2	Initial project cost	$1,250,000
3	Yr 1 cash flow	$100,000
4	Yr 2 cash flow	$250,000
5	Yr 3 cash flow	$400,000
6	Yr 4 cash flow	$450,000
7	Yr 5 cash flow	$470,000
8	NPV	$47,968

Table 8.5 Cost–benefit analysis using net present value with a 5% discount rate

	A	B
1	Discount rate	5%
2	Initial project cost	$1,250,000
3	Yr 1 cash flow	$100,000
4	Yr 2 cash flow	$250,000
5	Yr 3 cash flow	$400,000
6	Yr 4 cash flow	$450,000
7	Yr 5 cash flow	$470,000
8	NPV	$148,575

The return on investment is $148,575 ($1,398,575/$1,250,000) over five years with a 1.12 benefit–cost ratio. The selection of an appropriate discount rate is one of the most important decisions that must be made when calculating the NPV. These two scenarios show that the choice of a discount rate can make a difference when deciding whether to proceed with a project. With a ten per cent discount rate, the project may not be approved as it has a benefit–cost ratio of slightly less than one, but with a five per cent discount rate, the benefit–cost ratio exceeds one and is more likely to be approved.

Another commonly used approach to evaluate a proposed project is the IRR. The focus of this technique is on the breakeven cash flow level of a proposed project. The advantage of this approach is that it does not require a discount rate to be selected as the output of the analysis is a rate of return derived from the annual cash flows. If the

Table 8.6 Cost–benefit analysis using internal rate of return

	A	B
1	Initial project cost	$1,250,000
2	Yr 1 cash flow	$100,000
3	Yr 2 cash flow	$250,000
4	Yr 3 cash flow	$400,000
5	Yr 4 cash flow	$450,000
6	Yr 5 cash flow	$470,000
7	IRR	8.6%

IRR is higher than the discount rate/market rate, then the project may be one worth pursuing.

The easiest way to calculate an IRR for a project is to use the IRR formula in Microsoft Excel© as shown in Table 8.6. The format for the IRR formula in cell B7 is: =IRR(B1:B6) which instructs Excel to calculate an IRR for the cash flows shown in cells B1 through B6. The IRR for the example project is 8.6 per cent, suggesting that if the current discount rate is ten per cent then the project might not be worth pursuing because the IRR is less than the current market rate. However, with a five per cent discount rate this is a more feasible project from a financial perspective—because the IRR is greater than the current market rate.

What Is the Size of the Impacted Area?

The last critical factor to consider in doing a CBA is deciding on what benefit area to measure. This is a judgement call and should be based on the size of the area impacted by the placemaking project. It will be dependent on the type, scale and location of the project. As with the time period, the spatial area used should be consistent across all benefit categories. However, this may not always be possible due to limitations with available data. If data are available, it would be advisable to examine several spatial extents—one within a few blocks of the project and the other at a broader neighbourhood or suburb scale.

Again, we use the three projects in Chapter 9 to illustrate how project scale can impact on the decision of what size the benefit area should be. For a small-scale project, the benefit area might only be a few blocks that surround the project, again bearing in mind that a CBA may not be required for these small projects. The decision on the scale for the medium-scale example is determined through the Centre Improvement Program guidelines—and is only the size of the area actually being improved. For large-scale development projects, it might be necessary to do the analysis at two levels—one at project boundary level and another at the neighbourhood, suburb or regional scale.

Returning to the Renew Newcastle project, we can see that the benefit area might vary by the type of benefit being measured. In some cases, the benefit area is the same as the project area, but in other cases, this was not possible and not appropriate given the benefits being measured. While it is important to be consistent across benefit categories, this is rarely possible particularly for projects that have benefits that span across a range of categories. Thus, it is important for those performing the CBA to be able to justify their choices for the size of benefit areas.

To conclude, there are a host of important decisions that must be made when doing a CBA for a placemaking project. The project type, scale and context will determine the decisions that are made with respect to what to measure, how it is quantified, the timeframe and the size of the area to examine.

Economic Modelling

Another method of evaluating placemaking projects is to evaluate a sample of completed projects and use that information as justification for future projects. It is also possible to use areas that while not part of an explicit placemaking project, have characteristics what would be expected from a placemaking initiative. This economic modelling approach forms the basis for the Valuing the Public Realm technique developed by Transport for London (see Boffa Miskell Limited, 2017) and by the Brookings Institution (Leinberger & Alfonzo, 2012).

While this approach can provide reasonable estimates of increased economic benefits attributable to placemaking initiatives, it is not a substitute for doing individual level proposed project analysis.

Furthermore, many jurisdictions now expect that a CBA will be done as part of the business case for most proposed projects as discussed later in this chapter.

The general approach for undertaking this analysis is provided below and is based, in part, on Leinberger and Alfonzo (2012). The first step is to identify the key factors that are important in making better places. There are a range of sources (e.g. Cohen et al., 2018; Millard et al., 2018; Robinson et al., 2017) that provide placemaking indicators ranging from those with a few indicators to others having a comprehensive set of more than 150 placemaking indicators (www.stateofplace.co/).

One relatively easy way is to use walkability as a proxy for determining "good places". There are a range of methods for determining walkability, but Walk Score© is one that is widely used, cost-effective and has been used extensively for research of this type (e.g. Carr, Dunsiger, & Marcus, 2011; Duncan, Aldstadt, Whalen, Melly, & Gortmaker, 2011; Gilderbloom, Riggs, & Meares, 2015). For any location, it examines: the walking distance to nearby amenities (e.g. shops, cafes, banks, parks, etc.); population density; block length; and intersection density. It is available for Australia and North America. For more details on Walk Score and its methodology, go to: www.walkscore.com.

The second step is to identify the locations of potentially walkable and non-walkable places within the area you wish to study. The selection of these areas can be based on local knowledge or more formally by using a set of criteria that are readily available (e.g. housing density, employment density, land use mix, etc.). Once the locations are identified, obtain the Walk Score values for each of the walkable and non-walkable areas.

The third step is to select the centre of the area and then draw a buffer around each centre point. The buffer should use the network distance (e.g. 1 km) along established footpaths and streets. It is important that the buffer be the same for locations. This easiest way to complete this task is to use geographic information systems (GIS) software.

The fourth step is to collect current property values, lease and rental rates and if available, retail sales data for all properties that are inside of each location's buffer area. This will be the most time-consuming step as obtaining these data can be challenging depending on your location.

Property value data should be the easiest of these to obtain as they are the basis for determining property taxes. However, lease/rental rates and retail sales data could be a challenge as there is typically no single source for these data. It may require some primary data collection through surveys or through web searches for each location to determine lease/rental rates.

The final step involves putting all the collected data into one file so that it can be analysed. The main question to be addressed is if there is any relationship between walkability using Walk Score© and property values, lease/rental rates and retail sales. This analysis can be done by using the statistical functions in Microsoft Excel© or with dedicated statistical software like SPSS©.

Using the analysis described above, Leinberger and Alfonzo (2012) found that "good places" as identified by high levels of walkability in the Washington, DC metropolitan area resulted in increased benefits in terms of property values, lease/rental rates and increased retail sales. Specifically they found that places with good levels of walkability had: (1) office rents that were $8.88/square foot/year higher; (2) retail rents that were $6.92/square foot/year higher; (3) retail sales that were 80 per cent greater; residential rents that were $301.76 per month higher; and (4) residential property sales that were that $81.54/square foot higher than those areas with a fair level of walkability.

Willingness to Pay

Another type of economic evaluation tool is known as "willingness to pay" or WTP. This tool is based on survey information where individuals are asked the maximum amount they would pay for a product. In the case of a placemaking project, the product could be how much they would be willing to pay for a certain amenity. For example, an individual might be asked how much they would be willing to pay for a shaded footpath or for additional benches in their local park.

There are two approaches to determining WTP—direct and indirect. The direct method involves asking individuals through an open-ended questionnaire the maximum amount they would pay for a specific product or service (Breidert, Hahsler, & Reutterer, 2006).

The indirect WTP method involves asking an individual their willingness to pay from a number of product alternatives as well as a "none" option. Unfortunately, regardless of the approach, there are issues with the accuracy of WTP. This stems from the fact that participants see it as a hypothetical exercise, not a real one and this introduces a hypothetical bias which can result in misleading conclusions.

Financial Analysis

While a CBA shows results as a single number or as a ratio, it may be important to know who benefits and who pays. This can be done by categorising those that benefit from the proposed project (e.g. local government, private landowners, the general public, etc.) and those that have to absorb the costs (e.g. local government). This type of analysis provides an important input to the financial analysis (FA) which is typically required as part of the project's business case. The FA examines whether the project is financially viable from the perspective of the project's investors. The key difference between the CBA and the FA is that the FA does not consider external factors such as social or environmental costs or benefits.

Depending on the type and scale of a placemaking project, it might be expected that property values and business activity will increase. If this happens, then: local government benefits because the amount they collect in rates will increase; property owners benefit because their land is worth more; and business owners benefit because of increased sales. In terms of costs, again depending on the scale and type of project, local government will be the entity paying for the project, or in some cases, the costs might be shared between local government and the affected landowners as in the case of the Centre Improvement Program discussed in Chapter 9.

What Is a Business Case?

Developing a business case for a placemaking project bridges the gap between the economic analysis and implementation. A business case is defined as: a justification for a proposed project or undertaking on the basis of its expected commercial benefit (www.dictionary.com[1]). As the definition implies, the preparation of business cases was historically confined to the private sector. However, preparation of business cases is now required for most public-sector projects. The New South Wales government (NSW Treasury, 2018, p. 5) provides the following definition:

> A business case is a documented proposal to meet the Government's objectives that is used to inform an investment and/or policy decision. It contains analyses of the costs, benefits, risks and assumptions associated with various investment and policy options linked to policy or program outcomes and informs future implementation, monitoring and evaluation.

Most state governments across Australia now have detailed guidelines and templates for preparing a business case (e.g. Building Queensland Frameworks,[2] NSW Treasury,[3] Economic Assessment for Victoria,[4] South Australia Public Sector[5] and the Projet Management resources in Tasmania[6]). While the business case requirements will vary depending on the type and location of the placemaking project, it should contain the following elements: the case for change; a cost–benefit analysis; a financial analysis; commercial analysis; and management analysis (NSW Treasury, 2018).

---

[1] https://www.dictionary.com/.
[2] http://buildingqueensland.qld.gov.au/frameworks/.
[3] https://www.treasury.nsw.gov.au/information-public-entities/business-cases.
[4] https://djpr.vic.gov.au/about-us/overview/the-economic-assessment-information-portal/i-am-looking-for-guidance-on-economic-assessment-for-a-particular-purpose/business-case.
[5] https://publicsector.sa.gov.au/documents/developing-business-case/.
[6] http://www.egovernment.tas.gov.au/project_management/supporting_resources/templates.

Conclusions

The focus of this chapter is on the economics of placemaking projects, but it is important to acknowledge that a significant part of many projects may not be able to be quantified in market terms. Economists have been working to develop methods for accounting for environmental benefits and improvements in well-being and livability, but more research is needed.

Key learnings from this chapter:

- CBA is an essential part of making a business case for placemaking projects. Its main strengths are that it is widely accepted and often required by decision makers. The main weakness is the difficulty in quantifying non-market benefits and costs such as enhanced environmental quality, well-being and/or liveability.
- Two important CBA considerations are timeframe and extent of area to assess.
  - The timeframe is critical because most costs are incurred at the start of the project, while benefits will accrue over many years as projects need time to develop and mature. The timeframe for a CBA should be based on project type (temporary or permanent), scale (small or large) and context (e.g. where the project is located, data available data). Regardless of the timeframe chosen, it is important to account for monetary flows over time when assessing a project's costs and benefits. NPV and IRR are two methods for doing this and can easily be done with Microsoft Excel©.
  - The extent of the area to be examined in a CBA will be dependent on the type, scale and location of the project. The spatial area should be consistent across all benefit categories, and if possible, it is advisable to examine several spatial extents—one within a few blocks of the project and the other at a broader neighbourhood/suburb scale.
- Other methods used to economically assess placemaking project include Economic Modelling and Willingness to Pay. However, these methods are not as common as CBA.

- Another critical aspect involved when assessing a placemaking project is the financial analysis which examines whether the project is financially viable from the perspective of the project's investors. The key difference between the CBA and the FA is that the FA does not consider external factors such as social or environmental costs or benefits.
- The analyses discussed in this chapter are typically required when making a business case for the project. A business case provides the justification of a project and includes: the case for change; a CBA; a financial analysis; commercial analysis; management analysis; and risk analysis. The business case bridges the gap between the economic and financial analyses and project implementation.

References

Boffa Miskell Limited. (2017). *A Value of the Urban Realm Toolkit for Auckland*. Boffa Miskell Limited and Auckland Design Office City Centre Unit, Auckland Council, 1–71.

Boffa Miskell Limited and Auckland Design Office City Centre. (2017). *A value of the urban realm toolkit for Auckland?* Case Study Research into applying the Transport for London VURT Methodology in Auckland, New Zealand. Auckland: Boffa Miskell. Retrieved from http://knowledgeauckland.org.nz/assets/publications/Value-of-the-urban-realm-toolkit-for-Auckland-Boffa-Miskell-2017-part-1.pdf. Accessed 29 Apr 2019.

Breidert, C., Hahsler, M., & Reutterer, T. (2006). A review of methods for measuring willingness-to-pay. *Innovative Marketing, 2*(4), 8–32.

Carmona, M. (2019). Place value: Place quality and its impact on health, social, economic and environmental outcomes. *Journal of Urban Design, 24*(1), 1–48.

Carr, L. J., Dunsiger, S. I., & Marcus, B. H. (2011). Validation of Walk Score for estimating access to walkable amenities. *British Journal of Sports Medicine, 45*(14), 1144–1148.

Cohen, M., Gajendran, T., Lloyd, J., Maund, K., Smith, C., Bhim, S., & Vaughan, J. (2018). *Valuing creative place making: Development of a toolkit for public and private stakeholders: Stage 1: Literature review 2018*. Sydney: NSW Government.

Duncan, D. T., Aldstadt, J., Whalen, J., Melly, S. J., & Gortmaker, S. L. (2011). Validation of Walk Score® for estimating neighborhood walkability: An analysis of four US metropolitan areas. *International Journal of Environmental Research and Public Health, 8*(11), 4160–4179.

Flanagan, M., & Mitchell, W. (2016). *An economic evaluation of the Renew Newcastle project.* Final report prepared for Renew Newcastle Limited. Center of Full Employment and Equity, Newcastle: University of Newcastle.

Gehl, J. (2017). *The value of place.* Unpublished report.

Gilderbloom, J. I., Riggs, W. W., & Meares, W. L. (2015). Does walkability matter? An examination of walkability's impact on housing values, foreclosures and crime. *Cities, 42,* 13–24.

Hensher, D., & Wang, B. (2016). Productivity foregone and leisure time corrections of the value of business travel time savings for land passenger transport in Australia. *Road & Transport Research: A Journal of Australian and New Zealand Research and Practice, 25*(2), 15–29.

Leinberger, C. B., & Alfonzo, M. (2012). *Walk this way: The economic promise of walkable places in metropolitan Washington, DC.* The Brookings Institution, 9.

Millard, T., Nellthorp, J., & Ojeda Cabral, M. (2018, June 25–29). *What is the value of urban realm? A cross-sectional analysis in London.* Paper presented at the International Transportation Economics Association Conference, Hong Kong.

New South Wales Treasury. (2018). *TPP18-06 NSW Government Business Case Guidelines.* Sydney: New South Wales Government.

Robinson, S., Barkham, R., Carver, S., Gray, H., Siebrits, J. Holberton, R., … Marini, R. (2017). *Placemaking; Value and the public realm.* CBRE Consulting.

Savills. (2016). *Spotlight development: The value of placemaking.* London: Savills World Research.

SGS. (2011). *Economic evaluation of 'renew' projects.* Final Report. SGS Economic and Planning, Melbourne.

Smith, R. G., Jorna, P., Sweeney, J., & Fuller, G. (2014). Counting the costs of crime in Australia: A 2011 estimate. *Research and Public Policy Series, 129.* Canberra: Australian Institute of Criminology.

Stern, M. (2014, May 30–31). Measuring the outcomes of creative placemaking. In *The role of artists & the arts in creative placemaking.* Baltimore, MD—Symposium Report (pp. 84–97). Washington, DC: Goethe-Institut and EUNIC.

9

Project Implementation

Sébastien Darchen, Laurel Johnson, Neil Sipe and John Mongard

Introduction

There is sparse literature on the implementation of placemaking in Australia. The literature that exists tends to focus on state-led megaprojects that aim to create a "sense of place" (Shaw & Montana, 2016) or the close association between placemaking and place branding as emphasised in the work of Richards and Duif (2018) on placemaking for small cities. Mongard (September 2018) notes that placemaking is best implemented through a networked planning and design process which involves collaborative design incorporating all types of

---

S. Darchen (✉) · L. Johnson · N. Sipe
The University of Queensland, Brisbane, QLD, Australia
e-mail: s.darchen@uq.edu.au

N. Sipe
e-mail: n.sipe@uq.edu.au

J. Mongard
John Mongard Landscape Architects, South Brisbane, QLD, Australia

© The Author(s) 2020
D. Hes and C. Hernandez-Santin (eds.), *Placemaking Fundamentals for the Built Environment*, https://doi.org/10.1007/978-981-32-9624-4_9

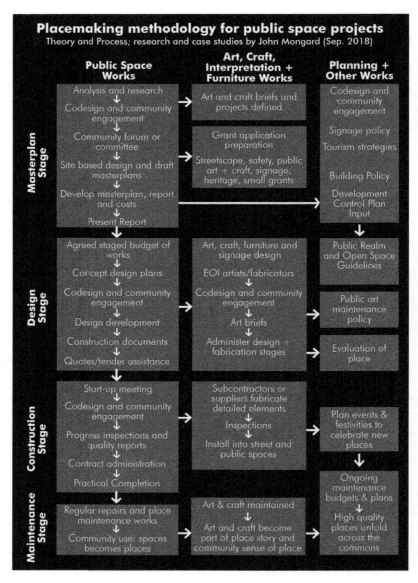

Fig. 9.1 Placemaking methodology for public place projects (*Source* John Mongard Landscape Architects, Place Practice Procedures [2018])

engagement with users and dwellers. People create places for themselves: other actors such as urban designers and placemakers have a role in facilitating meaningful places arising from development projects. The development process is often depicted as a linear process in project management and planning processes, however, "place" best emerges from an iterative and cyclical process of user engagement and set within a network of interactions (see Fig. 9.1).

In this chapter, we analyse the implementation framework in three Queensland case studies (small scale, medium scale and large scale). The purpose of this exercise is to investigate the range of implementation challenges at different scales as a way to highlight the diversity of placemaking activity in Australian cities. If we consider the 5Ps framework (People, Process, Product, Programme, Place evaluation) presented in Chapter 2, this chapter on project implementation focuses on the process, product and programme. In relation to the 5Ps framework, it is important to define the scope of this chapter. This chapter on project implementation focuses on the process but also on the tangible outcomes of a placemaking project. This chapter will unpack relative power dynamics that manifest between public and private actors, and the impact of operational strategies, and the resources that are available in successfully implementing a placemaking project.

What Is an Implementation Framework?

In this chapter, we refer to the term "implementation framework". An implementation framework includes the different components that will make the implementation of a placemaking idea possible. We have identified five main components: governance (the arrangements that manage and deliver placemaking), stakeholders (who is involved and what are their interests), resources (how the placemaking initiative is funded and resourced), timeline (time between the initial idea and the project completion) and maintenance. The maintenance of the place is an important point to consider in the implementation framework.

Governance

It is important to note that placemaking initiatives are characterised by various governance arrangements. In North America and in Canada specifically, Business Improvement Areas (BIAs) have played a central role in revitalising central business areas such as in central Toronto and Vancouver (Darchen, 2013). The aim of the placemaking process is then to create a safe and clean environment where businesses can thrive. This type of initiative is characterised by governance arrangements that are of a private type (Darchen & Tremblay, 2013). This means that there is limited consultation with the civil society on the project's objectives. Placemaking initiatives of that kind are mostly driven by Business interests. Placemaking also happens through regeneration processes, we can then use the term regenerative placemaking; according to Pollock and Paddison (2014, p. 85), creating an attractive city through the reinvention of the city has become part of the rhetoric of regeneration. Those type of placemaking initiatives participate in the re-aestheticisation of city centres. We consider governance for placemaking as being site-specific and related closely to the public/private nature of the project and its spaces. We concur with the definition of governance in Chapter 10. As we show in the analysis of the three placemaking case studies, the system of place governance is determined by the site-specific system for delivery. Governance in an ideal process is co-created with the dwellers, users and stakeholders involved in the placemaking project.

Stakeholders

In the Australian context, based on the different placemaking projects he has led, John Mongard (December, 2018) identifies the following stakeholders who can engage in placemaking activities, they do not always hold the title of "placemaker"; they can be place facilitators, community planners, engagement consultants, town planners, landscape architects, developers, local government and state government. Table 9.1 presents these and other placemaking stakeholders. While not each of

Table 9.1 Stakeholders in placemaking

Stakeholder type	Their interest in placemaking
State government	Funders, design guidelines, identify places and potential places of State interest and initiate placemaking activity at those locations
Local government	Local government officers identify places and potential places and initiate placemaking activity at locations such as local shopping centres, public spaces; duty of care and risk management for public space, enforce building and planning regulations; activate private and public space; broker placemaking partnerships with business owners and operators, artists and designers and community members
Community planners	Co-design with community and other stakeholders for placemaking outcomes
Engagement officers	Consult with community and other stakeholders about placemaking either before, during or after design process
Town planners	Assist in the identification of sites for placemaking intervention, develop regulations and rules for siting of buildings and structures, parks and public spaces
Landscape architects	Design outdoor areas to harmonise the natural and built environment in places at different scales
Private land developers	Brand identity and promotion for developments, creation of quality places to attract investment
Business owners and operators	Enhance the profile of an area and the experience for customers and visitors to that area to increase business income
Artists and designers	To generate ideas for embellishing sites and precincts to create memorable and meaningful places. Site analysis, community engagement, design generation
Residents	To experience high-quality public and private places that evoke pleasure
Tourists and visitors	To have an authentic experience of a place, even if the visit is short

Source Mongard (December, 2018)

these stakeholders is present in all placemaking activity, the table is a useful reminder of the breadth of interest in placemaking endeavours.

Many different types of urban professionals can engage in placemaking activities. In very simple terms, John Mongard (September 2018) defines the role of a "placemaker" as simply to be able "to walk in the shoes of the dweller". A dweller knows, feels and remembers a place intimately (Heidegger, 1971). Dwellers are people who inhabit an area regularly (residents, workers, business owners, visitors), and they are the most important stakeholder in any placemaking project. As explained by Mongard, the placemaking process should involve dwellers at each step of the placemaking project if the place is to be imbued with the meanings and experiences of local people. Mongard usually sets up an interactive co-design process named "Set-up shop". The process brings together teams of relevant experts who talk and brainstorm with stakeholders and dwellers over an intensive period, resolving key issues, actions and visions and collaborating on future plans. Venues for engagements on main streets are usually vacant shops, parks or footpaths. This co-design process repeats at each stage of the placemaking process, allowing people to engage on ideas for space and details, as well as on the overall needs and visions. The placemakers undertake this process on site: this experiential way of working allows dwellers and placemakers to envisage futures within the space or place to be improved and within a process open to all the senses (Mongard, September 2018). Related to the stakeholders in placemaking processes is the theme of "Power in Placemaking" explored in more detailed in Chapter 5.

Resources

This point is linked to the point presented above on the governance of placemaking. Often the governance arrangements and the funding mechanisms are interconnected in placemaking processes. For example, placemaking initiatives led by BIAs will be typically funded through a levy collected every year from businesses that are part of the association or the benefitted area. In this chapter, under the term resources, we investigate the different bodies/stakeholders/institutions participating in the financing of placemaking initiatives. Importantly, a business case is generally prepared for placemaking initiatives. Each of the cases will overview the business case process. What is notable is the diversity of approaches to preparing a business case. Some placemaking is purely opportunistic, while the medium- and larger-scale activities generally require a detailed business case to justify the investment. Typically, the funding is a mix provided by different institutions; in the three case studies presented below, we provide examples of the different sources of finance for placemaking.

Timeline

The timeline refers to the time frame for the placemaking from inception through to its implementation. This time frame encompasses the engagement and conceptualisation of the placemaking project, the implementation and the evaluation and maintenance of the project. Mongard (September 2018), through his extensive practice of placemaking, defines five stages of placemaking for a public space project, spanning the planning, design, construction and maintenance stages over a progressive time frame. Placemaking initiatives to revitalise regional centres usually span periods of 3–15 years, while innovative private development placemaking in new living places may take 5–10 years to complete. These holistic placemaking projects devolve into smaller place projects and events. Typically, a main street placemaking project might take 2–5 years to undertake, while smaller projects such as public art installations form 1–2-year projects.

Maintenance

We define maintenance as the action of maintaining the "place" created through the placemaking initiative. Maintenance is managed through guidelines, codes and policies and is implemented by gardeners, building staff and other construction staff engaged by private and public bodies. Maintenance can be a significant issue and if it is not factored into the long-term placemaking intervention. Mongard notes that renewed places require regular funding and care. Placemaking should aim for an enduring outcome: to last generations, if not hundreds of years. Once built, the monitoring and maintenance responsibility of the place project generally falls to the local government, the businesses that benefit from the initiative, and sometimes to the dwellers who regularly inhabit these places. Businesses on a main street are often the ones to keenly monitor the quality and maintenance of the placemaking. Local government are charged with maintenance, renewal and repair of most of the public places in Australia; however, Mongard (September 2018) notes that there is an increasing trend for private developments to carry out these roles where community and body corporate titling encompasses public realms. Where this directly and positively benefits particular dwellers, who have a direct say on the place, this often leads to better maintenance and quality.

Placemaking Occurs at Different Scales

The scale of a placemaking project will determine the process, product and programme required to enact it. Small projects have smaller spaces, and often fewer constraints and stakeholders. Large projects have more complexity and interactions. The larger the project, the more difficult it can be to achieve good placemaking. We consider three different scales. Our case study for small-scale placemaking is a permanent art-led place project on a city footpath, by the artist Chris Trotter. Other small-scale placemaking encompasses projects such as the revitalisation of a laneway, a pocket park or more temporary initiatives such as temporal installations, food trucks, festivals and events. Medium-scale placemaking refers to larger place initiatives such as a main street, a town centre precinct, a large park or a cultural precinct such as an events or arts hub. Medium-scale projects can have an economic impact on a larger geographic area and a broader community (e.g. Suburban Centre Improvement Program in the Gold Coast analysed in the second case study). Large-scale placemaking initiatives refer to the development of communities, districts and neighbourhoods. Sometimes, this placemaking can trigger regional renewal, such as The Vibrant Towns of

The Scenic Rim project led by John Mongard (2016). The Brolga Lakes project in Queensland is analysed in our third case study and represents a large new place being created for a thousand dwellers.

Small-Scale Placemaking

The small-scale case study relates to the work of a public artist who is active in both urban and rural settings. He often "makes places" in high profile "main street" environments in these settings. The public artist is Christopher Trotter whose work is small scale and small site placemaking. He is best known for his kangaroo sculptures on George Street in Brisbane's central business district. Those sculptures are highly regarded for their playfulness and appeal to international tourists. Chris describes his design motivation as bringing wildlife to the city in a shared space to signify the importance of sharing the environment, even in fast-paced urban locations. The work also references the way that First Nations people shared space and resources with the colonial settlers in the city's early settlement (http://www.trotter.com.au/trotter/City_Roos.html) (Fig. 9.2).

Fig. 9.2 Chris Trotter's kangaroo sculpture in George Street, Brisbane (Photos by Neil Sipe, 2019)

Stakeholders and Governance

A small-scale public art project will encounter a range of stakeholders and governance arrangements, particularly if it is located in an urban setting. Many of these settings are complex and require the artist to be skilled in engagement, negotiation and coordination and to be able to develop strategic partnerships. For example, the kangaroo sculptures in Brisbane required the artist to coordinate with the Queensland Police Service, Brisbane City Council's engineering and road departments as roads needed to be closed and underground utilities located and protected during the installation phase. The footpath was disrupted as the sculptures were secured in situ. Generally, for small-scale placemaking projects the stakeholders are local government elected officials and staff, business owners and operators, the creative community and the general public. Traditional owners and Aboriginal artists are increasingly engaged in placemaking activities and they are important stakeholders. The interests of local government include the quality and type of image that is presented and how well that image represents the area. They are also concerned with public risk and associated duty of care matters such as tripping and injury hazard, universal access and clear public throughways. Sometimes, public artists will negotiate with a local government-appointed community advisory panel that will filter the work for community interests. Other times, public artists negotiate directly with elected officials and staff. For smaller local governments, the public artist may be required to generate a contract for the placemaking activity as these councils may not be familiar with the contractual arrangements for small-scale placemaking activity. Public art agents have recently developed to represent the artist in public and private placemaking projects. The agents will manage the process. They may broker the relationship between the artist and the client, organise the contract and insurance, outsource the construction and installation of the work. The public art agent has some appeal to the placemaking funders as they are interested in minimising their risk in a placemaking project. This can be frustrating to sole-operator artists who may find it difficult to compete with the public art agents.

Resources

In the case of Brisbane's kangaroo sculptures, the public artist participated in a competitive tender let by Brisbane City Council. Tenders can be either selective (a few artists only) or open to all. For other projects, the artist initiates the placemaking idea and takes the idea to the relevant local government and the community for their consideration. Artist-initiated placemaking requires entrepreneurship, patience and the ability to persuade key stakeholders that the placemaking idea has value.

Some local governments, particularly smaller ones, are opportunistic in the resourcing of small-scale placemaking initiatives such as public art projects. They may, for example, access Commonwealth, state government or other public funds through grant schemes related to regional arts funding, community building, main street improvements and even disaster recovery initiatives. Publicly funded projects generally have a broader community objective for their investment such as public space activation or streetscape improvement in the "high street" or to mark a significant event or time in the history of a place. Public art for placemaking may also be funded by private sector developers seeking to enhance the profile and presentation of their site/building/enterprise.

Developing the business case for a public art project is typically not done by the artist, but rather by the funding agent. The business case includes a cost–benefit analysis of the public art investment. It is difficult to quantify the value of public art in placemaking, though retrospective review of business activity including expenditure in the local area before and after the installation of the public art is possible. Other forms of value demonstration are a count of visitations to the public art that can be measured through social media "hits", including photos of the public art that appear on Facebook, Instagram and other social media outlets and an analysis of words associated with those images. For example, the small scale and colourful "Brisbane" signing the Southbank Parklands, adjacent to the central business district is an example of a highly valued public art installation that generates considerable social media activity, particularly for visitors to the city.

Timeline

The timeline for this project took nine months from concept design through design development to fabrication and installation. Typically implementation of public art projects will be variable and related to the requirements of the funder. For example, a public art installation that is publicly funded will need to meet the requirement of the grant and contract. Timelines can be short and that creates pressure for the artist, local government and installers. Temporary placemaking actions such as festivals and events also create time pressure for organisers.

Maintenance

To optimise their value, maintenance of small-scale public art installations is vital. Maintenance is a consideration for the public artist at the design and construction stages. The costs of maintenance will be factored into the budget. In the case of Trotter's sculptures, the ongoing maintenance rests with Brisbane City Council, the owner of the space.

Medium-Scale Placemaking

The case study for the medium-scale placemaking is the Centre Improvement Program (CIP) introduced in 2000 by the City of Gold Coast, Australia. This model of placemaking focuses on the improvement of spaces around existing local businesses. It was inspired by the City of Brisbane's (CIP) program. The aim for the Gold Coast was to have a type of revitalisation that was more structured than before with a specific type of funding mechanism. This revitalisation scheme, known as CIP, evolved from 2013 into "City Placemaking". This revitalisation programme was a bit broader and included different types of funding mechanisms.

Based on the CIP initiative, medium-scale placemaking can happen at the main street scale (e.g. CIP) but will have economic benefits beyond the main street. CIP initiatives are characterised by a high cost–benefit ratio (e.g. approximately 35:1 for the Burleigh Heads CIP)

(City of Gold Coast, 2014). The Gold Coast Council has undertaken CIP initiatives at Chevron Island, Paradise Point and Burleigh Heads. In the case of Burleigh Heads, the improvements included extended footpaths at the street corners, narrowing intersections for pedestrian safety, shade trees, artworks, seating and lighting. Artworks and furniture were included to add richness to the centre. These improvements significantly enhanced the alfresco dining opportunities in Burleigh Heads (City of Gold Coast, 2014).

Stakeholders and Governance

CIP initiatives are undertaken by Gold Coast City Council with a primary focus on creating economic benefits for the business that participate in the programme. The CIP has been used by the Gold Coast Council for ten years. The key components of this programme include:

- Consultation with the local landowners and business community to help shape the design and inclusions; and
- The local landowners pay one-third of the costs through a levy that is applied for ten years.

The governance is similar to the Canadian BIA model explained above. Business interests are driving the process. However, as we explain in the section on resources, there is a contribution from taxpayers which is a differentiation with the BIA model. The revitalisation process is led by the CIP team made of seven professionals: an architect that serves as the executive coordinator; three landscape architects; one urban designer; one community liaison business development officer; and one community liaison business officer. Another landscape architect was added to the team in 2013 when the CIP became the City Placemaking program. The CIP team is technically part of Gold Coast Council, but it operates independently in terms of developing a revitalisation programme. The programme is done jointly with the business owners who will directly benefit from the upgrading. The CIP team produces a report on economic evaluation and effectiveness for each project they undertake (see City of Gold Coast, 2014).

Resources

In the case of Burleigh Heads, the total cost of the improvements was $1,477,870 of which $300,000 was payable over ten years (22% of total) by the taxpayers. Funding for CIP projects is a share with 50% of funding provided by the Council and 50% by the affected landowners.

But with the latest City Placemaking program, smaller tactical urbanism projects were included: the range there are between $15,000 and $150,000 with most of the tactical urbanism projects around the $50,000 mark (Interview 1). Those smaller projects were fully funded by the Council. With the City Placemaking program, the Council aimed at diversifying its revitalisation efforts to reach areas in the city that would not be upgraded with the previous CIP.

Timeline

The timeline for the Burleigh Head's implementation was short as the works were completed in two stages: Connor Street: April 2003 and West Street—December 2003. The CIP timeline also included an evaluation phase after the works were completed to find out about the cost benefits of this placemaking initiative. Evaluation has been undertaken ten years after work completion (City of Gold Coast, 2014).

Maintenance/Evaluation

In the ten years since the CIP's first project in Burleigh Heads, the total return to the community for three projects was approximately 13 times more than the initial investment. This indicates a strong community benefit. The CIP was responsible for increasing the appeal of each centre, which improved the rental return to landlords, increased the profits of traders and expanded the number of local employees (City of Gold Coast, 2014, p. 8). These benefits totalled $80 million: $17 million in rent paid to landlords; $16.7 million in trader profits; and $42.2 million increase in wages.

Although Burleigh Heads would have undertaken some level of change in response to broader retail trends, the CIP was instrumental in unlocking and bringing forward an extensive amount of development potential and employment. The extensive redevelopment of Burleigh Head's Connor Street has been instrumental in creating an expansive dining precinct that was not previously available (City of Gold Coast, 2014, p. 9).

Large-Scale Placemaking: Brolga Lakes Residential Development

The Brolga Lakes project is a large-scale sustainable community that incorporates an innovative planning mechanism—a Biodiversity Offset Area (BDOA). Rural land will be rehabilitated to create 71 hectares of habitat targeted at koalas and birds. A development entitlement on the balance of the land will become a sustainable development for up to 1000 dwellers and will create a new template for peri-urban living in Australia. An initial development approval was granted in 2015 and then was further developed and refined in 2018–2019 with the goal of improving the urban design and placemaking aspects of the project. The first stage of the project is under construction.

With its innovative provision of energy-efficient homes, and its on-site water, waste, food and power systems, Brolga Lakes will create a place surrounded by revegetated bushland and wetlands that embraces natural ecological systems within the design, construction and maintenance of the place (Fig. 9.3).

Governance and Stakeholders at Brolga Lakes

The planning approval process actively engaged Council officers and leaders in order to embrace the innovative nature of the placemaking project. A team of consultants led by John Mongard Landscape Architects (JMLA), and EcoUrban Pty Ltd is undertaking the ongoing placemaking process.

Fig. 9.3 Brolga Lakes, aerial view of site adjacent to Ramsar Wetlands (*Source* EcoUrban, 2018)

A think tank studio was set up by JMLA to brainstorm the placemaking. Over a period of six months, the studio became a forum for ideas and futures, with the team, the client and potential builders and collaborators. The dedicated room allowed an iterative progression of the placemaking plan and concepts to be debated, creating a robust project oriented to its environmental and place goals. The site and its low-density rural residential surroundings currently do not have any community focus or place. The Brolga Lakes masterplan, which embodies the placemaking strategies, provides a strong framework for public commons and places, event spaces and community networks which can emerge over time within the site and its natural setting (John Mongard Landscape Architects, 2018). To assist the placemaking process, a research hub has been created on site as a collaboration between Brolga Lakes and the University of Queensland. The research hub will, amongst its works, seek to gauge the perceptions and the values of people who buy and then live at Brolga Lakes and compare the nature of the placemaking to conventional suburban developments. Will having dual home frontages and minimal fences facilitate sociability? Will the creation of home clusters surrounded by a variety of commons create more opportunities for community life and casual encounters?

Brolga Lakes is being developed using community title ownership. This governance system allows private ownership of land for homes as well as group control within the large communal open space areas that make up the balance of the land. Community titling enables innovative placemaking and ecological initiatives to be created within such places, particularly where local authority mechanisms and typologies do not exist for such emerging types of peri-urban development. Community titling will also allow the community of dwellers and residents to be actively involved in the future decision-making and maintenance of the place (Fig. 9.4).

Resources

Brolga Lakes is privately funded. The unusual BDOA arrangement requires the rehabilitation and ongoing maintenance of 80% of the site

Fig. 9.4 Brolga Lakes masterplan, commons and living areas (*Source* John Mongard Landscape Architects, February 2018)

as conservation forests and koala/wildlife habitat, established within a five-year period. This is a significant resource requirement. In the initial stage, 77 lots are being built within the network of existing lakes. Careful planning is required to ensure that the balance of the land can be progressively rehabilitated. A large site nursery has been established upfront to grow over half a million trees. This resource was set up to create an affordable system to successfully implement the BDOA, and to combine with the provision of a central food and garden plants production hub for future residents.

In such projects, there are substantial upfront planning, development and infrastructure costs. These weigh more heavily in the initial stages when the income from sales of land is yet to flow. Eighty per cent of green common areas allocated within Brolga Lakes has to be constructed and carefully apportioned across all stages of the development. Financial planning and budgeting must be part of the placemaking process: without these activities, there will neither be the time, or the funds set aside for the creation of quality places.

Feasibilities occur along the way to ensure that the development can meet its qualitative and quantitative goals and values. An important concept in Brolga Lakes is "the transfer of hard infrastructure into green infrastructure". In a conventional suburb, most of the infrastructure is hard: roads, kerbs, drainage pipes, and stormwater structures. In this peri-urban model, the infrastructure is designed to be "soft" and "green": grass swales, overland water and gullies, no kerb and channel. In Brolga Lakes, the character of the peri-urban place is defined by soft/green infrastructures, which shifts resources and funds away from conventional civil construction, towards more ecologically sustainable construction.

Timeline

Brolga Lakes has been through a lengthy planning stage of seven years due to its unusual peri-urban form and BDOA planning mechanism. This planning stage included two years of placemaking focused urban design. This placemaking affected the form of the housing, lots and common open spaces, particularly by introducing concepts of social ecology and climate change resilience. The design and construction stages have overlapped, since early works included setting up the nursery, waterway rehabilitation and bulk earthworks for the first stage. The design of streetscapes, greenways and places within the community hub has been undertaken at a broad level to establish feasibility and scope, and then particular place areas are detailed further according to time priorities. In a large development such as this, time is money and construction, and the placemaking is closely tied to private funding programmes and income generation.

The community title process will ensure that over time, there is a broader level of resident engagement in the place as it emerges. This has occurred with a similar project established 15 years ago—the Ecovillage at Currumbin in the Gold Coast hinterlands. It has similar titling and peri-urban form to Brolga Lakes, and Ecovillage residents have developed an active decision-making process and community-based web networks. The placemaking led to a high level of communal values with public spaces creating much richer environments for living than in conventional suburbs, which are not led by placemaking processes or values. Recent engagement with Ecovillage residents has shown that there is a high level of appreciation for the placemaking that occurred during the building process.

Placemaking within private developments has to ride the course of time, money and construction. Without the intention to make place during the design and construction phases, the place visions and goals may not reach fruition. Placemaking needs to be a paradigm, a philosophy and a process that drives a whole development towards place. People make place for themselves: development teams can only facilitate its emergence. Placemaking requires skills and tasks bedded across the development process, timeline and budget.

Maintenance

Place maintenance at Brolga Lakes will be done jointly by the community and Birdlife Australia. Common open spaces that are part of the community title body corporate will receive levies for ongoing place maintenance. A levy will also be raised to manage the conservation areas in perpetuity: this levy will assist Birdlife Australia with rehabilitation, interpretation and educational tasks. The future dwellers, the residents of Brolga Lakes, are the long-term facilitators of the unfolding place: their combined body corporate levies, in lieu of conventional house and land rates, provide the financial mechanism for place management into the future. This model provides more direct control for a community to manage its own places and resources.

Conclusion

A key factor for implementing high-quality placemaking is that the placemakers engage with both the users and the place context. This should occur ideally within an experiential process. Placemakers are facilitators who can put themselves in the shoes of a dweller, and they help people to imagine and make their future places. By adopting a curatorial responsibility for the place, placemakers can create processes that move space towards place. The design and implementation of a project must respond to the values of a place and dwellers. Place implementers help people to draw out and create meaning in their places, but they can only do this authentically in a process that engages dwellers all the way through the project. The enduring value of placemaking requires a commitment to maintain the quality of the place into the future.

Funding and time management are important elements of any placemaking project. Good places rarely result from a low resources base. Small place projects such as the Chris Trotter sculpture rely on good budgets, a good place-based idea and strong curation, in order for such installations to be robust and lasting works. The Gold Coast case study shows that placemaking can influence beyond the project and evolve over time into larger projects: the place initiative evolved towards a complete City Placemaking program with a variety of funding mechanisms. Timelines for implementation typically focus on the design and construction stages, but they often neglect the maintenance and evaluation parts of the project. Placemakers are required to have many skills, but central to the implementation is the intention to facilitate authentic, meaningful places.

Table 9.2 Roles of placemakers

Placemaking	Placemaking implementers
People	Engage the users and dwellers of the place from inception through to maintenance
Place	Engage and work with the place context, history, landscape in a collaborative and experiential way
Process	The values of the place and its people together drive the design through a networked and iterative process.
Product	Facilitate and curate the placemaking elements to ensure that meaningful places and experiences are created for dwellers
Programme	Maintain the quality and meaning of the place throughout the place project and programme
	Manage the budget, timeline and process to ensure placemaking can be implemented with high quality and maintained into the long-term

A commitment to the values of the place is critical to successfully implementing placemaking, as illustrated in each of the cases in this chapter. For example, in Brolga Lakes the placemakers envisage a future for the site that responds to the site's ecological values. The underlying principle of ecological repair and revitalisation drives the place design and its implementation. In all cases, engagement with the site (its history, landscape, users) reveals the values of the place and those values underpin the design and its implementation. Related to this message is the role of placemakers as facilitators who bring meaning to a place. The placemaker's role is to assist dwellers to make sense of the place through the design of the space and its placemaking elements. Table 9.2 is presented here to link these place implementation messages to the broader placemaking framework presented in Chapter 2 and are the key learnings from this chapter.

References

City of Gold Coast. (2014). *Centre improvement program: Economic evaluation and effectiveness review*. City of Gold Coast: RPS Australia East Pty Ltd.

Darchen, S. (2013). The regeneration process of entertainment zones and the BIA model: A comparison between Toronto and Vancouver. *Planning Practice and Research, 28*(4), 420–439.

Darchen, S., & Tremblay, D. G. (2013). The local governance of culture-led regeneration projects: A comparison between Montreal and Toronto. *Urban Research & Practice, 6*(2), 140–157.

Heidegger, M. (1971). *Poetry, language, thought.* New York: Harper and Row.

Interview 1 with Executive Coordinator, City Place Making, City Development (City of Gold Coast), November 2018 at UQ.

John Mongard Landscape Architects. (2016, July). *Vibrant Towns of the Scenic Rim, Stage One Beaudesert, Main Street Mount Tambourine and Boonah, for Scenic Rim Regional Council, Brisbane, Australia.* Retrieved from https://www.scenicrim.qld.gov.au/council-services/infrastructure/projects. Accessed 29 April 2019.

John Mongard Landscape Architects. (2018, February). *Brolga Lakes masterplan and placemaking.* Brisbane, Australia.

Mongard, J. (2018, September). Placemaking: Theory and process, research and case studies by John Mongard, Brisbane, Australia.

Mongard, J. (2018, December). Place and meaning: A critical discussion, article on place theory developed for teaching and research at QUT and further developed for placemaking teaching at University of Queensland, Brisbane, Australia.

Pollock, V. L., & Paddison, R. (2014). On place-making, participation and public art: The Gorbals, Glasgow. *Journal of Urbanism: International Research on Placemaking and Urban Sustainability, 7*(1), 85–105.

Richards, G., & Duif, L. (2018). *Small cities with big dreams: Creative placemaking and branding strategies.* London and New York: Routledge.

Shaw, K., & Montana, G. (2016). Place-making in megaprojects in Melbourne. *Urban Policy and Research, 34*(2), 166–189.

10

Leadership in Placemaking

Lara Mackintosh

Introduction

Leadership in placemaking requires often assumed skills. The resources available to placemakers typically demonstrate how leaders can implement projects, initiate ideas and run workshops. However, the development of leadership skills and how these can be learnt are not typically discussed. There are many different ways of considering, enabling and implementing placemaking, and the anticipated goals may be different for each of the stakeholder groups. So how do placemakers navigate their way through this complex management process? What are the skills required to enable engaging, effective and successful placemaking for all, or at least most? Leading a team is challenging, and in placemaking, it often requires an adaptive, reflective approach. This chapter on leadership begins with a background on leadership models, before introducing a new framework for leadership in placemaking.

L. Mackintosh (✉)
School of Arts and Sciences, University of Notre Dame,
Fremantle, WA, Australia
e-mail: lara.mackintosh@nd.edu.au

The third part of the chapter invites you to critically reflect on the case studies presented throughout this book. This reflection is focused on common strategies that are employed, the different types of situations that may arise during a placemaking project and the skills required to engage with all stakeholders to reach an outcome. The chapter concludes by inviting the reader to review your own capabilities and biases, understand your leadership role in placemaking and support leadership in others.

Background and Theory

An examination of leadership in placemaking requires a different perspective; one that takes a broad look at all stakeholders involved, observing and interpreting behaviour and actions. As discussed in this book, the contexts in which placemaking occurs are varied and include the environmental context, both natural environment (Chapter 3) and First Nations perspectives (Chapter 4); the social context, at the scales of the community (see Chapters 1 and 5); and political context of the place, influenced by the governance systems of place (see Chapters 6 and 11), the economic standpoint of a project (see Chapter 8) and the capability to "make place" (Chapter 9). All of these elements impact the capacity of the place to thrive (Chapters 7 and 8). Leadership in placemaking requires an understanding of these different contexts and skills in reading and responding as these contexts change. This may differ from the views on leadership held by those involved in placemaking, and therefore, it is important to acknowledge different theories about leadership that have led to these views.

Traditional Theories

Traditionally, leaders have been considered to have certain traits such as determination, integrity and confidence (Northouse, 2018), and that leadership skills can be learnt. A leader-centric approach recognises that there are specific leadership styles and behaviours that contribute to the success of a team or project or result in meeting performance outcomes and targets (Haber, 2011). In such approaches, leadership is unidirectional; a leader has a personal influence on the followers, who are passive in the projects and activities. In placemaking, the followers are considered the stakeholders, who belong not to a single organisation or institution, but to a number of community groups.

Contemporary Frameworks

Placemaking projects offer an opportunity to explore the different leadership approaches that can be taken. Contemporary leadership can be task-based or focus on the relationships within the projects. Leadership is guided by subjective perception and values, related to specific projects and situations, rather than driven by objective values such as economic performance. The behaviour of leadership, participants and communities respond to the social and environmental contexts and situations, informed by an understanding of why certain behaviour occurs in certain contexts. Socially pre-determined formal hierarchies are not necessarily assumed.

Contemporary frameworks place importance on leadership as a process requiring communication in which the leader is representative of diverse communities and in which authenticity is seen in the values shared by all stakeholder (Northouse, 2018). This type of leadership can be seen within the emerging discipline of placemaking. Two frameworks in particular—transformational and situational—are considered relevant to placemaking practices and projects.

Transformational Leadership

First defined in 1978 by James McGregor Burns, transformational leadership focuses on engaging and connecting (with stakeholders) in order to raise motivation for change. Howell and Avolio (1993) further defined transformational leadership as authentic when the focus is on the collective good and leaders transcend their own interests for the sake of others (Howell & Avolio, 1993). Transformational change is relevant in placemaking, where change is often the desired outcome, and it is the role of leadership to manage, direct and coordinate this change. Transformational leadership is often focused on the transformation of the followers. Bass (1985) saw transformational leadership as means of raising followers' motivation by increasing awareness of, and value of, goals. In doing so, self-interest is transcended and higher levels of needs are addressed (Bass, 1985). Northouse (2018) identifies four transformational leadership factors found in transformational leadership. Leaders have idealised influence as strong role models whose ethical and moral conduct are respected by the followers. Inspirational motivation is achieved when leaders inspire commitment to shared visions through authentic communication and engagement. Followers who are intellectually stimulated to be creative and challenge their own beliefs and values, as well as that of the leader and the organisation, are more likely to transform. Transformational leaders find ways to listen to individuals in a supportive environment. These factors can be seen in others models of transformational theories, where a clear shared vision transforms norms and values through a process founded on trust (Bennis & Nanus, 2007), and leaders model a way forward by challenging the process and enabling others to act (Kouzes & Posner, 2017). In placemaking, it is possible that those in leadership roles are members of the stakeholder groups, with vested interest in the outcomes of the projects. Therefore, the transformation that takes place may also occur in the leaders as well as the followers.

Situational Leadership

Paul Hersey and Kenneth Blanchard began developing their model of Situational Leadership in 1969 with the life cycle of leadership theory (Hersey & Blanchard, 1979). This model focuses on how a leader can adapt their style to suit different situations. It relies on the leader's ability to evaluate followers, assess the followers' capability and capability in achieving the given goal and change the level of support or direction provided (Goodson, McGee, & Cashman, 1989). Of interest to placemaking is the different kinds of support given by leaders. This support can range from guidance and directions (task-oriented) to socioemotional support (relationship-oriented); and address the readiness level, the ability and willingness, of the followers to perform the task, function, objective. Situational Leadership Theory recognises that readiness of level of followers within organisations may change and requires a different approach. This is also likely in placemaking projects, where the readiness of stakeholders may fluctuate depending on the stage of the project, the influence of external factors and changes to the type and number of stakeholders involved at any one time.

The Role of Leadership—In Communities, Organisations and Projects

Leadership within organisations, local governments and placemaking practices can make or break a placemaking project. If leadership relies on an individual, or a single approach, this places more long-term projects at risk. Additionally, placemaking projects can comprise complex stakeholder groups, with multiple levels of governance and different capabilities and capacity for change. These aspects of placemaking can make it difficult to apply leadership theories developed for business models and organisations. When looking at placemaking case studies, the leadership model can be identified by examining how the leadership role leads change and how that change is evidenced. Those projects that take a top-down approach are more likely to be in the traditional model, where a leader, or a leadership team, directly influences the project and the nature of the outcomes. Leadership may be more transformational when a change of stakeholder values and vision is the result. However, in placemaking the situation of the project—the context, stakeholders and/or their capacity—is dynamic and the behaviour of those in leadership roles must adapt and respond accordingly. Additionally, the leadership role itself can be dynamic, and different stakeholders and representatives may hold a leadership role at different points within a placemaking project. This shared role can shift agency within a project and build stakeholder capacity, to strengthen the networks within communities and share positive outcomes and benefit.

Understanding how dynamic leadership is recognised and how the transformation of both stakeholders and place can be accommodated is the focus of the leadership model presented below. This is considered important in placemaking projects where the implementation is staged and occurs over time; the outcomes of the project are far-reaching and long-lasting, or the stakeholders and communities benefiting are diverse and complex.

Research examining leadership models in Australian Higher Education has provided an alternative model. Typically, higher education institutions are complex, multi-layered institutions subject to significant and regular change and are considered similar to the placemaking in which multiple stakeholders with diverse needs and capabilities require a dynamic and responsive approach. One such model is distributed leadership.

Distributed Leadership

Distributed leadership focuses more on the environment in which the leadership occurs, instead of focusing on other structural, hierarchical and directive approaches of leadership. Learning (to lead) is at the core of this model and critical to building institutional capacity for leadership and change. Distributed leadership also recognises the contribution of the different participants can make to leadership in developing the motivation for continued improvement (Jones, Harvey, Lefoe, & Ryland, 2012).

The findings from Jones' research have informed the development of a leadership matrix in which the dimensions and inputs that enable and support distributed leadership are defined (Jones et al., 2012). This matrix captures the dynamic nature of leadership roles in complex organisations; the importance of critical self-reflection at all levels; the changing relationships from individual to collective identity; and the shift in power as the culture moves from one of control to one of autonomy. These dimensions can also be found in placemaking projects, as evidenced in examples from other chapters. Additionally, the values and practices of distributed leadership provide guidance to actions that can support change and growth (Jones et al., 2012). These values—trust, respect, recognition, collaboration and reflection—are typical of leadership models. However, when aligned with the practices of leadership—self-in-relation, social interactions, dialogue through learning conversations and growth-in-connection—the focus on relationships and interactions is made explicit. The values alone focus on the traits needed by individual leaders, and leaders' practices on behaviours observed. Focusing on relationships and interactions in large higher education institutions enables practices to shift towards a relational distributed leadership, in which the emphasis shifts from leaders to leadership (Jones et al., 2012). The matrix that aligns these values and practices supports the implementation of a distributed leadership approach alongside and within the more structured and hierarchical systems of higher education institutions. This structure is important in distributed leadership, when the roles of leader and follower are more clearly defined, those in the roles are easily identified and the interactions that take place, and the changes in relationships, are clearly visible. The self-enabling reflective process embedded in the distributed leadership model leverages off this visibility. This cyclical process requires the identification of where and how the approach can be best applied, and replanning based on reflection of action taken. If the actions, and the impact of those actions, are not clearly visible in the behaviour of those involved, reflection is more difficult.

The hierarchical structures and systems evident in higher education institutions are not necessarily as well formed in placemaking, if at all. The role of leadership in placemaking projects can be obscured and unclear. It is possible that more than one person may assume the role and it is likely that confusion, and conflict, may arise. To better understand the leadership roles in placemaking, the experiences of placemakers have been used to identify the different structures and systems of placemaking and the different strategies that are employed by leadership in placemaking projects and activities. In 2018, working with the authors of Chapter 6, we interviewed eight key placemakers and place leaders in Western Australia. The interviewees included placemakers from within local governments, private companies, state government developers and local community groups.[1] We found that the role of leadership varied within the different organisational structures, and that each role meant that the leadership contributes differently to the project.

Those within the institutions and organisations responsible for land development, referred to in this chapter as development managers, identified that placemaking sat across departments and agencies within a hierarchical, silo-ed structure. Placemaking is seen as the responsibility of those delivering an integrated built fabric, as well as a financial investment and a marketing opportunity. This responsibility may be distributed dependent on the decision-making capacity of the agency and the management requirements of the project at that point. In managing placemaking, the role of leadership requires meeting multiple objectives, such as the value of experience and the value of land and investment. In doing so, developers provide the financial capital to invest in, and to raise the value of, placemaking.

As local governments take a leadership role in placemaking, the hierarchical process and regulatory procedures, previously seen as barriers, are described as contributing to expertise and knowledge that can be used to facilitate and support placemaking. The agency of local government in making decisions can be used to work with stakeholder and manage community projects and networks. The leadership role taken by local government builds on their expertise and uses the procedures to bring disparate community groups together, navigate through regulation and implement pilot projects. Local governments provide the

---

[1] The interviews ranged from about 30 minutes to 1 hour in duration. Using a semi-structured approach, the same set of questions were asked to each of the interviewees with follow-up questions typically focusing on Western Australian examples of placemaking. The questions for the first half of the interview focused on the value of placemaking and the second half on leadership within placemaking. Chapter 6 draws on the values of placemaking presented in the interviews. Interviewees were selected to compose a cross-section of placemaking activity in Western Australia including in the context of local community organisation, local government urban planning and placemaking (in both inner suburban and outer suburban contexts), major private investor developments and major state government developments. There were overlaps between these contexts in the examples.

management capacity and political capital to implement and facilitate placemaking.

When interviewed, the community-based placemakers describe their organisational structure as under-arching, with the role of advocating for the community and enabling others in placemaking. The strength of community organisations lies in their local expertise and understanding of the areas and what has happened in the past. This provides the catalyst for change and directs the focus of the projects. The leadership role seems to be one of advocacy and representation, ensuring not only that communities are heard but also that they are disconnected from the politics and logistics (of implementation) of placemaking. Community organisations provide the social capital to motivate and direct placemaking.

The structure of the consultancy is not as critical as the structure of the project itself. A placemaking consultant described how she sits alongside many of the stakeholders, across all levels, providing advice and analysing the different situations as they emerge during the project. The leadership role for consultants often sits within the design and implementation stages of a project and involves getting people from different backgrounds, and with different roles, to embed placemaking as a principle of their business practice. This requires consultants to provide the knowledge capital that builds on a wide range of experiences to inform and direct placemaking.

Placemaking Leadership

The different views of placemaking, and leadership, have become evident in the different organisational structures when viewed through the lens of distributed leadership. As such, the distributed leadership model has informed the development of a more dynamic leadership approach in which the different leadership roles can be accommodated and all stakeholders are empowered to engage and contribute to placemaking projects regardless of organisational structure. The challenge in this approach is building the capabilities and capacity of the stakeholders and leadership to recognise the different situations which may occur

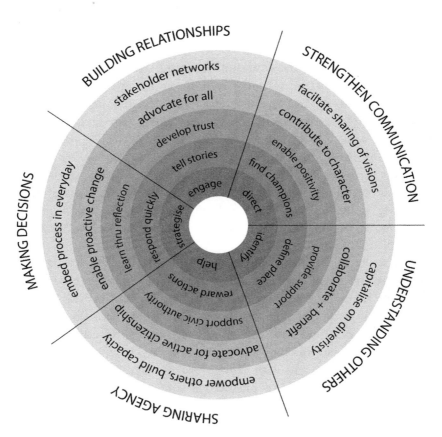

Fig. 10.1 Leadership in placemaking reflective tool (Image by Lara Mackintosh, 2018)

in placemaking and to take advantage of the opportunity to provide support through guidance and direction when appropriate.

A Leadership in Placemaking Reflective Tool, illustrated in Fig. 10.1, has been developed to assist placemakers to overcome this challenge of reading the many situations that arise during placemaking projects and to strengthen their skills in responding accordingly. This tool brings together the types of actions that may take place within placemaking projects and the different ways in which engagement can occur. The types of action, referred to here as Domains of Action, are building relationships, strengthening communication, understanding others, sharing agency and making decisions. These domains are placed equally around the circular diagram, as each Domain has equal value within the tool.

The Domains of Action have emerged from analysis of the seven interviews, in which placemakers from different disciplines and backgrounds describe their experiences of engagement and their relationships with stakeholders in placemaking projects. These five Domains arose from responses given to six key prompts for discussion—providing examples of projects placemakers had been involved in; ways of measuring good or successful placemaking; strategies for managing diverse stakeholder; developing a shared goal/vision; advice for someone entering the field of placemaking, and advice for those wishing to make a proposal or implement a placemaking project. When analysing the responses to the prompts in the interviews, reference to the actions and interactions that took place in placemaking projects and practices was looked for. The responses were coded according to different types of activities and practices that occurred. The similarities in these activities formed the categories for the five Domains of Action.

The interview responses were further coded, to identify the types of behaviours within each of these Domains. In the response from all stakeholders, common types and patterns of engagement were evident in the Actions that were discussed. Within each of these placemaking Domains, five levels of engagement are defined. While informed by the orientation of support developed by Hersey and Blanchard as part of their Situational Leadership Theory, the definition of the levels of engagement been adapted to placemaking based on analysis of the responses presented in interviews. These levels of engagement are scaled from <u>primarily task-oriented</u> at the centre—focused the tasks required to reach the desired outcome—to <u>relationship-oriented</u>—focused on the actions required when interacting and relating to others in a placemaking project.

There is no intended hierarchy to these Domains, and each is seen as equally valid and valued within placemaking. As such, the model is circular, with Domains equally spaced around the circle. Within each

Domain are five concentric rings, each allocated to a level of engagement. The task-oriented levels at the centre focus on the tasks required to reach the desired outcome and often require those in leadership roles to be communicating effectively as they actively engage with others. However, engagement can extend beyond task achievement, exploring alternative solutions and requiring active collaboration with others. Given parameters can be challenged, requiring those in leadership roles to foster relationships between others and respond to the actions of others. The outermost, relationship-oriented level of engagement requires those in leadership roles to step back from active participation in achieving the given tasks, focusing instead on facilitating others to build new relationships and strengthen existing connections between and within stakeholder groups.

Building Relationships

This domain acknowledges the role of leadership in building relationships during the placemaking project. Task-oriented leadership in this domain (towards the bottom of the list below and the centre of the circle diagram) requires placemakers to bring stakeholders together through curated activities that prompt and build networks. Relationship-oriented leadership encourages stakeholders to form and build their own networks, looking beyond existing relationships, to include all stakeholders.

> **More Relationship-Oriented Process to Building Relationships**
>
> Stakeholder networks provide opportunities for stakeholders to build their own networks
> Advocate for all stakeholders
> Develop trust, and sense of authenticity, getting [to] a level of comfort
> Tell stories, take the time to understand communities, tell their stories, where they're coming from
> Engage with different stakeholders
> **More Task-oriented**

Strengthening Communication

This domain recognises the importance of the roles of leadership when communicating with, responding to and managing stakeholders. The task-oriented leadership adopts a more passive approach—listening and disseminating information that may have been already determined. The relationship-oriented approach requires the leadership to engage more actively, facilitating, and contributing to, the communication of shared vision and understanding, self-determined by all stakeholders.

> **More Relationship-Oriented Process to Strengthening Communication**
>
> <u>Facilitate sharing of visions</u> and understanding
> <u>Contribute to character</u> of place through storytelling, the broader context
> <u>Enable positivity</u>, self-directed and determined modes of communication
> <u>Find</u> (and promote) <u>champions</u> of place
> <u>Direct</u>: communicate clearly defined roles, expectations and visions
> **More Task-oriented Process**

Understanding Self and Others

Regardless of their stakeholder group, those in a leadership role may contribute to the development of the understanding of place and project in different ways. A task-oriented approach requires the leadership to understand existing places, through sharing experiences. A relationship-oriented approach ensures that the different stakeholder groups contribute to the project respectfully, meaningfully and regularly to include all stakeholders of all capacities and skills.

> **More Relationship-Oriented Understanding Self and Others**
>
> Recognise and <u>capitalise on diversity</u> (values, capacities, skills, motivations)
> <u>Collaborate + benefit:</u> collaborate with mutual trust and respect; work with others for mutual benefit
> <u>Provide support</u> to communicate shared visions consistently, early and often
> <u>Define place</u> quality through experiences, sense of belonging, meaning, beauty and inclusion
> <u>Identify</u> successful places, an iterative process of sharing values.
> **More Task-oriented Understanding Self and Others**

Sharing Agency

It is the role of leadership to develop the agency of stakeholders, their capability and willingness to contribute to change through placemaking. A task-oriented leadership approach includes taking and modelling respectful participation, in which the differences in capacity, capability are recognised and accommodated. A relationship-oriented approach actively builds on this, encouraging others to be respectful and considerate and empowering stakeholders to support and sustain the places they have created.

> **More Relationship-Oriented Process to Share Agency**
> Empower others, build capacity empower stakeholders to be sustainable through building capacity and skills
> Advocate (and support) for active citizenship and change the power relationships within a project
> Support civic authority through ownership, stewardship and control
> Reward actions and contributions to engender public commitment to change
> Help each other come together to learn and share, to achieve change
> **More Task-oriented Process to Share Agency**

Making Decisions

Placemaking is a dynamic process, with changing circumstances and situations occurring throughout a project. It is the role of leadership to recognise these changes and support stakeholders as they respond. When task-oriented, those in leadership contribute to the discussions and negotiations needed for a shared vision, which remains consistent throughout the project. Relationship-oriented leadership will find ways for stakeholders to respond to changing situations as they occur, empowering stakeholders to regularly reflect and review.

> **More Relationship-Oriented Process to Making Decisions**
>
> <u>Embed process in everyday</u> practice by aligning with the interests and motivations of the stakeholders
> <u>Enable proactive changes:</u> through requests for help
> <u>Learn through reflection:</u> engage in an iterative process to reflect on the shared vision and review its continuous alignment with actions
> <u>Respond quickly</u> to change through flexible, agile and responsive processes
> <u>Strategise:</u> develop a shared strategic vision early, with everyone and across all levels
> **More Task-oriented Process to Making Decisions**

Jones et al. define the values of distributed leadership and aligned them with certain practices of leadership (Jones et al., 2012). The practices—self-in-relation, social interactions, dialogue through learning conversations and growth-in-connection—refocus the values—trust, respect, recognition, collaboration and reflective practice—from traits and behaviour to relationships and interaction. While the Domains of Action and Levels of Interaction emerged from the interviews conducted, the values and practices of distributed leadership are evident in the Reflective Tool described here. Distributed leadership in placemaking requires those in leadership roles to read situations as they arise and support the processes underway without necessarily becoming an active participant, shifting the level of engagement from task-oriented to relationship-oriented. The leadership sits alongside the project, observing, evaluating and helping others to respond to situations as they occur. Different leaders emerge at different times throughout the process, in response to different situations. However, in order to do so, placemakers must be able to read dynamic situations and identify the potential for leadership in others.

Identifying Leadership in Placemaking

The role of placemakers, seen here as a leadership role, is fluid and can be found within the stakeholder group(s) or from external partners, professionally involved in the project for a specific time. At times, the person, or groups of people, who have the capability to read the situations, to encourage emerging leaders to come forth and to deflect barriers, may not exist within the stakeholder groups of the project. Experts are brought in as lead consultants, to guide and advise the placemaking process. Alternatively, the expertise required to progress the project in certain situations may exist within one or more of the stakeholder groups. An individual or team in a leadership role may at times actively lead the process, but at other times may step aside to allow other leaders to come to the fore. Those in leadership may have a direct relationship with the project, benefiting from its long-term success. Alternatively, they may not have a stake in the project beyond the realisation of the outcome of the project.

Using the Leadership in Placemaking Reflective Tool

The different types of stakeholder interviewed—development managers, local government, community and consultant—were prompted to discuss the approaches they used in placemaking projects. Four common themes emerged from these discussions, each reflecting the Domains of Action and Level of Interaction in different ways. These common themes—consultation strategies; project types; experiences of placemaking; and barriers to placemaking—are examined below. The Placemaking Reflective Tool is used to demonstrate how distributed leadership within the different stakeholder organisations is approached. The Domains of Action in Placemaking Tool are looked for in the themes discussed, to demonstrate how the tool can be used to recognise and respond to the different situations that occur in placemaking.

Consultation Strategies

The focus of the consultation strategies for the development managers, local government and community representatives is on strengthening communication to build relationships, understand self and others and share agency. The communication strategies mentioned include more relationship-oriented activities and interactions such as using different modes and messages to target different audiences. In building relationships, the leadership focuses primarily on engaging with different stakeholders to build networks.

> …try and communicate with the community … all those different messages for different … different target audiences.

The community stakeholder interviewed focused on relationship-oriented networks in which leadership proactively prepares stakeholders to participate and lead.

> …rather than just coming up with a boring old plan that gets put on the shelf, we want to encourage the people to get involved and become positive and do their own stuff.

For the consultants interviewed, as placemaking leaders they are focused on the task of developing understanding, reflecting the nature of most consultancy agreements.

> … we do all the usual stuff like personas and getting people to walk a mile in other people's shoes and needs mapping, and all of that sort of thing.

Community leaders discussed more relationship-oriented approaches, getting people together early to understand their motivation for involvement and participation. When discussing consultation strategies, there was little mention of approaches to share agency and build capacity to contribute to change. Nor were decision-making processes discussed.

Project Types

The discussion of the projects by the stakeholders focused mostly on the decision-making process. For development managers and consultants, leading these processes requires a task-oriented approach. These projects can be large scale projects, in which the shared vision is applied consistently across the project. These project visions can be driven by core business objectives, which may be commercial or strategic.

> ... you're looking at the whole town centre rather than a project and saying ... how can we get this place to really buzz. We're looking at the whole town centre and saying where would be the places that are the real hubs of activity, but also understanding how people would ... why people would want to go there and how they'd move around.

Smaller, guerrilla-type projects, which often exist outside core business, offer a more relationship-oriented approach for leadership, in which a process of review and reflection responds to changing situations.

> Often what you do is kind of bespoke because it has to suit that place, and there-fore it's not necessarily completely tried and tested. So, it could go wrong, and when it goes wrong it's in public. So, you kind of have to have that dialogue, take people along with it to manage ... they understand that it's a trial or a prototype or whatever it is.

For local government and community, the projects discussed are also task-oriented when private sector or community lead, trial or prototype projects. When community leads projects, engagement and participation can become different as community stakeholders "practice and have a go".

Placemaking Experiences

The experiences discussed by the placemakers from local government and community were focused on strategies that shared agency. The leadership roles took relationship-oriented approaches, prioritising needs of the wider community and encouraging bottom-up strategies that were self-sustaining and authentic.

> If it's something that's come from bottom up and it's been a lot more around the community and business driven initiative, in my opinion,

> I feel like those groups have a little bit more authenticity when they then go out to ... other people and try to attract them to ... to do placemaking initiatives.

When mentioned, the decision-making process that leads to these placemaking experiences was also relationship-oriented, empowering stakeholder to influence decision-making processes through supportive relationships.

> Councils shouldn't be problem solvers, in my view, we should be a participant in a process that helps solve problems and ... but that could be led by the community, that could be led by the private sector or developers or ... or whatever.

The leadership role discussed by the consultant was task-oriented, involving the "curation of a strong vision enforced through a strategic approach". The experiences described by the developer leadership focused on communication and networking strategies, partnering with other stakeholders, to share events, describing the placemaking experience as "a journey" in which all involved are "learning together".

Barriers to Placemaking

Many of the barriers described by the stakeholders are task-oriented and relate to difficulties in sharing agency and decision-making processes that make it difficult to be responsive. This was reflected in all four of the stakeholder groups, particularly when referring to current policies and procedures and the politicisation of placemaking projects. A development manager identified the need to "take the learnings and be able to amend our policy settings". In this case, this relationship-oriented approach would change the power relationships and support active citizenship in placemaking. The community placemaking leaders noted that "volunteer energy and spirit can be really hard to keep going" and suggested a relationship-oriented reward-based approach that would sustain change by empowering stakeholders to be self-supporting.

Examples of Leadership in Placemaking

Analysis of the placemaking strategies discussed in interviews has tested the parameters of the domains and levels of interaction of the Leadership in Placemaking Reflective Tool. Case studies and examples from other chapters within the book are used below to demonstrate how the different situations within a dynamic distributed leadership can be recognised. You are invited to extend this examination to critically reflect on other case studies presented throughout this book, using the Leadership in Placemaking Reflective Tool. Reflecting on the experiences and practices described, the Domains of Action can be used to identify and clarify the potential of actions taken. Reflections on the levels of interaction—from task- to relationship-oriented, can be used to understand the different placemaking practices and leadership roles.

Small-Scale Placemaking

In Chapter 9, Project Implementation, an example of small-scale placemaking is given, where a public artist makes places in high profile main street environments. In this case study, the artist takes on the leadership role. The steps taken by the artist required to coordinate and construct these places rely on relationship-oriented communication as a common vision is shared among the community and with local and state government departments. Collaboration with the community stakeholder required the artist to identify the shared benefit of the artwork, especially when initiating the project. This required the artist to understand his own practices as well as the stories of others in the community. While such public art projects often have the capacity to advocate for others, this relies on the strong relationship between the artist and the community. Where multiple stakeholders are involved, this advocacy can support agency of stakeholders as they take active roles in the placemaking project. However, timelines, risk management and budgetary constraints can result in a more task-oriented process in which those managing these resources make decisions, shifting the leadership role to local government and/or private owners.

Collective, Self-Build Placemaking

In Chapter 11, The Systems of Place Agency, the work of "guerrilla" architect Santiago Cirugeda is used to demonstrate active interaction as placemaking. In his leadership role, the architect initiates projects in which the stakeholders build their own networks, strengthening relationships within and across the designer stakeholders, who create and certify the project, and the community who construct the projects. In doing so, the project responds to the community's needs as the architect works with creative peers across disciplines. Horizontal decision making enables multiple stakeholders to engage proactively in change. Collective financing and participatory construction empower stakeholders to become involved. Agency for change is shared as built structures are designed to match the skill levels of the community builders. The designer makes decisions for the project strategically, exploiting gaps in regulation and responding quickly to situational changes. In order to do so effectively, however, the architect must understand the limitations and capacities of the community and authorities and adapt the design of the project to suit. While seeking to "reclaim the city for the general public" in order to navigate and subvert existing authorities, the architect must use direct communication to define expectations and visions.

Empowering Placemaking

Chapter 14, The ART of engagement, discusses how public art can bring communities together and makes them think about key issues. In this way, placemaking capitalises on the diversity within communities. Nursey-Bray discusses the role of place in street art, leading to a deeper understanding of self and others and contributing to the discourses on, in this case study, Indigenous Peoples in cities. Indigenous street art "is a powerful tool used to reclaim, intervene and decolonise urban spaces" building capacity through empowerment. Local government decision-making processes have become relationship-oriented as they care for and maintain the public artworks. Members of the general public and passers-by engage with the artwork as they read the stories told in the work, achieving the tasks of advocating for all members of the community and telling their stories. In some of the art projects discussed, where the leadership has facilitated a development and sharing of a vision, communication is strengthened. Agency for positive change is shared as the indigenous community is empowered and their capacity to make positive change is increased.

In these case studies, the leadership role changes throughout the project depending on the involvement of different stakeholders and the opportunities to share the role easily. Leadership in these projects can be difficult to define, as it is shared among the members of the community, authorities and others.

Learning Leadership Through Experience

The experiences projects and practices described and discussed by the placemakers and evident in case studies illustrate the dynamic nature of leadership in placemaking. However, the ways of developing the skills to become aware of the changing situations, to respond, and help others to respond to these changes, are less evident. When asked to share advice to students seeking to become placemakers, the responses were similar across the different stakeholder groups. While building discipline knowledge is critical to leadership in placemaking (development managers), understanding the essence of place and people (local government), of their vision, values and identity (community) is considered core to know what drives people's behaviour and the capacity of the place—"what the place can and can't do". Placemakers must be strategic thinkers, to be open to different practices and perspectives and able to operate between professions, laying out a road map for change. Leadership in placemaking requires strong relationship building skills. Placemakers that respectfully listening to people, and place, and are empathetic, can pull people and ideas together without imposing their own vision on others. These skills of knowledge building, respectful communication and strategic, critical thinking are recognised as critical non-technical skills in tertiary education and leadership programs, but are difficult to teach in formal situations, and assessment of these non-technical skills is complex. The placemakers interviewed were aligned in their thoughts on how such skills can be learnt—through experience and active participation in communities and places.

Through experience and critical reflection, placemakers can learn to recognise the changes in situations, the dynamic roles within placemaking, and the different scales of interactions as they occur.

> I can spend half an hour in a space that I think I know and learn more about how people use that space but also pick up on things I hadn't seen before.

Communication and sharing experiences can lead to a common understanding of context and project.

> [placemaking] generally requires people to be really open to collaboration, ... putting their views to one side and thinking in a really open-minded way of what other people are saying and their views ... so having a curious sort of mind is really helpful and that inquisitive nature around ... keep asking the question why, like, why ... so, why do you think that, or why do you say that, is really important.

The placemakers identified another core skill critical to leadership in placemaking—that of personal resilience. Leadership requires placemakers to be prepared to challenge the status quo, having confidence in themselves and their abilities to understanding people and project. Listening to the voices of stakeholders requires an ability to look beyond the emotion to understand the heart of the project. One of the interviewees referred to a memorable moment from the TV show *Parks and Recreation*, which demonstrates how placemakers could react to challenging situations

> when someone is yelling at her all she hears is someone caring very loudly ...

As placemakers, we seek to support placemaking through the development of leadership and the ability to drive placemaking. You are invited to review your own capabilities and biases, understand your leadership role in placemaking and support leadership in others using the Leadership in Placemaking Reflective Tool. I believe this tool has the potential to challenge current practices and support the development of critical reflection in placemaking by using this tool in several ways.

- Analytically, to identify and define distributed leadership in placemaking exemplars and case studies. Doing so will deepen your understanding of placemaking and strategies for success. Additionally, you will be developing your skills in reading and understanding the diverse situations that occur during placemaking. Strengthening situational literacy in this way supports meaningful communication.
- Reflectively, to understand your own placemaking practices and your leadership role. You are encouraged to look critically for assumptions made during placemaking projects and question your own values and responses. Often such reflection is difficult, yet challenging practices and assumptions is often the catalyst needed for your own transformation.
- Regularly, as the dynamic nature placemaking projects requires a dynamic approach to leadership. Regular analysis of situations and roles and reflection of practices and values will enable you to document a project as it develops, grows and changes.

References

Bass, B. M. (1985). *Leadership and performance beyond expectations*. New York, NY: Free Press.

Bennis, W. G., & Nanus, B. (2007). *Leaders: The strategies for taking charge* (2nd ed.). New York, NY: Harper and Row.

Goodson, J. R., McGee, G. W., & Cashman, J. F. (1989). Situational leadership theory: A test of leadership prescriptions. *Group & Organization Studies, 14*(4), 446–461.

Haber, P. (2011). Progressive leadership: Models and perspectives for effective leadership. In K. A. Agard (Ed.), *Leadership in nonprofit organizations: A reference handbook* (pp. 312–320). Thousand Oaks: Sage.

Hersey, P., & Blanchard, K. H. (1979). Life cycle theory of leadership. *Training & Development Journal, 33*(6), 26–34.

Howell, J. M., & Avolio, B. J. (1993). The ethics of charismatic leadership: Submission or liberation? *Academy of Executive Management, 6*(2), 43–54.

Jones, S., Harvey, M., Lefoe, G., & Ryland, K. (2012). *Lessons learnt: Identifying synergies in distributed leadership projects*. Sydney, NSW: Australian Government Office for Learning and Teaching.

Kouzes, J. M., & Posner, B. Z. (2017). *The leadership challenge: How to get extraordinary things done in organisations* (6th ed.). San Francisco: Jossey-Bass.

Northouse, P. G. (2018). *Leadership: Theory and practice* (8th ed.). Thousand Oaks: Sage.

11

The Systems of Place Agency: Adaptive Governance for Public Benefit

Jillian Hopkins

> Site-specific adaptive governance is a catalyst to align spatial and operational agendas and ensure sustained commitment to public benefit over a project life.
>
> Jillian Hopkins

Introduction

This paper explores how regulatory systems and site-specific governance influence place production and decision-making to drive public benefit. Through a series of Australian and international case studies, this paper will unpack relative power dynamics that manifest between public and private actors and the impact of project brief and operational strategies in successful project implementation. The "spatial agent"

J. Hopkins (✉)
School of Architecture, University of Technology Sydney,
Sydney, NSW, Australia
e-mail: jillian.hopkins@uts.edu.au

© The Author(s) 2020
D. Hes and C. Hernandez-Santin (eds.), *Placemaking Fundamentals for the Built Environment*, https://doi.org/10.1007/978-981-32-9624-4_11

(Awan, Schneider, & Till, 2011; Lorne, 2017) understands key decision-makers across tiers of government to leverage associated power structures and to "make things visible" to the parties involved (Awan et al., 2011). Since these government systems and structures of power are site and city specific, this paper is not a survey of government frameworks, nor is it a how-to manual for design practitioners. Rather it aims to provoke critical conversation between government and activist actors to consider how systems and processes of governance can enable alternative models of city-making. The opportunities for both governments and activists to influence change through, and despite, the existing legislative and regulatory systems, and methods of leveraging governance structures to do this, will be explored. This paper will argue that project governance is the mechanism for defining public value agendas (Macchia & Hopkins, 2019), "injecting quality" (Carmona, 2014) and maintaining this agenda over the life span of a project (De Magalhães & Carmona, 2009). The nexus between design concept and operational governance will be considered as a site of opportunity, and the potential role of government in this process explored.

The placemaking discourse, whether grassroots or top-down, is at its core, a demand for public value. Whether at the scale of a parklet or pop-up performance space or the building, park or precinct, projects that are owned, built by or intended for the public can and should place public value at the core of design and operational decision-making. "We individually and collectively make the city through our daily actions and our political, intellectual and economic engagements" (Harvey, 2003, p. 939). The mechanisms in which a city builds and maintains places for the public directly correlate with its value for that public. Tactical placemaking (bottom-up activism) commonly emerges in locations where government structures have failed to maintain or deliver adequate public value (Hou, 2010), for example under a freeway, on derelict tracts of land or in sections of the city where affordability or infrastructure has otherwise excluded civic engagement (Lydon & Garcia, 2015). In these cases, the community become bottom-up activists in reaction to top-down neglect. By contrast, places that have not been neglected, but rather recently developed, are often entrenched in public–private partnerships, commercialisation, over-densification and other counter-public mechanisms of "destructive neoliberalism" (Harvey, 2003). In Sydney, the integration of private actors in public projects has become the source of satire (Stitch, Cilauro, & Gleisner, 2015), international bemusement (Joabour, 2015), academic critique (Shaw & Montana, 2016) and even intergovernmental conflicts (City of Sydney, 2019) but is sustained despite such criticism. If spatial agents are to influence these large-scale urban precincts and public projects as they are under development, then the corresponding tactics must also scale up. Whether from within government, or in reaction to it, effective place agents must engage with the site-specific political, economic and operational interdependencies to provoke alternative outcomes.

Contemporary city-making in the neoliberal economy claims to balance the competing interests of a profit-driven market with public benefit, but time and again public interests are compromised or traded off in favour of economic growth (Shatz & Dallas, 2016; Travers, 2018; Yarina, 2017). If we accept that this neoliberal model is counter-public and needs to shift, then we must also consider what the alternative models might be and, more immediately, how this shift might be activated. The scaled precedents cited in this paper explore how an understanding of legal and political constraints can be leveraged to create viable models of placemaking to produce the new urban commons and active democratic participation called for by Harvey (2003). In these precedents, the governance structures for procuring, designing and operating place ultimately define its public value. Sustained and aspirational governance has the organisational power to resist and diversify current growth-centric trends, to propose alternative financial models and to set precedents for future projects. With public value embedded in project governance, decisions around time, financing and design must shift to a long-term, human-centric approach to place. A tactical project is elegant in its high speed, low cost and maximum engagement (a pop-up park could be constructed literally overnight using found objects and motivated volunteers), but as projects scale up in cost or complexity, time frames must be resituated to incorporate everyday use and long-term maintenance. Project governance is one mechanism to consider the whole of life perspective from project inception through project brief, procurement, delivery and operation.

Defining Key Terms

Formal government and site-specific governance systems (and actors) impact place production, given that "Public spaces are the loci of complex interactions among multiple stakeholder whose decision and activities affect place qualities" (Zamanifard, Alizadeh, & Bosman, 2018, p. 155). <u>Government</u> is here defined as the (shifting) political climate and (pre-determined) regulatory system within which a place is situated. Government is defined by regulatory instruments (policy, legislation, development control plans, land classification, deeds), political frameworks (local, state, federal leadership) and the processes of government departments and agencies controlling or influencing the site. In public projects, government often operates in multiple modes, as landowner, developer, design client, project manager, certifier and operator (OVGA, 2013). For public sites, government systems are often complex and abound in competing interests, and while government may be lobbied or leveraged to make change, election cycles are often shorter than a project life cycle.

By contrast, <u>governance</u> is considered here as site-specific and mutable, with the actions (and systems) of governance determined by the actors involved. Governance is process-led, active and usually sustained beyond (and outside) political terms of office. Place governance may be determined by boards, trusts, acts of parliament (networks) or within the terms of reference and procurement arrangements of a specific project (processes). In the context of this paper, governance is considered as the site-specific systems for inception, procurement, delivery and operation of a public place (Carmona, 2017; Zamanifard et al., 2018). As the formal mechanism through which project ambitions are defined, measured and sustained, project governance directly impacts the delivery of public value (Macchia & Hopkins, 2019). Governance may derive from self-initiated organisational structures (such as Holzmarkt or Recetas Urbanas collectives) or formal governing mechanisms like the Opera House Trust (Sydney) or the International Building Exhibition (IBA) (Germany). While government is at times unwieldy, governance can be interactive and flexible in the right conditions. Rather than rigid (or safe) rules, governance systems can be negotiated and even co-created with stakeholders (Carmona, 2014) and are both momentous and vulnerable in this mutability. Public and quasi-public projects must often slip between formal government mandates and adaptive governance processes to achieve the best outcomes. Recognising that certain types of power are embedded in both government (political vision, financial, regulatory power) and governance (human-centric, process-driven, creative power), the effective place agent learns to navigate these different systems and leverage the slippages and ambiguities to effect positive change.

Leveraging Place Governance for Public Benefit

Using a series of international and Australian case studies, this paper proposes six ways to leverage governance structures to achieve public benefit for public places. Project governance is by its nature site-specific, inherently flexible and opportunistic, considered over time and driven by a public agenda. The tactics to leverage such governance structures may be subversive or cooperative depending on site-specific politics and power dynamics and are defined as follows: (1) revealing hidden complexities: exposing conflicts and spatial opportunities; (2) subverting government regulations: identifying and exploiting legal loopholes; (3) defining site-specific systems: sustaining collective agendas; (4) freeing government constraints: enabling emergence and transgression; (5) structuring public ownership: adapting for a life cycle legacy; and (6) earning public trust: consistent demonstrations of public value decision-making. These selected precedents deliberately range in scales from a walking performance (Political Equator), to a community circus (Recetas Urbanas), collective arts precinct (Holzmarkt), post-industrial urban park (Landschaftspark) and UNESCO listed cultural institution (Sydney Opera House). Each precedent demonstrates site-specific complexities, contested terrains, power structures and governance systems that influence the design and operation of place. In each project, multiple actors have negotiated, maintained or inhibited public benefit, including architects and landscape architects, government planners, site owners, the

Trusts or Boards who govern the site, politicians, activists and communities. Not surprisingly, the most successful projects occur when these actors have negotiated shared agendas around public benefit and maintained these consistently over the project life cycle.

Revealing Hidden Complexities: Exposing Conflicts and Spatial Opportunities

Artist and architect Teddy Cruz uses tactical projects to reveal hidden complexities in contested territories. His work is embedded in the regulatory systems that govern place with a view to subvert or convert these conflicting conditions into provocative opportunities. Two projects reflect this approach: firstly, the Political Equator performance (Cruz & Fonna, 2017) in which he mediates two governments to install a temporary official border crossing in a culvert drain between US/Mexico contested territories and secondly, the San Diego skaters underpass project (Cruz, TedTalk, 2013) in which the project team navigate complex interdependencies of ownership to build a skatepark under a freeway. Teddy Cruz leverages his two roles as a dual-citizen activist and professional academic to negotiate outcomes. In Political Equator, the project outcome is a filmed one-day public performance. The processes that enabled that single day involved complex extended negotiation with formal actors at Homeland Security (USA) to access the culvert drain from the San Diego bio-reserve and with Mexican border officials to set up and operate a temporary checkpoint and stamp passports on arrival at the informal settlement in Tijuana. As an American academic and a Mexican national, Cruz was uniquely able to mediate between government actors to unpack the layers of regulation embedded in this ambiguous borderland site. Cruz transformed the site into a passage for performance and thus exposed its complexities: the US-funded opening in a secure border (via the culvert unwittingly constructed by US road authorities); the physical discomfort of an unsanctioned border crossing; and the arbitrary (walkable) distance that divides and defines cultural and national identity. Cruz uses architectural (spatial) design, negotiated governance and community participation (the walking public) to expose a hidden network of inequality at the site of influence. The project is less about outcome, than it is using processes to expose conflict. His active engagement with government officials to sanction the event (that in other contexts would be illegal) uses project governance as a tool for systematic subversion.

Cruz's work deals with sites of ambiguity that are neglected or in conflict due to their border conditions, in between governments. This includes territorial borders but also occurs at boundaries where local and federal landholdings converge or where site conditions (like an overhead transport corridor) create leftover tracts of land. In the San Diego skateboard project, Cruz uses his architectural skill set to visualise the complex land ownership that governs a contested site under a San Diego freeway. He recounts how the teenage skaters first attempted an occupation and began self-building their skatepark, only to be evicted two weeks later by police. A systematised approach was required, so the skaters developed what Cruz describes as a "critical process" or adaptive governance. They first "recognise(d) the specificity of political jurisdiction" (Cruz, 2013), including underlying land ownership, political governance and influences by adjacency. The skatepark site was positioned between multiple owners, the port authority, airport authority, two city districts and transport review board, closely bounded by Caltran freeway territory. To influence these powerful landholders, the skaters consolidated into a formal, legally recognised non-government entity, which in turn enabled them to negotiate permission from the various stakeholders to build their skatepark (Cruz, 2013). Both these projects combine regulatory research and visualisation of site-specific conflicts with the establishment of an organised governance to negotiate consents (Carmona, 2014). These provocative projects use systematised, and generally legal, methods to subvert and overcome regulatory constraints.

Subverting Government Regulations: Identifying and Exploiting Legal Loopholes

While Cruz cleverly works within the system, "guerrilla" architect Santiago Cirugeda tests the legal limits of the city through active intervention. His collective self-building projects act first and seek permission later. Cirugeda takes subversive action with full knowledge of the laws that would otherwise prevent it, using legal loopholes to work around prohibitive regulations. Cirugeda's early architectural projects involved building a series of micro-playgrounds and amenities on sites where regulations are ambiguous. A playground perched on a mobile dumpster is both portable and permissible; unregulated airspaces in urban laneways are sites for clipping and hanging extendable storage units; vacant lots are venues for occupation (Iker, 2012). Cirugeda has since scaled up his micro-experiments to (self) build a community circus precinct, school classrooms, and to occupy an abandoned cement factory (Cirugeda, 2014). His work carries a deliberate agenda to resist regulatory frameworks and reclaim the city for the general public. It has arisen from contextual conditions: the financial crisis in Spain; "Occupy" events across the country; and the global guerrilla urbanism movement (Hou, 2010). Through contextual necessity, Cirugeda has established an "insurgent" (ibid.) practice with his creative peers, exemplifying how "each epoch, produces its own understanding of space and experiences it accordingly" (Borden, Kerr, Rendell, & Pivaro, 2001, p. 6, after Lefebvre). With "space as social (re)production" (ibid.), individual authorship is discarded for collective practice. The resulting tactics for placemaking (occupation, self-building, collective effort) are in direct reaction to the "lived reality" of the epoch (Groth & Corjin, 2005).

In subverting existing authorities, Cirugeda deliberately establishes alternative governance models. His processes are both consistent and methodical, if not always legal. These include horizontal decision-making, interdisciplinary and professional collaborations, collective financing, participatory construction and an architectural style to suit the self-building typology and situation. Cirugeda's understanding of the legal parameters and planning frameworks enables him to creatively work around the issue of approvals—such as reinventing the school build as an educational workshop or building temporary structures then seeking approval later. His architectural aesthetic of exposed bolts and assemblages is driven by necessity but is equally preparing for a future argument with local authorities. His school and circus projects are elevated on angular, brightly coloured steel frames like giant spiders, appearing deliberately on the move. These lightweight frames can be erected quickly by unskilled volunteers, require limited footings and can support prefabricated or salvaged structures. Although Cirugeda likens these anthropomorphic frames to an "ugly friend" (Cirugeda, 2014), they also represent a systematised response (governance) to the challenges of self-building, by being temporary (for future deniability), immediate (for quick and stealthy occupation of place), reusable (in case of authority dismantlement and relocation), cheap (for the activist's budget), articulated (for architectural flare) and participatory (for community engagement). In the absence of regulatory authorities, Cirugeda accepts the role of certifier and project engineer and the liability that entails (ibid.). Cirugeda thus creates a parallel form of governance that achieves arguably the same intentions (safety and structural stability) without the red tape of the state. It could be argued that his professional accreditation enables him to assume that role for such a project. He works frequently with other architectural collectives and thus informally shares the associated risk through collaborative problem-solving.

These complex tactical projects expose the unjust, outdated governance structures of a place and then fill the resulting void with their own alternative, flexible modes of governance. Although relatively small in scale, these tactical and temporary approaches reveal existing conditions and become testing grounds for future larger-scale public and community projects. For Cirugeda, his legal loophole "plug-ins" was the premise for his self-built circus, school projects and (arguably unsuccessful) cement factory occupation. For Cruz, his engagement with the San Diego skateboarders and the convoluted collection of landowners and stakeholders that controlled an otherwise abandoned in-between place, informed the Political Equator and related studies into scarcity, innovation and restrictions across borders. For Cirugeda, government regulations are understood so to be overcome and transplanted with a self-governing, collaborative governance model. For Cruz, what seems to be rigid government control of a site is a negotiable condition, where borders are more fluid than not. In both cases, Cirugeda and Cruz see governance as a mechanism to their aspirational outcomes (freedom and social innovation, respectively), and both recognise the site specificity, and often fragility, of these governance structures.

For Cirugeda, an overzealous local council can obstruct an occupation, for Cruz, the unofficial compliance of border officials adds gravity and legality to his migratory performance. At the temporary and micro-scale, mediating project governance requires nimble, negotiation skills and may occupy 80% of a project. At larger scales, these idiosyncratic governance structures recur and their obstructive potential is magnified over time and project complexity.

Defining Site-Specific Systems: Sustaining Collective Agendas

Such alternative models of project inception, delivery and operation tend to emerge where mainstream city-making has been neglected or made unviable (Groth & Corjin, 2005). The projects work around or in spite of the lack of government buy-in and often where the boundary condition creates a no-man's land (ibid.). At the Holzmarkt (Woods Market) in Berlin, a collective art community was established on the waterfront, at first on the abandoned industrial site and then again when private interests into planned urban regeneration folded. The neglected industrial site was occupied in 2000 by Club 25, a venue renowned for hosting "the best parties in town" (Oltermann, 2017). Club 25 was itself an act of placemaking, as the clubbing subculture actively occupied an otherwise abandoned warehouse. It was operational for a decade and combined an inclusive open-door policy with a fluid sense of time (all weekend parties were common) to create a quasi-public place. Club boundaries shifted in summer to absorb external areas. Restrained spatial design (limited adaptive re-use of industrial structures) and behavioural de-regulation induced the collective sense of permissible transgression that Club 25 was famous for. When a public–private partnership to regenerate the waterfront precinct was supported by the Berlin government, new high-rise developments promised to demolish the club and alter the precinct. Club 25 owners Juval Diezigier and Christoph Klenzendorf were part of the public outcry to resist the perceived gentrification of the waterfront. "We wanted to disable the mechanisms of the race-to-the-bottom economy"

(Oltermann, 2017, web). The public–private partnership prevailed over their activism, but when the developer later pulled out, Diezigier and Klenzendorf adapted from protesters to proponents, claiming "If your position is that you are always against everything that is changing in this city, then you'll eventually get overrun and left behind. You have to learn to use the system to your advantage" (Oltermann, 2017, web). Withdrawal of the private investor (after protracted negotiations) opened up an opportunity for disruptive placemaking: Holzmarkt resulted.

From the outset, the site governance established the rights and ambitions of the collective. The project financing, by a Swiss superannuation firm, ensures the collective cannot be sold off. Strict legally binding mechanisms, including 99-year rolling leases, are controlled by a consortium of twenty-five separate companies (from the collective), each with equal voting rights. Negotiations with transport and rail landowners also secured long-term land rights on adjacent lots. Programming is controlled to preference art, culture and music venues and avoids oversaturation of other uses. There is one bakery, one brewery, some bars and restaurants. Restaurants are tucked into the back of this site, while public orchards, playground and the live music venues occupy the riverfront. Any rules are intended to maximise civic engagement. The landscape is collectively operated, businesses are encouraged to trade services within the precinct, and living on site is prohibited to prevent private interests clouding governance (Oltermann, 2017). From a design perspective, the built outcomes are derived from their use rather than aesthetic concerns. Like Cirugeda's exposed structures, the architecture of the Woods Market expresses the collective and the latent layers of site that went before it. Photos are not permitted at events to ensure the place is experienced rather than captured, and the spatial outcomes are equally nebulous. Temporary installations for events and exhibitions lead to regular physical modifications of the site. The spatial outcomes are less consistent than in a commercial precinct, for example with regulated material palettes or style codes, but the result is more adaptable for its use because of this.

Despite these counter-commercial features, Holzmarkt is not devoid of commercial interests as it struggles to operate alternative space economics (McCann, 2002). The precinct financing is an alternative public–private model; leveraging a superannuation investment to secure public ownership, profits from the precinct are fed back into the collective to support maintenance and upgrade. The open-door policy has been modified in practice to regulate behaviour and ensure a safe, respectful site, for example stag events or other heavy drinking groups are prevented entry. The prevalence of creative activist projects, like Club 25 and now Holzmarkt, are appropriated for Berlin's mainstream "creative city" marketing campaign (Colomb, 2012). Holzmarkt thus mediates the open market, the collective and the state. When Harvey makes his claim to "roll back the wave of destructive neoliberalism", he accepts that alternative, more inclusive models for city-making would be imperfect, indeed even "continuously fractious, but based upon distinctly different political economic practices" (Harvey, 2003, p. 941). Although imperfect, this coordinated collective has established its own site-specific governance and "political economic practices" and so begins to operate in effective parallel to its commercial counterparts. It is uniquely placed to influence (or shift) broader economic models.

Freeing Governance Constraints: Enabling Transgression

Recognising that high-quality places are a combination of economic, social and spatial factors (Carmona, 2014), the most effective public places align spatial design tactics with site governance structures (De Magalhães & Carmona, 2009). While deterministic programming can activate a place in a specific moment, complex public projects must operate within the everyday and over time to achieve public value. An enduring public place should not rely on programming for activation, but rather provide a set of conditions that enables a range of (unpredictable) activities to occur. Through freeing prohibitive constraints on behaviour and embedding this approach into the long-term strategy for place operation and maintenance, project governance can enhance inclusivity, interaction and demarginalisation (after Langhorst, 2014). Landschaftspark Duisburg-Nord is a brownfield renewal project developed during the 1990s in Duisburg, Germany, to create a public park and commercial precinct in a former industrial site. The subtle design, by Peter Latz and Partner, responds to the rambling "ruin" that went before. Existing industrial infrastructure is carefully retained, new paths are unobtrusive crushed gravel, and existing paths and paved areas are retained as remnants. Deliberate localised landscaping enhances and supplements the wild "emergent ecologies" that were already flourishing during the site's abandonment. These "emergent ecologies …. [are] the most authentic elements …of urban nature (on site)… the physical expressions of human and non-human processes that are not controlled by human maintenance regimes" (Langhorst, 2014, p. 1113). Plants and visitors creep through the industrial remnants unmolested by onerous regulations, evoking the "sublime" of a modern ruin (Langhorst, 2014) and all the potential pasts and ambiguous futures that it entails. A visitor's negotiation between this relatively uncontrolled natural environment and non-human industrial systems becomes an act of agency.

The project actively counters the passive and precise designs of a "professionally curated landscapes" to deliver a process-led approach of infill and enhancement. "The ongoing interaction of human and non-human processes in ruins yields continuously changing conditions and experiences, antithetical to the attempts to create an unchanging and 'perfect' landscape" (Langhorst, 2014, p. 1115). This is a project designed and operated with a complex sense of time, so that a day, a year and an era are all represented within its boundaries. The park is celebrated as unpredictable, inevitably dynamic and co-authored. Maintained systems (like storm water infrastructure or performance spaces) are paired with designed, yet discrete, planting systems to be "less about the construction of finished …works, and more about the … catalytic frameworks that might enable a diversity of relationships to… emerge" (Langhorst, 2014, p. 1120, after Corner, 1997). These "catalytic frameworks" combine imposed physical systems [scaffolding], governance structures [strategies], human and non-human interactions [agencies] and change over time [processes]. The frictions and interactions between these sometimes competing frameworks are what leads to the dynamic, and arguably authentic, experience of the park.

Langhorst explores how the post-industrial site as modern ruin and contested terrain is a catalyst for transgression. The human and non-human systems of the park are described as "precisely open-ended" rather than "vaguely loose" (Langhorst, 2014, after Berrizbeitia, 2001) to distinguish deliberate governance from a more randomised approach. At Landschaftspark Duisburg-Nord, regulations are restrained, but not passive. Activities are enabled, rather than not prohibited. The distinction here is that freeing up prohibitions puts the onus on the visitor to engage with place in their own unique, unstructured way, rather than modifying behaviour in anticipation of rebuke or in protest of accepted norms. In the typical city park, "no smoking", "no skating" and "no climbing" are common signs, as a means of mitigating and even sometimes punishing (through fines) behaviour that is deemed transgressive or antisocial. At Landschaftspark Duisburg-Nord, visitors are encouraged instead to treat the park as they wish. "Flexible, imaginative uses are tolerated, and where they occur frequently, spatial conditions might be adapted to accommodate them… activities… are mostly tolerated… Very few areas are off limits" (Langhorst, 2014, p. 1119). Graffiti, climbing pegs on industrial silos, teenage hideouts or secret vegetable patches scar the physical landscape, but these human marks are seldom removed and occasionally even enhanced, much like the emergent (non-human) ecologies they complement. This hands-off governance empowers people to occupy place, to adventure, to explore and, if required, to alter the park in that process. The potential to uncover diverse activities creates engagement, and thus, the park is activated without imposition by the state. The "open-ended" governance enables authenticity.

Behind the "emergent" design methodology is an equally dynamic governance structure that has led to and sustained this commitment to unfettered public space. A transformative public-focused agenda was established at the project inception and carried through into design procurement, delivery and finally the operation of the park. While Langhorst doesn't describe the specific governance structure, there are a number of telling points that public benefit was paramount in project decision-making and delivery. Firstly, the project was established by the IBA as part of a 10 billion DM investment into regional programmes, over 10 years (Langhorst, 2014). Both the budget and the decade-long time frame indicate a serious commitment of resources, established to outlive changing governments. Understanding that this project would develop and sustain over generational time (rather than political time) is accepted at the outset. This project is then described as the IBA's figurehead project, suggesting a political imperative for high performance. Secondly, the initial planning process is described as an "open forum". Top-down planning and grassroots initiatives were combined, planning and design decisions were decentralised to enable diverse responses, and stakeholder engagement and community collaboration were embedded from the inception (Langhorst, 2014). Alternative models for procurement, partnerships and idea generation were supported, suggesting an overall openness to innovation from the outset. Thirdly, the successful scheme is described as embracing the "IBA's process-driven, functional transformation of complex landscape structures with an inevitably high proportion of unpredictability" (Langhorst, 2014, p. 1117). To have such a bold, complex project brief established even before engaging the principal designer suggests earlier professional partnerships and a clear "process-driven" agenda. The "unpredictability" promised by the winning scheme speaks to the visionary, leadership of the governing body. Finally, the procurement of a then [emerging] landscape architectural firm suggests a commitment to new ideas and innovation.

This combination of competent project inception and visionary briefing led to the selection of an appropriate and capable design professional to undertake the project and the ultimate delivery of the physical outcome. These design processes are then directly supported by the park's "precisely open-ended" governance structure during its operation. The spatial and (emergent) ecological agendas of the site are in sync with its (non)maintenance strategy, (de)regulations and resulting human (mis) behaviours. There are evident parallels between the exploratory processes that drove project decision-making and the complex clarity of its physical manifestation in the park. The individual professionals behind the IBA's outward profile were evidently able through their governance systems, to establish and maintain a collective agenda consistently through the project life, despite changes in staff or political climate.

This collective agenda inherently promotes public access, freedom of behaviour and longevity or emergence of place over time. These themes are embedded throughout the project design and its operation and therefore difficult to dislodge or dilute with commercial or political pressure from outside the process, ensuring a more sustained legacy of place.

Structuring Public Ownership: Adaptive Governance for Life Cycle Legacy

The enduring place establishes and sustains a public legacy over the whole project life cycle from inception through to operation. The Sydney Opera House is a sterling example of embedded public ownership and the alignment of spatial and operational agendas over time. Beyond its aspirational beginnings and convoluted proceedings, the visionary project completely changed and continues to change the spatial, social and economic landscape of Sydney. Other pens have described the 233 entrants to the international design excellence competition, the character and vision of the winning Danish Architect Jorn Utzon, the state-run public lottery that paid for the $102 M construction, the massive overruns that led to the project being 14 years in construction and 15 times over budget and the government's eventual replacement of the architect (Pitt, 2018). Although it is not the purpose of this paper to delve deeply into the long finished construction of this fascinating building, a few points are of interest to the place agent looking to learn from such a benchmark: (1) the visionary government and government officials that endorsed and drove the project, (2) the risk accepted by government to innovate and the knock-on effects this had for Australia, in particular, the concrete industry, (4) the highly successful public engagement strategy through a long-term public lottery, (5) the design excellence competition, and its governance, that enabled an international (relatively emerging) architect to enter and win the project, and (6) the impact of changing government and political terms on project success.

Accessibility is a persistent theme across the design and operational governance of the Opera House. In its 2007 listing, UNESCO described the Sydney Opera House as a place of "outstanding universal value for its achievements in structural engineering and building technology… a great artistic monument and an icon, accessible to society at large" (UNESCO, 2007, web). The combined visitors to the site are estimated at 8.6 million annually of which a mere 1.45 million people (16%) are paying ticketholders (Sydney Opera House, 2017) and the remaining 84% are international and local visitors walking into, around and over the building. Despite this heavy footfall and contemporary counter-terrorism concerns, the Opera House Trust has supported remarkably high levels of physical public access. Entry thresholds to the site and the building rely on geographical and spatial cues over regulated security checkpoints. A walking visitor arriving from the ferry or bus terminal at nearby Circular Quay or through the Botanical Gardens can walk along the public waterfront, climb the enormous external stairs that cascade down the exterior plinth, then on arrival at the top, stroke the tiled sails, enter into the mid-level foyer, circumnavigate the main hall to reach the purple-carpeted harbourside foyer and even use the public amenities without payment and (except for special events or shows) without security checkpoints. Visitors arriving by car, or passing through the undercroft bar, proceed under the main plinth at sea level, to ascend into the dramatic concrete underbelly, leading the visitor up the grand stair to the ticket office foyer then up into the main mid-level foyer and so on. While bag, ticket and ID checks are added at key points if there are shows, the overall sense is free and public accessibility. Commercial ventures are limited to discrete locations (two restaurant bars in the undercroft, and one off the main promenade) and their aesthetic highly refined. It is also possible to circumnavigate the building on its headland and to climb under and over the main plinth 24 hours a day, with the even deeper interior access available 7 days. The tourist is welcomed to the site without a ticket, and the thresholds of control are as close to the actual theatres as possible to encourage this sense of public ownership. Security cameras are discrete, and the fences are few. The physical thresholds neatly align with operational security lines without the need for additional barriers, queues or guards. This seemingly recessive security is a deliberate act of governance that preferences a friction-free public experience.

The sense of public ownership evoked by the building is not a coincidence; it stems directly from the clearly defined terms of governance outlined in its charter and mandated by the Conservation Plan, Utzon Design Principles, Management Plan (UNESCO, 2007) and Reconciliation Action Plan (Sydney Opera House, 2017) to ensure the site continues to evolve. The stress on public value manifests in a venue that simultaneously supports high-end cultural events, like symphonies and ballets, alongside children's theatre, school spectaculars and community choir events (at reduced rates). As a result, children across the state and many Sydney-siders have once performed in this iconic building and at the very least have watched a friend or family member do so, and once the backstage has been breached, these Sydney-siders become true public owners of the place. Opera House programming is deliberately diverse; the Sydney Symphony Orchestra, Australian Ballet, and Opera Australia are regular events, alongside the Baby Proms series for toddlers and Bangarra contemporary indigenous dance performances. In 2017, indigenous curator and creative executive, Rhoda Roberts was appointed Head of Indigenous Programming at the Sydney Opera House in the first dedicated position of its kind to ensure this commitment to indigenous performance is maintained (Opera House, 2017). The playlist has also expanded in recent years to include public lectures (the Festival of Dangerous Ideas), burlesque and circus performances and contemporary live concerts (Bjork, Crowded House, Nick Cave, Mary J. Blige) inside the main concert hall or on the external stairs. These outdoor events (both free and paid) break down the (elite) cultural barriers of performance spaces.

Forty-five years later, the social legacy of the Sydney Opera House has transcended construction and financial challenges to achieve lasting public value. Even though the building is World Heritage listed and was recently recognised by Deloitte's as a social asset worth $4.6 billion (Pitt, 2018), site governance must still fight for its continued public value. In 2018, a prominent Sydney business and radio personality negotiated to project a racing advertisement onto the sails. The Opera House CEO vehemently spoke out when, defending the cultural importance of the place with her declaration that "the Opera House is not a billboard" (Chaser, 2018). The state government overruled the CEO and public protests, and the racing ads went ahead: even strong public governance is subject to erosion.

Earning Public Trust: Demonstrating Consistent Public Value Decision-Making

Public ownership, once undercut, is difficult to retrieve. Public land, once commercialised, is rarely restored. Around the headland from the Opera House, is the Barangaroo development located on a prominent state-owned site on the south-western harbour foreshore of Sydney. The urban renewal project was established as a public–private partnership in 2003 to transform an industrial maritime port. This previously forbidden site sparked the collective imagination of urban thinkers and designers at its outset with over 80 entries to the initial open design competition, but this engagement quickly devolved into a highly privatised process. At Barangaroo, the decisions that compromised public governance of place, once started, were compounded (Joabour, 2015; Pham, 2015). These decisions included: (1) co-awarding the design, to combine the competition-winning urban design scheme and local firm, with a large-scale design development firm who later went on to document, develop and even purchase offices on the site, (2) excluding local government and the city's Lord Mayor from the decision-making by establishing the "special purpose" Barangaroo Delivery Authority (Pham, 2015, after Acuto, 2012), (3) reduction in the ratio of public open space promised and an extensive height increase to key office towers immediately fronting the harbour, (4) the concurrent mass sale of the public housing located in the immediately adjacent Rocks precinct and the nearby Sirius, a beloved brutalist tower and social housing remnant, (5) demolition of the maritime watchtower, the one remaining industrial remnant on the site, and (6) finally, the permission for and high-speed delivery of a massive multi-storey casino tower at the site centre, dedicated to an exclusive international high-roller market.

Beyond the curious prevalence of gambling within Sydney's state projects, it is interesting to note the appropriation of placemaking practices

(Brenner, 2015) to appease the public while these non-public negotiations were occurring. The public park was completed first in the project staging, and the rest of the precinct is regularly "activated" with pop-up markets, temporary installations in the "community" undercroft and an indigenous art programme integrated into project scaffolding and facades. Without devaluing the individual quality of these works, the placemaking tactics were more about programming and socialising the site, than establishing the long-term cultural integration that a site of this scale should demand. The placemaking gestures were applied too late to inform how the site is used, to curtail the commercial footprint or to restore privatised land to the public asset portfolio. Despite compromised public benefits, the project was awarded the American Institute of Architects Prize for Excellence for its design. While the delivered outcome meets certain industry expectations and indeed remains a spectacular geographical location, the missed opportunities for significant urban green space (Pham, 2015), public harbour access and an integrated indigenous land response do not deliver the extent of public value that could be expected for such a prominent and rare piece of land.

Repeated inconsistencies and compromises in project governance erode public trust and set precedents for other state significant sites to follow. Overdevelopment and under-delivery of public benefit are now a topic for televised satire (Stitch et al., 2015) and outraged private conversations but go largely unchecked in the current political climate. Those that did protest about the processes at Barangaroo [the Lord Mayor, the winning architect turned City Councillor, Sydney Morning Herald journalists, the Greens party] were silenced as "silly", "obstructive", "lacking vision" by the elected ministers, former prime minister, radio shock jocks and prominent casino owner driving the decision-making and subverting existing planning laws (Joabour, 2015). The constant quashing of alternative viewpoints in the media and the speed with which planning laws were reorganised to suit the commercial interests of the project entirely excluded the general public from engaging with decisions about the future of the significant public landholding. The lack of genuine debate, combined with repeated spatial compromises, promoted economic interests over social, spatial and cultural place outcomes.

Reflections: Governance in Government and Place Agents in the Public Sector

Recognising that a democratic city should support a diverse set of spatial conditions as a backdrop for living, these projects are a reminder of the role of government in securing and sustaining public value. While activist projects are nimble provocations for innovation, top-down public-sector systems and actors can, and should, contribute to public-focused city-making practices. In London, the non-profit group, "Public Agency", recruits and advocates for design professionals in the public sector, working alongside the 2012 Social Value Act to reframe how Britain assesses public value beyond cost. In Australia, government architects are producing public documents to promote place-based practice, including the "Better Placed" policy in NSW (GANSW, 2017) and "Government as a Smart Client" in Victoria (OVGA, 2013). These documents propose an integrated approach to establishing, procuring and assessing design for public projects and provide tactics for doing so. "Better Placed" was instrumental in mandating "good design" into the NSW Environmental Planning and Assessment Act in 2017. Meanwhile, community and non-profit advocates equally influence government practice. For example, the Community Design Collaborative, supported by the Pennsylvanian Institute of Architects in Philadelphia, matches design professionals with community groups to deliver the first 10% of a project in a pro-bono capacity, filling a strategic void left by mainstream government, particularly around charter schools. Such gaps in government will only transform if dedicated, public-focussed professionals take up the challenges of the bureaucracy (Landry, 2005).

Realigning public benefit to public places is a task that requires multiple tiers of effort, over time and across scales. Government, in this context, has the potential to become an influential player in setting up the conditions for change. Rather than producing blunt instruments of regulation or building ever-nebulous commercial partnerships, governments can establish a networked approach with public benefit at its core. Cross-disciplinarity and embedded creativity as an asset (Landry, 2005) and facilitating stakeholder interrelationships (Carmona, 2014) are such tactics.

Key Learnings for the Place Agent:

Learning from the projects represented here, the place agent, whether embedded in the top-down system or working at the grassroots level, has genuine power to challenge existing regulatory systems through adaptive governance. Consistent project governance that leverages political and regulatory conditions can drive public benefit through all stages of placemaking. Such adaptive governance has the potential to effectively counter neoliberal models of development with viable alternatives and to integrate spatial design with operational governance to produce genuine public benefit. The corresponding shift towards social value in the UK has implications for how governments price their assets and suggests that diversified funding models (beyond the public–private partnerships) will continue to emerge in grassroots and government sectors (refer Architecture for Humanity's exceptional list of alternative funding models, Stohr, 2012). As the tactical placemaking movement evolves into highly organised acts of place production by collectives and activists, public-minded place agents in government make headway in policy leadership. The cross-pollination of these tactics and governance models has the potential to make genuine shifts in the established regulatory systems for place production and operation to drive better, more enduring public value.

References

Awan, N., Schneider, T., & Till, J. (2011). *Spatial agency: Other ways of doing architecture.* London and New York: Routledge.

Borden, I., Kerr, J., Rendell, J., & Pivaro, A. (2001). Things, flows, filters, tactics. In *The unknown city*. A Strangely Familiar project (pp. 2–25). Cambridge, MA: MIT Press.

Brenner, N. (2015). Is "tactical urbanism" an alternative to neoliberal urbanism? In Post. *Post: Notes on modern and contemporary art around the globe.*

Carmona, M. (2014). The place-shaping continuum: A theory of urban design process. *Journal of Urban Design, 19*(1), 2–36.

Carmona, M. (2017). The formal and informal tools of design governance. *Journal of Urban Design, 22*(1), 1–36.

Chaser (The). (2018, August 10). *That's the biggest billboard in Sydney mate*. Retrieved from www.smh.com.au/video/video-entertainment/video-entertainment-news/thats-the-biggest-billboard-in-sydney-mate-the-chaser-20181008-58nld.html.

Cirugeda, S. (2014). *Rebel architecture: Guerrilla architect*. Directed by Ana Naomi de Sousa. Al Jazeera. Retrieved from https://www.youtube.com/watch?v=674N2SnaAfs.

City of Sydney. (2019, March 4). *Extraordinary council meeting on the Waterloo Estate development*. Agenda and Papers. Retrieved from https://meetings.cityofsydney.nsw.gov.au/ieListDocuments.aspx?CId=133&MId=3156.

Colomb, C. (2012). Pushing the urban frontier: Temporary uses of space, city marketing, and the creative city discourse in 2000s Berlin. *Journal of Urban Affairs, 34*(2), 131–152.

Cruz, T. (2013). How architectural innovations migrate across borders. In TedGlobal talk 2013. Retrieved from www.ted.com/talks/teddy_cruz_how_architectural_innovations_migrate_across_borders.

Cruz, T., & Fonna, F. (2017). *The Political Equator*. In "Visualizing Citizenship: Seeking a New Public Imagination", Yerba Buena Center for the Arts Exhibition. San Francisco, CA. Retrieved from ybca.org/whats-on/visualizing-citizenship.

De Magalhães, C., & Carmona, M. (2009). Dimensions and models of contemporary public space management in England. *Journal of Environmental Planning and Management, 52*(1), 111–129.

Government Architect of New South Wales. (2017). *Better placed: An integrated design policy for the built environment of New South Wales*. Crown Copyright. NSW Government, Sydney.

Groth, J., & Corjin, E. (2005). Reclaiming urbanity: Indeterminate spaces, informal actors and urban agenda setting. *Urban Studies, 42*(3), 503–526. In Hamdi, N. (2010). *The placemaker's guide to building community*. London: Routledge.

Harvey, D. (2003). The right to the city. In Debates and developments. *International Journal of Urban and Regional Research, 27*(4), 939–941.

Hou, J. (Ed.). (2010). *Insurgent public space: Guerrilla urbanism and the remaking of contemporary cities*. New York: Routledge.

Iker, G. (Ed.). (2012). *Negotiating legality: Projects by Santiago Cirugeda*. In Mas Context, Ownership, Issue 13. Spring 2012. Retrieved from http://www.mascontext.com/issues/13-ownership-spring-12/negotiating-legality.

Joabour, B. (2015). The rise and rise of Barangaroo: How a monster development on Sydney harbour just kept on getting bigger. *The Guardian*. 30 September, 2015. www.theguardian.com/australia-news/2015/sep/30/the-rise-and-rise-of-barangaroo-how-a-monster-development-on-sydney-harbour-just-kept-on-getting-bigger.

Landry, C. (2005). *The creative bureaucracy: The original think piece*. Retrieved from www.charleslandry.com/themes/creative-bureaucracy/.

Langhorst, J. (2014). Re-presenting transgressive ecologies: Post-industrial sites as contested terrains. *Local Environment: International Journal of Justice & Sustainability, 19*(10), 1110–1133.

Lorne, C. (2017). Spatial agency and practising architecture beyond buildings. *Social and Cultural Geography, 18*(2), 268–287.

Lydon, M., & Garcia, A. (2015). *Tactical urbanism: Short-term action for long-term change. The streets plan collaborative*. Washington: Island Press.

Macchia, P., & Hopkins, J. (2019, March). Procurement for public value: Reflections from GANSW. *Architectural Bulletin*.

McCann, E. J. (2002). The cultural politics of local economic development: Meaning-making, place-making, and the urban policy process. *Geoforum, 33*, 385–398.

Office of the Victorian Government Architect (OVGA). (2013). *Government as 'Smart Client': Guidelines for building procurement processes*. Edition 01. Victorian State Government, Melbourne.

Oltermann, P. (2017, April 30). The party city grows up: How Berlin's clubbers built their own urban village. *The Guardian*. Retrieved from www.theguardian.com/cities/2017/apr/30/berlin-clubbers-urban-village-holzmarkt-party-city.

Pham, K. (2015). *Vanity unfair—Examining the impact of development authorities on the designation and development of public space: Barangaroo case study*. In State of Australian Cities Conference. Paper presented at the 2015 State of Australian Cities Conference (SOAC) No (Vol. 7, pp. 9–11).

Pitt, H. (2018). *The House: The dramatic story of the Sydney Opera House and the people who made it*. Sydney: Allen & Unwin.

Shatz, L., & Dallas, R. (2016). Participatory, technocratic and neoliberal planning: An untenable planning governance menage a trois. *Australian Planner, 53*(1), 37–45.

Shaw, K., & Montana, G. (2016). Place-making in megaprojects in Melbourne. *Urban Policy and Research, 34*(2), 166–189. https://doi.org/10.1080/08111146.2014.967392.

Stitch, R., Cilauro, S., & Gleisner, T. (2015). *Keep out—Public property*. In Utopia (television satire). Season 2. Episode 3. Directed by Rob Stitch. First aired in September 2015. Australian Broadcasting Corporation (ABC) Television.

Stohr, K. (2012). Financing sustainable community development. In Architecture for Humanity (Ed.), *Design like you give a damn* [2] (pp. 56–73). New York: Abrams.

Sydney Opera House. (2017). *Our story*. www.sydneyoperahouse/ourstory; and *Sydney Opera House reconciliation action plan*. Retrieved from https://www.sydneyoperahouse.com/content/dam/pdfs/rap/SOH_RAP_2017-19.pdf. Accessed February 2019.

Travers, T. (2018). Taxing power. In London School of Economics & Alfred Herrhausen Gesellschaft (Ed.), *Shaping cities in an urban age* (pp. 179–186). London: Phaidon.

UNESCO. (2019). *Sydney Opera House World Heritage listing 166* (established 2007). Retrieved from whc.unesco.org/en/list/166/.

Yarina, E. (2017). How architecture became capitalism's handmaiden: Architecture as alibi for the high line neoliberal space of capital accumulation. *Architecture & Culture, 5*(2), 241–263.

Zamanifard, H., Alizadeh, T., & Bosman, C. (2018). Towards a framework of public space governance. *Cities, 78,* 155–165.

12

DigitalXPlace

Andrew Toland, Melissa Cate Christ and Julian Worrall

> For it is only today now that our fascination for this technology has waned and its promises sound hollow, that culture and society are being defined by the digital condition in a comprehensive sense. … It is this hybridization and solidification of the digital – the presence of the digital beyond digital media – that lends the digital condition its dominance.
>
> Felix Stalder, *The Digital Condition* (2018)

A. Toland (✉)
School of Architecture, University of Technology Sydney,
Sydney, NSW, Australia
e-mail: andrew.toland@uts.edu.au

M. C. Christ
School of Design, Hong Kong Polytechnic University,
Hung Hom, Hong Kong

J. Worrall
School of Technology, Environments and Design,
University of Tasmania, Hobart, TAS, Australia

© The Author(s) 2020
D. Hes and C. Hernandez-Santin (eds.), *Placemaking Fundamentals for the Built Environment*, https://doi.org/10.1007/978-981-32-9624-4_12

Introduction

Digital placemaking is an emerging area of research and practice that focuses on the use and effects of digital technologies within placemaking.[1] Its definition has evolved over time in parallel with the development of digital technologies and digital culture in the last ten years. Initially, its usage was primarily applied to the use of digital electronic multimedia technologies physically installed or projected in public locations (sometimes also described as media architecture) (Haeusler, Tomitsch, Tscherteu, & Van Berkel, 2012; Hespanhol, Haeusler, Tomitsch, & Tscherteu, 2017; Tomitsch, 2016). Increasingly, however, the term is being used to describe ways in which digital technologies might be used to extend traditional placemaking strategies, such as expanding community engagement or enhancing collaboration and communication amongst stakeholders[2] (Aurigi & De Cindio, 2008; Fredericks, Hespanhol, & Tomitsch, 2016; Latorre, 2011), as well as crowdsourcing information and mobilising participation. This latter definition is also closely related to the emerging field of urban interaction design, sometimes also referred to as urban IxD (Brynskov et al., 2014; Fredericks et al., 2016). Digital placemaking can also be considered part of the wide-ranging and rapidly burgeoning literature on the blurring of physical, digital, social and spatial experiences brought about by the proliferation of smartphones and social media platforms (Griffiths & Barbour, 2016; Kember & Zylinska, 2012; O'Neill, 2016; Travis & von Lünen, 2016).

Given the recent direction of the usage of the phrase in placemaking literature, we prefer to define the term in line with the current, more everyday language usage of the adjective 'digital' to refer to any

---

[1] It must be recognised from the outset that our commentary is focussed on issues of digital placemaking in the Global North. Both placemaking practices and the use of digital technologies are extensively deployed in the Global South (e.g., see Padawangi & Douglass, 2015), but are outside the scope of this paper.

[2] A striking further example of this can be found in Chapter 4 of this volume, where architecture students worked with Indigenous knowledge-holders to re-establish the traditional 'songlines' of a place using digital 3D-printed clay interventions.

condition or set of practices that implicates digital or computer technologies or communications, especially the Internet (Oxford English Dictionary, sense B4, 2018). In that sense, it can legitimately be applied to placemaking practices which place special emphasis on, or are primarily mediated through, digital technologies—an ever increasing set of placemaking practices. It would be foolish, given the place of technological change, to attempt to foreclose the range of possibilities to which the term might be applied. And it is important from the outset to acknowledge that practices which currently seem like the cutting edge of technologies within placemaking will quickly come to seem entirely anachronistic. As a result, all we can hope to offer in this chapter is a partial snapshot of a particular moment in time: the proliferation and pervasive use of digital devices and platforms make it impossible to offer a comprehensive overview or some cohesive model which might credibly be labelled 'digital placemaking'. Instead, we offer a number of cases which have caught our attention or with which we have personal experience that we hope the reader might also find instructive or interesting. We also offer some indications of the scope and possibilities of current placemaking practices to give a sense of the direction in which things might be moving.

One further preliminary point is necessary: the title of our chapter deliberately eschews the word 'placemaking'. Just as we wish to draw attention to the fact that digital practices are increasingly being normalised—seamlessly folded into the texture of everyday life—we may also want to re-evaluate the use of the word placemaking. This is because certain efforts of place*making* have come to be regarded as cynical attempts by private developers or state agencies to legitimise profit-making or urban redevelopment projects. Our title—and not without a certain sense of irony—borrows from the current fad for 'collabs' in the world of fashion (as in 'Takashi Murakami X Louis Vuitton').[3] The field of 'digital placemaking' has not escaped a tendency to appropriate

---

[3] A 2018 *New Yorker* piece mocked the trend with an acerbic list of parody collabs, culminating with 'Consumer Capitalism x Human Weakness': Tuck, Jake. 2018. "Hot New Fashion and Design Collabs," *New Yorker*, September 25, 2018. https://www.newyorker.com/humor/daily-shouts/hot-new-fashion-and-design-collabs.

the fashionability of new technologies into the placemaking discourse as a way to advance faddish claims or interventions. A more rigorous study of the effects of digital media and technologies on the age-old challenge of 'making' 'place' requires a much more careful and comprehensive theorisation of notions of 'the digital' in relation to notions of 'place'. Alongside our early caveat about the mutability of digital placemaking practices, we therefore offer a further caution around the fundamental terms of the discourse. Nevertheless, the imbrication of digital technologies and practices with the social, cultural and political-economic creation and re-creation of 'places' is now a fact of life.

Andorra Living Lab

The Andorra Living Lab offers a striking example of some of the techniques that might be considered as digital placemaking when applied at the scale of an entire country, albeit the tiny principality of Andorra. Located in the Pyrenean borderlands between France and Spain, Andorra has a population of 77,000 and covers 468 square kilometres—about two-fifths the size of Los Angeles. In 2014, the MIT Media Lab began consulting with the Andorran government about the principality potentially becoming the world's first 'smart country'. This goal would involve utilising big data for urban and transport planning, the development of a new 'innovation' district and various educational initiatives (MIT, 2017). Within this broader ongoing project, which falls squarely within the standard 'smart cities' discourse (Picon, 2015), the MIT City Science research group launched the CityScope Andorra platform. The platform was an iteration of the CityScope simulation tool that the group had been developing over a number of previous projects, such as the Cityscape Volpe platform, which was developed to test scenarios for the development of a 5.7 hectare former Department of Transportation site purchased by MIT in Cambridge, Massachusetts (Grignard et al., 2018). This early iteration used different Lego blocks to represent residential buildings, commercial spaces, roads, parks and other amenities. These blocks allowed representations of built space to be readily manipulated and reconfigured by participants in community planning and consultation workshops, just like a child's Lego set. The physical objects were then tied via sensors to a computer program running customised urban analysis software. When changes were made to the model, information about the impact of those changes (as calculated by the software) was displayed on a 2D screen as a set of analytical graphs and charts. This analytical feedback was projected back onto the surface of the 3D physical model in spatial form. The claim made by the researchers is that this tool enabled 'the rapid assessment of urban interventions which incorporates analytical and visualization components to enable dynamic or iterative, evidence-based decision-making between traditionally siloed stakeholders ranging from community members and government officials, to domain experts and technicians'. In addition, the researchers assert that 'The combination of a tangible user interface and real-time feedback facilitate consensus-building through collaborative experimentation allowing multiple stakeholders to address a wide range of interests simultaneously', allowing 'the planning process to become more transparent, data-driven and evidence-based' (Alonso et al., 2018, p. 259).

This initial Cityscape Volpe platform was developed into the CityScope Andorra platform in an even more ambitious manner. It presented Andorran citizens with a much more realistic three-dimensional physical model of the city and its surrounding landscape (Fig. 12.1). Onto this base model, time-based urban data such as human and vehicular movements could be projected (a condition described as 'tangible agent-based visualization'). Just like the earlier Volpe platform, users' design and planning suggestions could be simulated and analysed 'in real-time' (real-time in the sense of instantaneous feedback via the computerised urban analysis software), and the impacts then projected back onto the surface of the physical model. In addition, users were also provided with tablet devices running a customised augmented reality application that allowed realistic 3D digital models of proposed design interventions to be seamlessly overlaid onto the image of the physical model captured through the tablet's camera. The augmented reality app also allowed remote stakeholders to be present around the (literal) table of the physical Andorra model. The stated aim of the project was to test how an interactive digital and physical model would allow urban planners and

Fig. 12.1 Andorra Living Lab interactive model by the MIT Media Lab (*Source* Ariel Noyman, City Science group, MIT Media Lab [Creative Commons BY-SA 4.0])

stakeholders to test the computationally predicted effects of a number of variables: different mixes of residential and commercial usage; different densities and building heights; variations in the provision of parks and public spaces; different mixes of modes of transport, as Andorra is heavily car- and truck-dependent, with no railways or airport; different traffic configurations; and various levels of walkability (Grignard et al., 2018). Andorra is also significantly impacted by major spikes in tourism when large inflows of visitors come for specific events during festivals or the ski season: for example, more than 8 million people visited in 2016 (Actua, 2017). In this context, the 'agent-based' simulation, which allowed participants to view variations in vehicular and pedestrian flows caused by different design and planning scenarios, was presented as a significant additional tool enabling participants to understand the impact of different spatial configurations and planning parameters. The CityScope platform was introduced in Andorra in August 2017, and it has primarily been billed as a 'civic engagement tool', presented via means of demonstrations, workshops and classes (Grignard et al., 2018, p. 1940).

In both projects, the published information contains very little about the actual stakeholders involved or their specific responses to the technology. It is also not stated whether or not the stakeholders regarded the 'visualisation tool' as a useful way to either improve their understanding of the planning and urban design decision-making process and/or increase their level of participation and agency within that process. Also missing was an assessment of whether stakeholders felt the entire process could lead to better outcomes from a placemaking perspective. Digitally augmented physical urban models have been in use for a while in urban design and planning contexts, but they have often been used as tools of propaganda and persuasion for large-scale, top-down urban planning schemes. This is especially seen in rapidly developing cities in which multimedia technology is often used in an attempt to dazzle citizens and seduce them with techno-utopian images of urban futurity (Toland & Kilbane, 2018). In theory, building stakeholder participation into the feedback loop provided by digital sandbox-type models like CityScope offers the prospect of increased democratic participation in city-making processes. However, the risk of bedazzlement remains, where the spectacle of technology can mask a lack of genuine participation, especially where there is not a level playing field between experts and laypeople. At the same time, the simulated outcomes are dependent on the algorithmic coding of the computational urban analytical models. These models are a black box to participants and may contain assumptions and literally encoded values that may be of concern to stakeholders, but which may not often surface or be open for discussion in these situations.

Unsafe in the City

A contrasting case study which employs an everyday use of technology in its placemaking efforts is the 'Unsafe in the City' project. The project is a collaboration between the child development NGO Plan International, XYX Lab (the Space Gender Communication Lab) at Monash University and a spatial data technology company CrowdSpot. This project spatialised the accounts of sexual violence and harassment of 21,000 girls and young women in five cities around the world—Sydney, Madrid, Kampala, Lima and Delhi. Participants were asked to 'drop pins' in locations around their cities where they felt safe or unsafe, just as anyone might do when using a platform like Google Maps, as well as share stories about these places or occurrences. The project's leader, landscape architect Nicole Kalms, makes the point that geocoding and visualising 'hotspots' across the crowdsourced data allows patterns to emerge, forcing designers and planners to more closely consider the qualities of these urban spaces (Kalms, 2018). Urban parks, in particular, emerged as locations of particular concern. Even though design guidelines exist for creating safer parks, they have not necessarily been shown to improve women's perception or actual experience of security in these spaces. Kalms calls for involving women and girls themselves in participatory design processes to co-create safer spaces. In one example, she cites Vienna's redesign of parks after it was observed that facilities were predominantly directed towards boys, resulting in less park usage by 10- to 13-year-old girls, as well as older girls. These observations led designers to involve girls in local design workshops, ultimately producing gender-sensitive park designs for Einsiedlerpark and St. Johann Park in Vienna (Urban Sustainability Exchange, n.d.). Post-occupancy evaluation suggested that there was an increase in park usage by girls in the underserved age groups after the implementation of design ideas that were generated through the workshops. Although the workshops mobilised traditional participatory design practices, the use of digital tools to gather data on a city-wide scale allows urban problems and issues to be uncovered to which more traditional placemaking methodologies might then be applied. An earlier project by the XYX Lab and CrowdSpot, the Gender Equality Map (Monash University, n.d.), tested the approach later used in the 'Unsafe in the City' project. The project asked users to drop a pin within certain pilot areas around Melbourne wherever they experienced positive or negative experiences of gender equality (Women Victoria, n.d.). Examples included the provision of parents' rooms, pram accessibility, sexist advertising, the lack of women's sporting facilities or inadequate change-room amenities at local sports fields. While the level and quality of the engagement appear to have varied, reading through the postings and their locations begins to reveal an overall picture about the ongoing gendered nature of public space both in a broad sense and in very specific instances. While crime hotspot maps have existed for some time in many cities, the use of digital data collection and engagement methods to initiate changes in the way 'places' are 'made' with respect to a broader spectrum of gender-based concerns allows for more nuanced conversations around the relationship between gender, urban space, and design. The discussions can become less defensive, in the sense of being oriented around discourses of 'safety', and more inclusive, in the sense of placing design and space into wider discussions about persistent gender inequality in public life.

Hong Kong Stair Archive

Another way in which 'the digital' can contribute to placemaking can be seen in the Hong Kong Stair Archive (HKSA), a pilot project begun in 2014 by Melissa Cate Christ and supported by the Hong Kong Polytechnic University and the Hong Kong Research Grants Council. Conceived as a way to inventory and archive outdoor stairs in Hong Kong, it is part of Stair Culture, 'a long term research and curatorial project undertaken by Cate Christ/transverse studio in collaboration with various artists, designers, students, curators, and cultural and educational institutions as a platform to investigate the role of stairs in defining the character of Hong Kong as an urban landscape' (*Always at the Edge*, 2017, p. 49). Stairs, slopes and terraces are key parts of the pedestrian infrastructural system in Hong Kong, integral to the way residents navigate and occupy the city. However, beyond their role as simple pathways, they also enable, or perhaps force, residents to slow down and be more present and aware of their surroundings, of the place that they are in. This engagement can be because of the physical effort required to walk up a set of stairs, or the need to find and hold a railing to carefully descend another set, or because it is quite difficult to text or watch a video on one's phone while navigating a staircase (although we have certainly seen this happen, as well as accidents occurring because of it!). In this process, a higher level of eye contact occurs, especially when people commute and take the same route every day, or when primary school student monitors say hello to everyone that walks by, or when the elders in a neighbourhood install a makeshift seating installation at the top of a set of stairs. These actions enable a basic form of placemaking to occur, where residents identify their own place through these interactions with their neighbours and by noticing the environment around them. Part of defining Hong Kong's landscape with respect to stairs is to understand their role not just as pedestrian infrastructure, but also as important contributors to Hong Kong's cultural landscape and public space, a role which is taken for granted, or at least not explicitly understood, until their existence is threatened by development.

This situation became apparent through work which preceded the HKSA project, Cate Christ's teaching and research surrounding the proposal for an escalator along Pound Lane, a historic staircase in the neighbourhood of Tai Ping Shan. This initial work uncovered some key existing issues surrounding insufficient and hegemonic processes of public consultation and engagement (Tang, Lee, & Ng, 2012), the continuing challenge of acquiring heritage protection for cultural landscape elements and the need for a unified accounting system for stairs, such as the one that exists in Hong Kong to manage slopes and retaining walls (CEDD, 2018). Through both traditional and social media, as well as through a website, a public forum and an exhibition which documented the student work and academic research, a broader awareness of 'stair culture' was achieved, and a local concern group was formed (whose primary form of community and information dissemination is through Facebook and Whatsapp groups[4]), setting forth a model which was applied across other Hong Kong stairway locations in the HKSA project. This model integrated digital methods of data collection, representation, communication and storage/presentation such as: crowdsourcing through a mobile web application that has the format of an urban game; the use of GIS, a geospatial database and other digital tools to build an interactive online map as the interface for a digital

---

[4]Pound Lane Concern group Facebook page: https://www.facebook.com/groups/poundlanecg/.

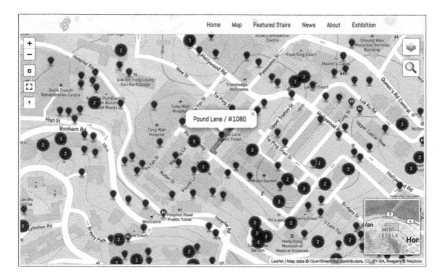

Fig. 12.2 Hong Kong Stair Archive Map (HKSA) online map, April 2019 (*Source* Melissa Cate Christ)

stair archive[5]; and the use of social media such as Facebook, Instagram and Twitter to promote, create and sustain a community around the research, including events such as panel discussions, workshops and an exhibition (Fig. 12.2).[6]

These methods of digital placemaking were utilized in tandem and as a necessary accompaniment to traditional 'in person' modes of communication and placemaking (such as posters, meetings and events) as a way to augment and increase the public's understanding, appreciation and use of the 'real' places: the ubiquitous stairs that are often overlooked as key contributors to the cultural and social landscape of Hong Kong.

As mentioned in the introduction, the use of smartphones, social media and the Internet is thoroughly integrated into how we communicate, schedule and occupy our time, and navigate through the

---

[5]HKSA map: https://hkstairmap.stairculture.com/?stairid=1291#19/22.28375/114.15039.
[6]Facebook page for Always at the edge of things and between places exhibition: https://www.facebook.com/alwaysathedge.

contemporary city. Because of this, every aspect of the HKSA was necessarily digitized in some way, at some point in the process, whether as a way to promote and get people to attend events, to navigate to a specific location, to document the stairs through digital photography or drawing in CAD or Illustrator, or how research data or event photos were shared on Facebook or posted on the website. All of these digital aspects contribute to making stairs places; however, the element of the project that was the most explicit about the use of digital technology to 'make place' was the urban game Stair Quest.[7] This 'serious urban game' was developed by Stefan Schmidlin and Mela Kocher from the Zurich University of the Arts for the HKSA's exhibition *Always at the edge of things and between places*,[8] which was supported by Connecting Space Hong Kong and the Hong Kong Arts Development Council. Termed a 'serious' game because of its mission to crowdsource data on Hong Kong stairs such as number of risers, whether there was a handrail or not, and photos, it was created at the height of the initial excitement about the potential of 'Pokemon Go' to draw people into the urban environment through games on their smartphones. Coming from the field of game design, Kocher and Schmidlin created a narrative hook for the game: a Spirit Dragon was split into over 3000 pieces and lodged in the stairs of the Central and Western District. To be rescued, teams needed to visit each stair to gather information and enter it into the game, gaining 'Spirit Dust' and naming rights for stairs where they gathered the most information, visited first, or got the most votes for their stairs' names or data. Set up as a collaborative game (as a way to verify information through multiple separate visits), the intent was to make gathering data a fun project for a group of friends, as it turned out to be much more enjoyable and easier to work in groups to count

---

[7]The game can only be played on a smartphone in the Central and Western District of Hong Kong Island. See https://quest.stairculture.com/ for info and to sign into the game using Facebook.

[8]*Always at the edge of things and between places*, webpage: https://stairculture.com/archive/exhibition/.

steps and puzzle over stair typologies. The data was stored in a database and then scraped to be included in the main geospatial database for the HKSA map.

Unfortunately, after the initial launch of Stair Quest through several workshops, the game did not attract many users. It, therefore, had less initial impact as a broadly used placemaking strategy in the sense of using it to get people to go to stairs in places they would not usually visit and to look at those stairs in a new way. Key challenges had to do with the limited time and budget to create the game, the lack of picture upload in the initial launch version of the game, the necessity to use Facebook to login, the restriction of the game to only Android and iPhones, and the need to make it a web application, rather than an app. Another challenge within the game itself is the difficulty of matching a stair in the map to your location, as most phone GPS devices are only accurate within 10–50 meters in Hong Kong, depending as well on the density and height of surrounding buildings. This was addressed by including the outline/polygon of the stair in the interface of the game along with a marker, but still led to some confusion. However, there has been continued interest in the game academically and within the field of game design and AR (MCCM book 2019; Kocher article/conference), and a second iteration of the game, along with a workshop and another round of crowdsourcing, was launched in May 2019 to focus on its utility as a research tool and its more streamlined integration with the HKSA map. It has, therefore, proven to be an invaluable part of crowdsourcing data and geo-referenced photos of the 3000+ stairs, particularly because it is inclusive of all members of society (albeit with a smartphone) who then get to better know an area of the city, the significance of stairs, and to feel part of a wider effort to preserve the city's heritage, all the while contributing to the HKSA. In summary, while a good portion of the HKSA project was conceived as a way to digitally connect residents and visitors to the physicality of the stairs in their places, the engagement enabled by elements such as Stair Quest allowed people to participate as a type of citizen scientist, contributing not just their presence, but also connecting to others and taking part in a wider community which values stairs as an important part of Hong Kong's socio-cultural heritage.

Post-disaster Christchurch

The recovery phase after disasters presents a situation in which the questions of place and its remaking become particularly acute. A destructive shock that damages or destroys the physical fabric of a city and displaces its inhabitants effects a reset of socio-spatial patterns, erasing the spatial underpinnings of the mental and social topography of urban places, and establishing a definitive temporal cleavage between 'before' and 'after' that motivates new actors and enables new ways of doing things to emerge. In such circumstances, there may be a more explicit reliance on the digital as a layer of the urban assemblage that, paradoxically, may be more robust, connective and enduring than the physical fabric of the city. In this way, the distinctiveness of the contribution of the digital dimension to (re)shaping places may be illuminated.

Christchurch, New Zealand, offers an interesting case of post-disaster placemaking in which digital tools and techniques have played a significant role in the reimagining and revitalisation of the city. The city was severely damaged in the earthquake of 22 February 2011, with 185 deaths, major damage and destruction to many significant buildings, and much of the central city subsequently cordoned-off and rendered inaccessible within the 'Red Zone', an area deemed too unsafe for public access. Within two years, 80% of the buildings of the central business district had been demolished. These events fundamentally altered the landscape of place—physical, social and mental—that constituted the city.

In the official responses to the post-disaster recovery of the city, a tension developed between the consultative approach taken by the municipal authority, Christchurch City Council (CCC) and the top-down agenda ultimately implemented by the national reconstruction authority established after the disaster, the Canterbury Earthquake Recovery Authority (CERA) (Wesener, 2015). From the outset, the CCC sought to involve the citizenry in rapidly devising a plan for recovery, making extensive use of digital techniques to facilitate and innovate effective consultation processes, in a situation in which entire sections of the physical city were off-limits. Notable amongst these was 'Share an Idea', a multi-channel initiative for community consultation to gather ideas for urban recovery, centred on an interactive website and proliferating across multiple digital platforms (Facebook, Twitter and YouTube) and physical media and spaces (news sheets, exhibitions and forums). Its positive, uplifting tone and inclusive design encouraged snowballing engagement, gathering 106,000 contributions over six weeks, approximately 21% of the city population. The quality of this initiative was later recognised with international awards for its innovation and effectiveness.[9] However, due to the transfer of effective authority for reconstruction from CCC to CERA in April 2012, the results and the CCC plan were effectively sidelined, engendering widespread distrust and disillusionment amongst many local communities, ultimately leading to a public demonstration protesting the lack of democratic accountability in the official recovery planning process (Carlton, 2013).

Bottom-up, self-organising initiatives represent an alternative type of community participation in post-disaster recovery, in which local and frequently newly formed groups work to build broader support and implement concrete interventions on damaged or abandoned sites. In post-disaster Christchurch, Gap Filler, Life in Vacant Spaces, Greening the Rubble and the Festival of Transitional Architecture (FESTA) are prominent exemplars of sustained community-led groups and initiatives that emerged in the aftermath of the earthquake (Bennett, Boidi, & Boles, 2013). The use of digital tools and technologies to gather and disseminate ideas, build support and implement projects is a notable dimension of these bottom-up initiatives.

Beyond facilitating engagement and implementation, in some of these projects digital technology is explicitly deployed to enable or enrich the experience of place. Specific examples include *Dance-o-mat* (2011), which set up a public dance platform using a converted laundromat washing machine as coin-operated digital jukebox, with

---

[9]Share an Idea won 'unanimous overall winner' of the Netherlands-based Co-creation Association's Co-creation Award in 2011, and the resulting plan developed by Gehl Architects from these responses won a major prize in Sweden's Virserum Art Museum's Triennal Architecture of Necessity Awards in 2013.

Fig. 12.3 An overview of the headline event of *Lean Means*, the 2016 iteration of FESTA Christchurch (Photo by Julian Worrall)

which anyone with a smartphone could become an open-air DJ; and *Super Street Arcade* (2016), which implemented a urban-scaled 'Space Invaders'-style arcade game using an urban screen on a building facade teamed with a body-sized joystick and button positioned across the street for pairs of passers-by to operate (Gapfiller, n.d.). These projects highlight the ludic potentials of digital augmentations to urban space and in their cultural semiotics suggest an openness to a youthful demographic often overlooked or disenfranchised in conventional urban improvements.

It is the example of FESTA, however, that provides a more substantial exemplar of the potentials of post-disaster placemaking under Felix Stalder's 'digital condition' described in the opening quote. Otherwise known as The FESTA, is a biannual event that gathers dozens of teams of design students, educators, artists and community groups to devise and build architectonic urban installations for one night of display and celebration in central Christchurch (Fig. 12.3). It has been described by Barnaby Bennett, one of its chief curators and advocates, as an 'activist experiment in city-making' (Bennett, 2018). The inaugural event, a nocturnal 'city made of light' entitled *Luxcity*, assembled 16 projects created by 350 students from across New Zealand, attracting an estimated 25,000 people on its opening night in October 2012 (Halliday, 2017). Subsequent iterations were held in 2013, 2014, 2016 and 2018 (the present author and a team of architecture students from the University of Adelaide contributed to the iterations in 2016 and 2018). Each iteration is themed around a topical urban issue, including participation, storytelling, identity, waste or food, and the event has continued to draw audiences in the tens of thousands and extensive participation from across the region, despite the increasing timespan since the disaster and the progress of reconstruction.

The primary objectives of the event have been to: encourage reoccupation of the central city; stimulate engagement and imaginative investment in alternative urban futures for Christchurch; and rebuild social capital and civic participation, stimulating longer-term change in who makes the city and how. These objectives, and its local community orientation grounded in the galvanising experience of disaster, position FESTA as a paragon of placemaking. However, through its set-up for creation and delivery linking academic networks in the fields of architecture and design with local communities based in Christchurch, the initiative has also served as a kind of sandbox and training camp for budding tactical urbanists across Australasia. The event has become the largest event on the architectural calendar in New Zealand, is covered in the national television and print media and has drawn attention and plaudits from around the globe.

While the emphasis at FESTA has been upon stimulating collective participation and sensorially rich embodied experiences in Christchurch's urban space, digital tools have been crucial for their implementation, effectiveness and reach. Primarily, these have been used to facilitate communication, coordination and dissemination. Digital tools and techniques are fully embedded in FESTA's own organisational and promotional machinery, while contributing teams routinely employ a panoply of social media platforms, including Facebook groups to coordinate activities, Twitter and Instagram accounts, complete with carefully curated hashtags, to disseminate images and information, and project blogs to record and reflect on experiences.[10] The aggregation of these channels can be understood as the digital layer of FESTA's placemaking operation, without which the scope and scale of both physical and social layers would be significantly altered and diminished. When combined with mediation and network effects, the (re)imagining of local urban places and the (re)formation of the constituencies that support them acquires a degree of geographic dispersal and entanglement that belies the compact topographic geometries suggested by the term placemaking. The example of FESTA suggests that the energies unleashed by disaster, married to the agencies enabled by the digital, can powerfully recast the social shape of place.

Conclusion

From a critical perspective, an examination of both the applications of, and the discourse around, digital placemaking reveal numerous problems, contradictions and tensions. Terms and concepts which appear to capture a zeitgeist and allow claims to be made about new ways of doing things—terms like 'the digital', 'placemaking' and indeed 'digital placemaking'—inevitably produce contested usages and meanings. The reality is that the increasing penetration of digital devices and platforms into the practices of everyday life is continuing to transform the web of relations between people, space and place. In these circumstances, the trope of digital placemaking is constantly at risk of being overtaken by actual events in which 'the digital' is just another ubiquitous tool. At best, digital placemaking captures an aspiration by designers and others to positively influence these new relations, but these efforts need to be set within a context in which it is understood that everyday socio-spatial culture is transforming with or without the contribution of

---

[10]The contributions to FESTA directed by the present author include *Cumulonimbus* (2016); and *Makkanika* (2018). Project blogs reflecting on the processes and outcomes are https://festa2016adl.wordpress.com/ and https://festa2018adl.wordpress.com/, respectively.

'designers' as such. Ultimately, the notion of 'digital' placemaking may come to seem anachronistic (like discourses about the 'cyber-' that once abounded in the not-too-distant past): in this contemporary moment, all placemaking inevitably demands an engagement with 'digital' technologies and practices. This recognition demands that we periodically return to interrogatee the central debates around 'placemaking' itself, an inherently slippery term, as well as how its deployment has come to serve various competing interests and agendas. At the core of this chapter has been an attempt to think through some of the complexities arising from the recent tendency to prefix claims about placemaking with the adjective 'digital' and to consider the ways in which certain strands of placemaking ideology and practice are themselves 'augmented' by this explicit connection with the digital. This approach is intended to cast a critical light on the dynamics within and around the discourses of both placemaking and the digital in order to sift for any genuine insights or transformations that might be created by conjoining the two.

DigitalXPlace in Essence

- Contemporary placemaking is by necessity 'digital' due to the ubiquity of smartphone and the Internet, but it will continue to also demand skilful deployment of traditional placemaking methods.
- Effective deployment of digital technologies requires an understanding of what new insights, engagements or representations they might allow within a broader matrix of placemaking techniques.
- Some of the most successful uses of digital tools for placemaking mobilise digital behaviours that are already part of people's everyday uses of technology, such as digital mapping applications, image sharing or event announcement and promotion.
- The constitution of place that emerges under the 'digital condition' is less about geographical propinquity and more about imaginative and affective engagement and selective affiliations and is therefore increasingly delaminated from locationally defined sites and communities, although it can often increase awareness about, and affinities for, specific localities.

References

Actua. (2017, February 28). *The number of visitors in Andorra increased again in 2016 and exceeded 8 million.* Retrieved from https://www.actua.ad/en/news/number-visitors-andorra-increased-again-2016-and-exceeded-8-million. Accessed 29 April 2019.

Alonso, L., Zang Y.R., Grignard A., Noyman, A., Sakai, Y., ElKatsha M., ... Larson, K. (2018, July). Cityscope: A data-driven interactive simulation tool for urban design: Use case volpe. In *International conference on complex systems* (pp. 253–261). Cham, Switzerland: Springer.

Always at the edge of things and between places. Melissa Cate Christ (Ed.). (2017). Hong Kong: Connecting Space Hong Kong and HKADC. Exhibition catalogue.

Aurigi, A., & De Cindio, F. (Eds.). (2008). *Augmented urban spaces: Articulating the physical and electronic city.* Aldershot: Ashgate.

Bennett, B. (2018, September 20). Feasting in the broken city. In *The big idea.* Retrieved from https://www.thebigidea.nz/stories/feasting-on-the-broken-city.

Bennett, B., Boidi, E., & Boles, I. (Eds.). (2013). *Christchurch—The transitional city pt IV.* Wellington, New Zealand: Freerange Press.

Brynskov, M., Carvajal Bermúdez, J. C., Fernández, M., Korsgaard, H., Mulder, I. J., Piskorek, K., ... De Waal, M. (2014). *Urban interaction design: Towards city making.* Amsterdam: Urban IxD Booksprint.

Carlton, S. (2013). Share an idea, spare a thought community consultation in Christchurch's time-bound post-earthquake rebuild. *Journal of Human Rights in the Commonwealth, 1*(2), 4–13.

Civil Engineering and Development Department (CEDD). (2018). *Slope safety system in Hong Kong.* Retrieved from https://www.cedd.gov.hk/eng/achievements/geotechnical/safety_system/index.html. Accessed 10 April 2019.

Fredericks, J., Hespanhol, L., & Tomitsch, M. (2016, June). Not just pretty lights: Using digital technologies to inform city making. In *Proceedings of the 3rd Conference on Media Architecture Biennale* (p. 7). ACM.

Fredericks, J., Tomitsch, M., & Stewart, L. (2017). Design patterns for integrating digitally augmented pop-ups with community engagement. *International Journal of E-Planning Research (IJEPR), 6*(3), 19–41.

Gapfiller. (n.d.). Website. https://gapfiller.org.nz. Accessed 11 April 2019.

Griffiths, M., & Barbour, K. (2016). *Making publics, making places.* Adelaide: University of Adelaide Press.

Grignard, A., Macià, N., Alonso Pastor, L., Noyman, A., Zhang, Y., & Larson, K. (2018, July). Cityscope andorra: A multi-level interactive and tangible agent-based visualization. In *Proceedings of the 17th International Conference on Autonomous Agents and MultiAgent Systems* (pp. 1939–1940). International Foundation for Autonomous Agents and Multiagent Systems.

Haeusler, M. H., Tomitsch, M., Tscherteu, G., & Van Berkel, B. (2012). *New media facades: A global survey*. Ludwigsburg: Av edition.

Halliday, J. (2017). FESTA festival of transitional architecture in Christchurch, New Zealand. *The Journal of Public Space, 2*(3), 177–186.

Hespanhol, L., Haeusler, H. M., Tomitsch, M., & Tscherteu, G. (2017). Cities of electronic clay: Media architecture for malleable public spaces. In *Media architecture compendium: Digital placemaking* (pp. 54–56). Stuttgart: Av edition.

Kalms, N. (2018, June 17). To design safer parks for women, city planners must listen to their stories. *The Conversation*. Retrieved from https://theconversation.com/to-design-safer-parks-for-women-city-planners-must-listen-to-their-stories-98317.

Kember, S., & Zylinska, J. (2012). *Life after new media: Mediation as a vital process*. Cambridge, MA: MIT Press.

Latorre, D. (2011, September 21). Digital placemaking—Authentic civic engagement. *Project for Public Spaces*. Retrieved from https://www.pps.org/article/digital-placemaking-authentic-civic-engagement.

Massachusetts Institute of Technology (MIT). (2017, October 13). *Small European nation becomes a "living lab" for urban innovation researchers*. Retrieved from http://news.mit.edu/2017/european-nation-andorra-living-lab-media-lab-urban-innovation-1013.

Monash University. (n.d.). *Gender equality map*. Retrieved from https://www.monash.edu/mada/research/labs/xyx-lab-monash-space-gender-communication-lab/gender-equality-map. Accessed 23 February 2018.

O'Neill, K. (2016). *Pixels and places: Designing human experience across physical and digital spaces*. New York: KO Insights.

Padawangi, R., & Douglass, M. (2015). Water, water everywhere: Toward participatory solutions to chronic urban flooding in Jakarta. *Pacific Affairs, 88*(3), 517–550.

Picon, A. (2015). *Smart cities: A spatialised intelligence*. Chichester, UK: Wiley.

Stalder, F. (2018). *The digital condition*. Cambridge, UK: Polity Press.

Tang, W. S., Lee, J. W. Y., & Ng, M. K. (2012). Public engagement as a tool of hegemony: The case of designing the new central harbourfront in Hong Kong. *Critical Sociology, 38*(1), 89–106.

Toland, A., & Kilbane, S. (2018). City mega-models as literal and figurative visioning tools. *Proceedings of the Institution of Civil Engineers—Urban Design and Planning, 171*(4), 166–176.

Tomitsch, M. (2016). Communities, spectacles and infrastructures: Three approaches to digital placemaking. In S. Pop, T. Toft, N. Calvillo, & M. Wright (Eds.), *What urban media art can do: Why, when, where, and how*. Stuttgart: Av edition.

Travis, C., & Von Lünen, A. (Eds.). (2016). *The Digital arts and humanities: Neogeography, social media and big data integrations and applications*. Cham: Springer.

Urban Sustainability Exchange. (n.d.). *Gender-sensitive park design at Einsiedlerpark and St. Johann Park*. Retrieved from https://use.metropolis.org/case-studies/gender-sensitive-park-design. Accessed 3 February 2018.

Wesener, A. (2015). Temporary urbanism and urban sustainability after a natural disaster: Transitional community-initiated open spaces in Christchurch, New Zealand. *Journal of Urbanism: International Research on Placemaking and Urban Sustainability, 8*(4), 406–422.

Women Victoria. (n.d.). *Gender equality map*. Retrieved from https://www.vic.gov.au/women/gender-equality/gender-equality-map.html. Accessed 3 February 2018.

13

Place Evaluation: Measuring What Matters by Prioritising Relationships

Dominique Hes, Cristina Hernandez-Santin, Tanja Beer and Shih-Wen Huang

Introduction

Placemaking is well documented for its role in fostering place attachment in increasingly dense, diverse and mobile communities, thus leading to positive impacts on health, community participation, civic behaviour and perceptions of safety (Anton & Lawrence, 2014; Billig, 2006; Kyle, Graefe, Manning, & Bacon, 2004). However, it has also been highlighted that placemaking projects can fail to achieve long-term benefits, often resulting in more superficial beautification projects with few long-term benefits. This can be called place-masking (Fincher, Pardy, & Shaw, 2016), or place-wash (Shaw, 2008), concepts outlined in more detail in Chapter 1.

This chapter explores the existing strategies to evaluate place from a socio-ecological perspective and argues that we need to go beyond

D. Hes (✉) · C. Hernandez-Santin · T. Beer · S.-W. Huang
Thrive Research Hub and Place Agency, Faculty of Architecture, Building and Planning, The University of Melbourne, Parkville, VIC, Australia
e-mail: Dhes@unimelb.edu.au

the easily measurable attributes of place and have greater inclusion of the intangible benefits of place. This evaluation needs to be across the aspects that are involved in placemaking at four different levels:

- the input—including people, time, resources, strategies applied as part of the process. It essentially documents "how" the placemaking initiative was developed. For example, to co-create a pop-up park through a design workshop with a local school, one would document the number of people, time and resources that go into organising said design workshop;
- the output—defined as the tangible elements resulting from the initiative. For example, the pop-up park itself and its design attributes;
- the outcome—which we define as indicators applied to the specific context of the place in a relatively short-term process. For example, this would include measures such as the number of visitors, the number of people engaged through the process or economic measures discussed in Chapter 8;
- the legacy (impact)—which, for placemaking, we define as the achievement of the overarching objectives of the process. For example, the conversations triggered by the consultation process leading to people taking active roles in developing the place into the future.

The input and the output are descriptive processes documenting what occurred. However, an evaluation process is interested in the outcomes and legacies that the project had—what is the impact of place on the stakeholders?

Choosing the indicators applied to assess this impact is critical to the ability to demonstrate the effectiveness of a placemaking process. Given that placemaking aims to trigger an emotional connection between the individual and the place (Cilliers & Timmermans, 2014; Trudeau, 2016), this chapter will argue that a place evaluation process should assess the relationships developed between the stakeholders and place. To be able to do this in a place-specific way, this needs to start from the community values including human and non-human values, both past and present. To achieve this, we developed the Four Dimensions of

Place Framework (FDP) as a strategy to identify key relationships that place processes need to support. Improvement in these relationships results in the benefits of placemaking discussed throughout the book—more investment, less crime, greater biodiversity, less vandalism, etc. The FDP provides a way to verify if the evaluation process is taking a holistic approach to place assessment. It does this by identifying indicators of positive relationships between the individual (self), the community, the natural environment and the human-made environment in which it is located. The main point being that if these relationships are evident, then the place is successful. Ways to measure these relationships are outlined with relevant theory and existing tools. Lastly, this chapter uses a case study to illustrate the FDP: The Living Pavilion (TLP) (1–17 May 2019), a temporary event space and placemaking project at the University of Melbourne.

Benefit of Evaluating Place

Evaluating how placemaking can positively contribute to urban environments is critical to inform both the continued development of the place and the way placemaking is done as a practice. Currently, there is no single tool which will critically, reliably, easily, holistically and meaningfully evaluate place projects, nor discern between those that are successful in achieving the desired place legacy from those that engage in place-masking.

In addition to avoiding inauthentic placemaking (see Chapter 1), there are further five benefits to evaluating place. The first is that evaluating a placemaking outcome can demonstrate the progress of an initiative and supports the justification for the budget. The second is the ability to compare places, facilitating learning and continual improvement. The third is that it allows prioritisation amongst a portfolio of projects. The fourth is the ability to clearly and simply communicate the intended outcomes for stakeholders such as investors, government and industry. Lastly, it provides an understanding of best practice which can inform the strategies to use for placemaking.

Tools for Place Evaluation

In a recent comprehensive review, Carmona (2019) identified over 20 ways through which place can lead to social, ecological and economic benefits as documented by 271 research-based studies. However, each study applied very different evaluation strategies often presenting a partial narrative of place benefits (i.e. studies focusing solely on well-being measures while other centred on economic return). Similarly, there are numerous tools available to practitioners to evaluate design projects, yet they are not holistic and often focus on one sector (recreation, canopy cover, biodiversity, activation, walkability and so forth) rather than the complex interrelated benefits of a place.

Over recent years, new Australian platforms such as Neighbourlytics and Placescore have been developed by placemaking practices as initial forays into the measurement of place. Internationally, there are hosts of indices and toolkits that seek to assess the quality of places (e.g. Place Standard, UN-HABITAT Public Space Toolkit, Happy Maps). In the market, there are over 75 indices, frameworks, guidelines and engagement tools that can inform place evaluation strategies.[1] However, the current approaches to evaluating place have various limitations:

- The process tends to be about assessment as an end product (i.e. creating a score) rather than or questioning how the evaluation can inform future redevelopment (facilitating the co-evolution of the place).
- These tools tend to use standardised indicators (i.e. mayor crime rates, population statistics, number of visitors) that tell little of the unique narrative of a particular place or the emotional connection developed between the visitor and said place.
- The evaluation processes tend to focus on the outputs and outcomes of the project failing to incorporate measures that link to the overarching objectives of place processes.

---

[1] The tools were collated in a matrix as part of ongoing effort led in by Place Leaders Asia Pacific and the Rating Place Project. The tools included in this chapter are listed in the reference section.

- Current approaches are not holistic and often only focus on human outcomes, yet we know that ecological or non-human elements are essential for human well-being (see Chapter 3).

Evaluation Is More Than Just Attaining a Score

Evaluation of place should be more than just an accounting exercise; it should contribute to a richer understanding of the place, empowering stakeholders to have agency over its development. The role of evaluation should not just be limited to scoring a place. The real value in evaluation is how it engages the stakeholders of that place in better understanding their values of that place and empowering them to work towards strengthening those values.

As such, this chapter discusses the benefits of evaluating place in terms of how the aspects of place contribute to improved social, ecological and economic outcomes. As is discussed in Chapters 2 and 3, it is critical to be able to assess the non-human and ecological aspects as they underpin the ability to thrive socially first, to enable desired economic outcomes second (Peattie, 1995; and, summarising the evolution of sustainability models Lozano, 2008). To summarise this argument: without air, water, soil, etc., there would be no trees, animals, food or people, and without people, the concept of money and the economy is irrelevant.

In looking at place and its impact on social, ecological and economic outcomes, it is really the richness of the relationship between place, human and non-human that determines its success. It is important to note though that an evaluation process based on relationships does not seek to undermine the role of economic evaluation. Place Economics is critical to holistic evaluation processes (see Chapters 8 and 9), and it is good practice in any organisation to collect information on financial performance of a project to ensure its ongoing viability and management. However, integrating indicators for relationships built and supported by a project increases the depth of the evaluation process, aligning to the overarching objectives of place practice. These relationship-based indicators comprise "intangible" and subjective measures that, while making it difficult to compare projects, provide a clear picture of the place-specific connections developed. Lastly, as concluded in Chapter 2, the current approach to placemaking tends to be very human and socially focused undermining the role of nature in achieving the sought after well-being and livability. It is for these reasons that the FDP was developed and will be outlined in the next section.

Four Dimensions of Place Framework (FDP)

The purpose of placemaking is to create meaningful relationships between users and spaces and to improve people's quality of life according to their needs and desires through the process meaning-creation (Cilliers & Timmermans, 2014; Trudeau, 2016). This definition of placemaking emphasises the two-way relationship between the physical space and people as being key to producing place. Space provides the canvas on which meaning and identity can be affixed and contested, and the characteristics of the place also shape people's attachment to the place as well as their relationship with others (Amin, 2012; Trudeau, 2016). This definition also highlights the relationship between the community and the self. Recognition, belongingness and sense of community all contribute to place attachment, and that in turn provides a "remedy against feelings of alienation and estrangement" (Aravot, 2010, p. 202). This conceptualisation of place suggests that space, community and self are the three critical components of place; and it is the relationship between these three that create great places.

One critical element that is not defined with enough depth in the above model is the role of the natural environment within place. It is well known that connection to our ecosystems—trees, animals, wind, water, sun, etc.—is critical to well-being (biophilia literature covers this extensively, see also the link between well-being and ecosystem services by Summers, Smith, Case, & Linthurst, 2012). Yet placemaking is often aimed at social and human development, not the natural environment, for example: How can people feel comfortable here? How can we reduce crime? How can we increase economic and social activity? How do we reduce loneliness? How do we create increased engagement in the community?

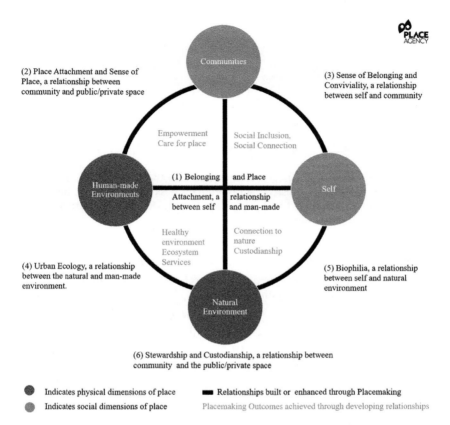

Fig. 13.1 Four dimensions of place framework for relationship-based evaluation (Image by Cristina Hernandez-Santin)

As such, we developed the Four Dimensions of Place Framework (FDP) shown in Fig. 13.1. It shows the main aspects of self, community, human-made environment and natural environment (in black), resulting in six relationship connections (1. Self and Human-made Environments; 2. Community and Human-made Environments; 3. Self and Community; 4. Natural Environment and Human-made Environments; 5. Self and Natural Environment; and 6. Community and Natural Environment) and the theories that underpin the value and expected legacy when supporting these relationship connections. Lastly, the image shows some of the expected place outcomes resulting from designing for the four aspects and 6 relationships (shown in grey).

INDEX	SELF AND SPACE	COMMUNITY AND SPACE	COMMUNITY AND SELF	NATURE AND SPACE	SELF AND NATURE	COMMUNITY AND NATURE
THRIVING PLACES INDEX	Y	Y	Y	N	N	N
GENSLER EXPERIENCE INDEX	Y	Y	Y	N	N	N
CALIFORNIA HEALTHY PLACES INDEX (HPI)			Y	Y	N	N
STATE OF PLACE INDEX	Y	Y				
A.T. KEARNEY'S GLOBAL CITIES INDEX (& GLOBAL CITIES OUTLOOK)	N	N	N	N	N	N
AARP LIVABILITY INDEX	N	Y	N	Y	N	N
BENCHMARKING CITY SERVICES	N	Y	N	N	Y	Y

Fig. 13.2 Sample of analysis of existing tools and their ability to measure relationship. Y=yes, N=no. This was a preliminary desk-based analysis and will be tested in the field through the Rating Place Project (Box 13.1) which is currently being developed with industry

From this, a process of how to measure the relationships was undertaken by looking at the various place-related evaluation tools on the market. Each tool was analysed evaluating its capacity to measure or provide meaningful information about the evidence for a specific relationship. Through a process of consultation and literature review, 75 tools were reviewed. Figure 13.2 represents a sample of this analysis where each tool was categorised for each relationship. The sections below further elaborate the attached theories that underpin these relationships and how to evaluate them with some of the place evaluation tools available on the market.

Self and Human-Made Environments

Having a bond with your lived environment, feeling acknowledged and accepted for your uniqueness and experiencing an emotional connection with the natural world, all contribute to well-being by providing a sense of "rootedness" (Fincher & Iveson, 2008; Hes & du Plessis, 2014; Scannell & Gifford, 2010). These positive relationships between you and the elements of place deliver benefits back to the place. That is, your perceptions and experiences of place influence the function and the meaning you give to that place. If these are positive, then you will be more inclined to invest the place (Cilliers & Timmermans, 2014;

Manzo & Perkins, 2016). The relationship between self and public/private space is called the "sense of belonging" encompassing history, ability to navigate, familiarity and access. Having good relationships results in what is termed "a sense of care" resulting in reduced graffiti, antisocial behaviour such as vandalism and abuse, and a sense of responsibility for the place leading to time and energy spent maintaining the place. A few of the tools that support the measurement of the strengths of these relationships are:

- Happy Maps captures crowdsourced and geotagged pictures quantitatively to build maps with measures of human emotions and perceptions in response to places.
- Walk Score App provides individuals with a walk score that examines the walkability of any home in a neighbourhood to nearby shops, cafes, schools and grocery stores.
- CrowdSpot engages with community to generate and map individual experiences of their city by focusing on issues such as bike safety, female safety and walkability.
- Lovability Index is a project conducted in Melbourne. Through a 7 question survey, a group of researchers were able to map the things that people loved the most about their neighbourhood. These questions are easily adapted to various contexts.

Community and Human-Made Environments

Beyond the self and space is the relationship between the collective group of stakeholders connected to that location (community) and the space. The key relationship that is created through the connection between the community and space is what is called "place attachment". Place attachment, as mentioned earlier, is the emotional and affective relationship people form with a place; though it is part of the relationship between self and space, it also impacts a sense of community. Conventionally, place attachment comprises of two components: place identity and place dependence (Davis, 2016; Heller & Adams, 2009). Place identity refers to beliefs, perceptions and thoughts about oneself in relation to a specific place. Place dependence refers to the ability of a place to satisfy a person's functional needs and wants.

Place attachment and a sense of community encourage people to take part in initiatives that protect and improve their communities (Manzo & Perkins, 2016; McMillan & Chavis, 1986). Conversely, when neighbours remain anonymous and do not stay long enough to develop an emotional connection with the place, they are less inclined to invest in home improvement or participate in neighbourhood revitalisation (Manzo & Perkins, 2016). Since placemaking is usually a bottom-up process, the characteristics and intensity of place attachment have been shown to influence the degree of community engagement (Junot, Paquet, & Fenouillet, 2018; Mihaylov & Perkins, 2014). Public participation and community engagement are critical in planning for lively and sustainable public spaces (Schlebusch, 2015). Public involvement in placemaking initiatives provides the most direct mean by which planning responds to community issues (Hou & Rios, 2003). The design of spaces is also critical in facilitating engagement through the types of places people can gather, connect, celebrate and meaning-making.

A few of the tools that support the measurement of the strengths of these relationships are:

- Neighbourlytics is a tool that can identify and map popular places in a neighbourhood such as main streets, parks and public places.
- Streets as Places toolkit provides a framework of quantitative and qualitative assessment which can inform, for example, the sociability of a place by assessing "street life" (quantitative) and "welcoming" (qualitative) attributes.

Community and Self

The key relationship between self and community is one of inclusion and conviviality through sense of belonging and encounter; the benefit is trust and contribution to place. Fincher and Iveson (2008) proposed recognition, encounter and the redistribution of resources as the three social needs for promoting a just diversity in urban life.

Their position assumes that in today's urban environment, which is characterised by increasing mobility and social complexity, most people would be constantly surrounded by people of different social backgrounds (Fincher & Iveson, 2008). Consequently, the ability to negotiate a relationship with "strangers" is a key to the ability to feel included and convivial, and the eventual outcome which they define as an improved quality of life (Fincher & Iveson, 2008). Furthermore, research has shown that people develop attachment to places that facilitate social relationships and group identity, and that the design and resulting characteristics of urban space affect the quantity and quality of interpersonal interactions (Amin, 2012; Scannell & Gifford, 2010). There is a need to design in place to meet, stand, chat, connect, support, sit, celebrate, contemplate, feel connected and included (e.g. design linking to different ethnic groups, history, shared experiences, etc.) and so forth to facilitate including and the feeling of connection to the community.

Connecting self to community, or inclusion, in urban spaces implies perception of safety, accessibility, visibility, integration and meaningful participation in social organisation; it is the opposite of disenfranchisement, marginalisation and social isolation (Hodgetts et al., 2008). Conviviality and inclusion are the outcomes when a positive relationship between the self and others has been achieved. Through encounters amongst strangers, convivial urban environment simultaneously acknowledges and normalises differences. "Conviviality is a social pattern in which different metropolitan groups dwell in close proximity, but where their racial, linguistic and religious particularities do not … add up to discontinuities of experience or insuperable problems of communication. In these conditions, a degree of differentiation can be combined with a large measure of overlapping" (Gilroy, 2006, p. 40).

A few of the tools that support the measurement of the strengths of these relationships are:

- Happiness Pulse utilises quantitative surveys from individuals to measure and assess the strength of an individual's well-being as it relates to their perceived community connections.

- Streets as Places toolkit is able to inform the comfort and image of place through subjective perceptions of safety, cleanliness and walkability coupled with crime statistics and sanitation ratings.
- EPOCH Measure of Adolescent Well-being is a tool that can identify individual happiness, engagement and happiness amongst other measures (Kern, Benson, Steinberg, & Steinberg, 2016).

Natural Environment and Man-Made Environment (Public/Private)

The relationship between natural environment and space is one where the built environment and public and private space are designed in such a way to enhance the non-human, natural environment. Non-human nature has benefits for self and community as well (see below) not just because it improves the health and vitality of people, but it also provides spaces to meet. For example, it provides places for shelter from the weather protecting from rain, sun, wind, hail, etc. Specifically, for the space itself, nature can provide amelioration of issues such as stormwater peaks, urban heat island and other extreme events expected to increase in the future (see Chapter 3). Beyond this, the integration of nature—trees, grass, gardens, habitats, etc.—increases resilience for the public–private spaces. For example, community gardens provide the ability to grow food in times of need, it provides places for people to learn how to grow food, and if the trees planted are productive trees, they can provide food for human and non-human stakeholders.

For non-human nature, the benefits of designing spaces to include and increase natural elements will mean the ability to create ecological niches; increased ecological services and access to soil, light and water means greater ability to restore, protect and even increase the viability of flora and fauna. In Auckland, for example, they are using rooftops to plant rare grass species to support rare short-range and flying fauna (Ignatieva, Meurk, van Roon, Simcock, & Stewart, 2008). This field of relationship has been called urban ecology.

More recent development within research on urban ecology views "cities as heterogeneous, dynamic landscapes and as complex, adaptive, socio-ecological systems, in which the delivery of ecosystem services links society and ecosystems at multiple scales" (Grimm et al., 2008, p. 756); this change incorporates the field of landscape ecology (McDonnell, 2011). As human-dominated systems, a shift from a traditional biophysical focus to a more social and interdisciplinary one is perhaps most logical in cities, and such studies are now increasing in numbers following landmark articles that identify humans as an important driver of environmental change from the local to the global level (such as Berkes & Folke, 1998 referred to in Elmqvist et al., 2013; Young & Wolf, 2006).

A few of the tools that support the measurement of the strengths of these relationships are:

- Smelly Maps, a sister map to Happy Maps, details streets by associated smell such as by the smell of emissions, food and nature.
- Streets as Places toolkit provides a mode to quantitatively and qualitatively assess the quality of natural spaces in cities.
- Biodiversity surveys. While there is no specific tool that can aid individuals in this, it is an effective strategy to assess the environment.

Self and Natural Environment

Humans depend on the services and resources provided by the natural environment (Rockström et al., 2009). It is critical that any development aims to design for the humans and non-human natural environment as outlined above (see also Chapter 3). In placemaking literature, the natural environment is conventionally regarded as an aspect of space, and it is discussed only in respect to its contribution to place attachment, liveability and environmental sustainability. Specifically, the literature describes the relationship between self and the natural environment as biophilia. In the biophilia hypothesis, Kellert and Wilson (1995) argue that people have an innate need to connect with life and lifelike processes, because throughout most of the human's evolutionary history people were intimately tied to the natural environment and other living beings (Hes & du Plessis, 2014). That need is a primal emotional response that associates certain aspects of nature with safety, security, food, water, survival and if present the result is a sense of satisfaction.

Recent medical and psychological research has shown that this remains even when technology and the built environment have largely severed people from nature (National Trust, 2019). People experience increased feeling of well-being, rejuvenation and connection when they are exposed to nature. The medical and psychological benefits have been extensively documented (Hes & du Plessis, 2014; National Trust, 2019). The biophilia hypothesis provides a foundation for the care of our natural environment. It moves beyond the conflict between economic development and ecological conservation in the mainstream sustainability discourse by arguing that connection with the natural environment is critical to people's well-being. This ethos is widely reflected in Indigenous cultures, which perceive the land and its non-human inhabitants as deeply embedded in both the community's use of natural resources and its spiritual nourishment leading to a sense of custodianship of the non-human (CoM & MSI, 2016).

Further, a sense of connection with nature has been empirically associated with environmental awareness as well as actions of stewardship and custodianship for nature. Connectivity with nature describes a sense of oneness and empathy with nature (Dutcher, Finley, Luloff, & Johnson, 2007). It has been theorised as the basis of environmental values, and several studies have linked connectivity to pro-environment and behaviours (Dutcher et al., 2007; Junot et al., 2018; Schultz, 2002). A place which has successfully developed a relationship between the self and nature will have healthier people who are more conscious of their role as carer for the natural world, which may be evidenced by greater pro-environment attitudes and actions. This is a virtuous cycle, which then means there is more vital and viable natural systems, creating more vital and viable selves.

A few of the tools that support the measurement of the strengths of these relationships are:

- Happiness Pulse surveys individual perceived well-being and, for example, can generate data on the amount of time spent in nature.

- CrowdSpot engages community to generate mapped experiences from surveyed individuals and could be utilised to assess individual relatedness to nature.
- Connection to Nature, a research-based index assessing individual connection to nature through documenting the ability to feel empathy for nature, stewardship, and relatedness to nature amongst others (Cheng & Monroe, 2012).

Community and Natural Environment

The relationship between community and the natural environment, if positive, is one of community custodianship and social well-being (see sections above, Chapter 3 and Junot et al., 2018). Research shows that where there is access to green space there is less crime and social dysfunction (Donovan & Prestemon, 2012). Further, if a community is highly active and engaged, then there are greater initiatives to look after the natural environment, such as community planting, clean-up, events for the natural environment (e.g. world migratory bird day) and so forth. Custodianship has been mentioned above in the relationship between self and the natural environment, but it is also a critical part of the community. For individual commitment and action will never create the quantum of benefit that a whole community can provide if engaged in care, nurture and contribution to the natural environment.

> Results suggest emotional connections with places contribute toward pro-environmental attitudes. Enhancing such connections is therefore likely to lead to increased environmental care and concern. (Budruk, Thomas, & Tyrrell, 2009, p. 824)

A few of the tools that support the measurement of the strengths of these relationships are:

- Happy Maps could be utilised to map how communities and nature interact informed by the lived experience of individuals in their communities.

- Neighbourlytics is a tool that could in the same vein as assessing community and space assess the relationship with nature and community.

Can We Have One Method to Evaluate Place?

The above discussion outlines how to evaluate the relationships and why they are important but still does not help with how to evaluate place consistently, reliably and holistically. The bad news is that there is no such tool or method, yet! There is no one tool which outlines the key aspects of place to measure, and there is not one tool that supports the ability to use evaluation as a process to underpin the ability to continue to co-evolve and create a place with its stakeholders. There is hope though, with the Rating Place Project which is being undertaken by a consortium of researchers in Australia (Box 13.1). They are working on the assumption that a consistent, holistic tool that supports co-evolution can be achieved through having a set of measures that are consistent across all places (place values) and various place-specific measures. The consistent aspects can be thought of as the heartbeat of a place, providing a basis to compare different places and so creating a baseline for place practice. The place-specific aspects in addition will support the ability of evaluation to do more than score. From the work carried out with 98 placemaking experts across three workshops in three locations (in two different CBDs and one in a regional town), the heartbeat aspects identified were: *Identity* (a place which is clearly distinct from other areas); *Accessibility* (an area that anyone can enter regardless of their situation and that is well connected via transport to other areas); *Belonging* (a place and community that people can relate to); *Sustainable* (that the area is both economically and environmentally viable allowing the place to function across various generations), *Atmosphere* (that the place has a good vibe, lively and amicable making people feel welcome), *Feeling* (which was defined by the participants as being able to generate an emotional connection with the people using the space—place attachment); and *Safety* (feeling safe while in the site).

> **Box 13.1 Rating Place Project (https://placeagency.org.au/rating-place/)**
>
> Rating Place is a research project that is drawing on existing industry knowledge and research to construct a robust framework to evaluate placemaking. Placemaking is understood as a process creating the capacity for people to emotionally connect to spaces through value-based design.
>
> The project is a unique collaboration between the Australian Centre for Architectural History, Urban and Cultural Heritage (ACAHUCH) and Thrive research group (University of Melbourne), University of Queensland, University of New South Wales, Deakin University and Curtin University/Notre Dame University.
>
> The Place Rating tool will allow practitioners and procurers to showcase their work in a manner that reinforces their credibility, provides baseline standards to place and brings recognition to their projects.

Applicability of the FDP—The Living Pavilion as a Case Study

In the previous sections, we have established the need to incorporate a larger range of "intangible" measures in support of more traditional evaluation approaches and that what is critical is the evaluation of the relationships developed, that is outcomes and legacies. In this section, we outline the process used to apply the FDP:

a. start from values and establish a variety of comparable and place-specific concepts for evaluation,
b. identify relevant relationships and verify holistic approach,
c. search the tool database,
d. if necessary extract relevant strategies from the tools and adapt to your specific project and context, and
e. apply your evaluation framework consistently at various intervals to understand the long-term legacy of a specific project.

The case study outlines how these steps were applied to develop the research strategy for a placemaking project entitled The Living Pavilion (TLP).

The Living Pavilion

TLP festival (1–17 May 2019) was a recyclable, biodegradable, edible and biodiverse temporary event space at the University of Melbourne's Parkville Campus, Melbourne, Australia. It was part of CLIMARTE's "Art+Climate=Change" festival (23 April–19 May 2019). The site selected was a small part of what will become the New Student Precinct (NSP).

Led by Dr. Tanja Beer (Thrive Research Hub—Melbourne School of Design) and Dr. Cathy Oke (Clean Air and Urban Landscapes Hub [CAUL] of the National Environmental Science Program), the project applied a participatory process to gather ideas, identify the values of this place and community and gather design and programming ideas. This was done through a Creative Development Workshop (9–11 July 2018, 30+ participants) and an ongoing collaborative process between the design and research team, the various project and programming stakeholders, the Indigenous reference group and artists, and the student volunteers and ambassadors of the project. The project was also informed by research conducted by the university with over 5000 students identifying their needs and desires. This contributed key opportunities for placemaking within the NSP (see the University of Melbourne, n.d.).

The creative placemaking approach was a scaled-up and very ambitious version of Dr. Beer's previous work in ecoscenography and seven years of other interventions (see "The Living Stage", n.d.). Each living stage was different emerging from local stories and opportunities. TLP responded to the site's heritage (pre- and post-colonisation) and became a platform to celebrate and expose the hidden stories of place. It aimed at reactivating and creating a new narrative for this part of the university as both an Indigenous place and a place for the students to be welcomed to the university—their home base. In its development, it also aimed to improve the relationships of the site with its ecological potential. To assess the project, the team developed a thorough research strategy and place evaluation framework (Fig. 13.3). The following sections will take you through the steps applied to develop this framework.

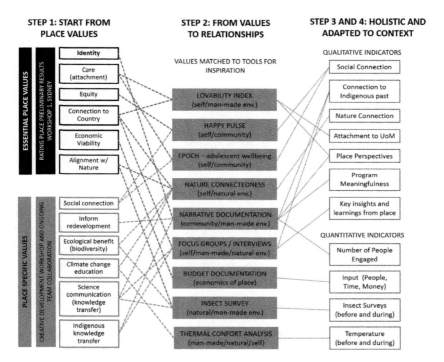

Fig. 13.3 TLP place evaluation framework. The image specifically shows the first four steps of the suggested process to develop your place evaluation framework (Image by Cristina Hernandez-Santin)

Step 1: Start from Values

One of the challenges of place evaluation is simultaneously allowing comparability and place-specificity. The aim was to use indicators that were comparable while avoiding the use of large-scale statistical measures that did not support the place narrative. For TLP, we referred to the preliminary findings of the Rating Place[2] Project to identify the place

---

[2]Note that the preliminary findings applied are specifically from the first Rating Place workshop conducted with 35 place experts and researchers in Sydney on 24 August 2018. The six indicators highlighted in this workshop differ from the unique aspects emerging from the collated views of 98 experts.

values as determined by the experts. Then, we supplemented these with place-specific values as determined by the stakeholders of TLP during the Creative Development Workshop (see Step 1 in Fig. 13.3).

Essential Place Values

Based on the results from the Rating Place workshop 1, held in Sydney, we identified six elements to evaluate a place:

- Identity, a place that is distinctive and shares a narrative;
- Equity, defined to incorporate accessibility, a diversity of experiences and dynamism that keep the site interesting and connected to the community regardless of their situation;
- Connection to Country, which the group defined as an emotional connection to nature, culture and history;
- Care (attachment), where evidence of sense of belonging and stewardship are visible;
- Economic Viability, where there is monetary and governance flows towards a place keeping strategy; and
- Alignment with Nature, ensuring that the site is adaptable and resilient to environmental changes (see "Rating Place Co-Developing a Rating Tool Workshop, Sydney", 2018).

Place-Specific Values

To determine the place-specific values, one must ask the local community and stakeholders: "what it is that you love about their place?" to find what they value, and what it is that they need or seek. These needs and values help to inform the ongoing plans for the evolution or redevelopment of their place. As mentioned above, TLP was a placemaking intervention that took place at a university campus in Australia. As such, the importance of education, student life, non-human users (ecology past and present) and the Indigenous history of site itself comprise four interacting narratives leading to the identification of six place-specific values.

Students participating in The Living Pavilion's Creative Development Workshop indicated how life on campus lacks a "sense of belonging", an issue that has also been more widely identified at Chancellery level (The University of Melbourne, 2018). This highlighted the need to include social connection as part of the evaluation framework as well as a consideration of how the project could inform further campus developments. Furthermore, the project's focus on Indigenous place and sustainability directed the addition of five more values. These included: informing redevelopment plans through a trial of key design ideas; quantifying the benefit of the installation for local biodiversity measures; sustainability and climate change education; eco-literacy for urban ecology concepts; and enhanced understanding and knowledge of Indigenous culture.

Step 2: From Values to Relationships

Step 2 involved finding the key themes of the project that were in alignment with place-specific and essential values and the tools to assess these. This included using a variety of existing tools and specialised quantitative and qualitative research methods. By understanding the values and objectives of TLP, we were able to identify four existing tools (lovability index, happy pulse, EPOCH measure for adolescent well-being and connection to nature) that could specifically address the relationship between self and the other three dimensions of place. These tools were then supported by additional research methods to draw out the place narrative (community) and the creation of two focus groups to specifically extract deep stories and experiences from the site users (see Step 2 in Fig. 13.3).

Step 3: Check for Holistic Integration of Your Measures

In step three, the aim was to ensure that all relationships were covered by the selected tools and evaluation processes. This includes providing a specific opportunity to reflect on the planned evaluation process and confirm that the human and non-human aspects were included.

While developing TLP place evaluation framework, this reflection allowed the research team to identify the gaps in the existing tools and, where necessary, to develop clear qualitative and quantitative indicators.

Step 4: Adapt to Your Specific Project and Context

When Implementing and evaluating place-based projects, it is important that the evaluation is place-specific, potentially requiring the tweaking of existing tools. For this case study, the research team had to adapt some standard statements from some of the tools make them project-specific. For example, adapting the EPOCH measure and the Connection to Nature Index (Cheng & Monroe, 2012; Kern et al., 2016, respectively), the team created place-specific statements for the project, such as: "I feel like a part of the University community"; "When I spend time at The Living Pavilion I feel a feeling of oneness with the natural environment"; or "The Living Pavilion has given me opportunities to relax and de-stress". This helped link the results specifically to the place initiative being assessed.

Engaging in this process for TLP resulted in the creation of a trans-disciplinary online-based survey instrument to collect qualitative data that could inform the future redevelopment of the area and placemaking initiatives conducted by the university. When paired with quantitative data (see Steps 3 and 4 in Fig. 13.3), the combination of indicators will help measure the outcomes of the project.

Step 5: Apply Consistently to Understand the Long-Term Legacy

The last step brings us back to the introduction of this chapter: an evaluation process that documents the input, output, outcome and legacy of a project. By working with an evaluation framework based on place values, measuring the relationships developed through the project it supports the project to achieve intended long-term impacts. The capacity is being created to allow the project to keep evolving. Table 13.1 outlines TLP evaluation framework through an input, output, outcome

Table 13.1 TLP evaluation summary on input, output, outcome and legacy

Input	Output	Outcome (including relationship-based indicators)	Legacy
People: Over 40 people participated as part of the design and research team, student cocreators and other collaborators	The landscape design of the temporary intervention 40,000 Kulin Nation Plants	The following things were quantified: Number of people engaged Economic Viability Insect & Pollinator Surveys biodiversity before and after event	Based on incidental narratives In setting up the potential you are allowing future relationships to emerge
Engagement achieved through a 3-day Creative Development Workshop 1 year in planning	60+ curated events responsive to place values	Individual connection to place Social Connection Nature Connection Connection to Indigenous past Attachment to the University	
Funded by Thrive Research Hub, The New Student Precinct and CAUL research hub		Place perspectives Design perspectives General feedback Place experiences Program Meaningfulness Engagement strategies Learnings by attendees	

and legacy model—effectively summarising the effort that went into the development of the project, including intervention results and relationship indicators. Lastly, it concludes with the potential strategies that determine how the legacy of the project was assessed. It is important to highlight that for established projects, the place evaluation framework could be reapplied at regular intervals (i.e. every 2 years). This provides an opportunity to reassess if the project continues to be aligned with the community values and to observe how the relationships supported by the place have evolved over time.

Conclusion

There are good reasons to evaluate placemaking projects. These are to support ongoing development, learning, transparency, reflection and evolution of the place. The evaluation approach can foster agency in the stakeholders involved by starting from their values, while also evaluating standard measures (heartbeats).

Key Insights from the Place Evaluation Chapter

- There are many tools to evaluate place but none of them offer a holistic approach.
- The power of evaluation is not just to score a place but to engage in the community to be involved in a place's continual evolution.
- What is critical is to measure how a place affects those of the place, the human and the non-human, if they are thriving, connected, involved the place is successful.
- The four dimensions of place are: self, community, human-made environments and natural environment.
- The six relationship connections that you look for to evaluate place are:

    1. self and human-made environments,
    2. community and human-made environments,
    3. self and community,
    4. human-made environments and natural environment,

5. self and natural environment, and
6. community and natural environment.

Tools Cited in This Chapter in Alphabetical Order

Connection to nature—Chen-Hsuan Cheng, Judith and Martha C. Monroe. (2012). Connection to nature: Children's affective attitude toward nature. *Environment and Behavior, 44*(1), 31–49.

CrowdSpot— http://crowdspot.com.au/.

EPOCH Measure of adolescent well-being—Kern, Margaret L., Lizbeth Benson, Elizabeth A. Steinberg, and Laurence Steinberg. (2016). The EPOCH measure of adolescent well-being. *Psychological Assessment, 28*(5), 586–597.

Happiness Pulse—Happy City (2010–2019) Happiness maps https://www.happinesspulse.org/.

Happy Maps—Good City Life (2016) Happy Maps http://goodcitylife.org/happymaps/index.php.

Lovability Index—Novacevski, M., Gray, F., and Garduno-Freeman, C. (2017). Lovability: Putting people at the centre of city performance. *Planning News, 43*(1), 22 and http://www.lovability.melbourne/.

Neighbourlytics—https://www.neighbourlytics.com/.

Placescore—PlaceScore (2018) founded by Kylie Legge in 2014. http://www.placescore.org/.

Place Standard—Place Standard, How Good is Our Place? created by Architecture & Design Scotland, NHS Health Scotland, Scottish Government. https://www.placestandard.scot/place-standard.pdf.

Public Space Toolkit—UN HABITAT (2015), Global Public Space Toolkit From Global Principles to Local Policies and Practice, Created in partnership with INU Retrieved from https://unhabitat.org/wp-content/uploads/2015/10/Global%20Public%20Space%20Toolkit.pdf.

Smelly Maps—Good City Life (2016) Happy Maps http://goodcitylife.org/smellymaps/index.php.

Streets as Places Toolkit—Project for Public Spaces—PPS (2015). Streets as Places Toolkit. Retrieved from https://www.pps.org/article/streets-as-places.
Walk Score App—https://www.walkscore.com/iphone/.

References

Amin, A. (2012). Strangers in city. In *Land of strangers* (pp. 59–82). Cambridge: Polity.

Anton, C. E., & Lawrence, C. (2014). Home is where the heart is: The effect of place of residence on place attachment and community participation. *Journal of Environmental Psychology, 40*, 451–461.

Aravot, I. (2010). Back to phenomenological placemaking. *Journal of Urban Design, 7*(2, August), 201–212. https://doi.org/10.1080/1357480022000012230.

Billig, M. (2006). Is my home my castle? Place attachment, risk perception, and religious faith. *Environment and Behavior, 38*(2), 248–265.

Budruk, M., Thomas, H., & Tyrrell, T. (2009). Urban green spaces: A study of place attachment and environmental attitudes in India. *Society and Natural Resources, 22*(9), 824–839.

Carmona, M. (2019). Place value: Place quality and its impact on health, social, economic and environmental outcomes. *Journal of Urban Design, 24*(1), 1–48.

Cheng, J. C. H., & Monroe, M. C. (2012). Connection to nature: Children's affective attitude toward nature. *Environment and Behavior, 44*(1), 31–49.

Cilliers, E. J., & Timmermans, W. (2014). The importance of creative participatory planning in the public place-making process. *Environment and Planning B: Planning and Design, 41*(3, June), 413–429.

CoM and MSI. (2016). *Caring for country: An urban application. The possibilities for Melbourne*. City of Melbourne and Monash Sustainability Institute. Retrieved from https://www.monash.edu/__data/assets/pdf_file/0006/720681/Caring-for-Country-Literature-Review.pdf. Accessed 27 Feb 2019.

Davis, A. (2016). Experiential places or places of experience? Place identity and place attachment as mechanisms for creating festival environment. *Tourism Management, 55*(February), 49–61.

Donovan, G. H., & Prestemon, J. P. (2012). The effect of trees on crime in Portland, Oregon. *Environment and Behavior, 44*(1), 3–30.

Dutcher, D. D., Finley, J. C., Luloff, A. E., & Johnson, J. B. (2007). Connectivity with nature as a measure of environmental values. *Environment and Behavior, 39*(4), 474–493.

Elmqvist, T., Fragkias, M., Goodness, J., Güneralp, B., Marcotullio, P. J., McDonald, R. I., … Wilkinson, C. (Eds.). (2013). *Urbanization, biodiversity and ecosystem services: Challenges and opportunities. A global assessment.* Dordrecht: Springer.

Fincher, R., & Iveson, K. (2008). Conceptualising recognition in planning. In *Planning and diversity in the city: Redistribution, recognition and encounter.* New York: Palgrave Macmillan.

Fincher, R., Pardy, M., & Shaw, K. (2016). Place-making or place-masking? The everyday political economy of "making place". *Planning Theory and Practice, 17*(4), 516–536.

Gilroy, P. (2006). Colonial crimes and convivial cultures. *A transcript of a video letter made by Paul Gilroy in London and screened at the Public Hearing "Debating Independence: Autonomy or Voluntary Colonialism".*

Grimm, N. B., Faeth, S. H., Golubiewski, N. E., Redman, C. L., Wu, J., Bai, X., & Briggs, J. M. (2008). Global change and the ecology of cities. *Science, 319*(5864), 756–760.

Heller, A., & Adams, T. (2009). Creating healthy cities through socially sustainable placemaking. *Australian Planner, 46*(2), 18–21.

Hes, D., & du Plessis, C. (2014). Reconnecting with nature, re-learning to be natural. In *Designing for hope: Pathways to regenerative sustainability* (pp. 45–71). Abingdon, Oxon: Routledge.

Hodgetts, D., Stolte, O., Chamberlain, K., Radley, A., Nikora, L., Nabalarua, E., & Groot, S. (2008). A trip to the library: Homelessness and social inclusion. *Social & Cultural Geography, 9*(8), 933–953.

Hou, J., & Rios, M. (2003). Community-driven place making: The social practice of participatory design in the making of Union Point Park. *Journal of Architectural Education, 57*(1), 19–27.

Ignatieva, M., Meurk, C., van Roon, M., Simcock, R., & Stewart, G. (2008). *How to put nature into our neighbourhoods.* Report by Landcare Research New Zealand Ltd., Manaaki Whenua Press, Landcare Research, Lincoln, NZ.

Junot, A., Paquet, Y., & Fenouillet, F. (2018). Place attachment influence on human well-being and general pro-environmental behaviors. *Journal of Theoretical Social Psychology, 2*(April), 49–57.

Kellert, S. R., & Wilson, E. O. (Eds.). (1995). *The biophilia hypothesis*. Washington, DC: Island Press.

Kern, M. L., Benson, L., Steinberg, E. A., & Steinberg, L. (2016). The EPOCH measure of adolescent well-being. *Psychological Assessment, 28*(5), 586.

Kyle, G., Graefe, A., Manning, R., & Bacon, J. (2004). Effect of activity involvement and place attachment on recreationists' perceptions of setting density. *Journal of leisure Research, 36*(2), 209–231.

Lozano, R. (2008). Envisioning sustainability three-dimensionally. *Journal of Cleaner Production, 16*(17), 1838–1846.

Manzo, L. C., & Perkins, D. D. (2016). Finding common ground: The importance of place attachment to community participation and planning. *Journal of Planning Literature, 20*(4), 335–350.

McDonnell, M. J. (2011). The history of urban ecology: A ecologist's perspective. In J. Niemelä, J. H. Breuste, G. Guntenspergen, N. E. McIntyre, T. Elmqvist, & P. James (Eds.), *Urban ecology: Patterns, processes, and applications*. New York: Oxford University Press.

McMillan, D. W., & Chavis, D. M. (1986). Sense of community: A definition and theory. *Journal of Community Psychology, 14*(1), 6–23.

Mihaylov, N., & Perkins, D. D. (2014). Community place attachment and its role in social capital development in response to environmental disruption. In L. Manzo & P. Devine-Wright (Eds.), *Place attachment: Advances in theory, methods and research* (pp. 61–74). Abingdon: Routledge.

National Trust. (2019). *Places that make us*. Report for the National Trust, Wiltshire, UK. [Online] Retrieved from https://nt.global.ssl.fastly.net/documents/places-that-make-us-research-report.pdf. Accessed 25 Feb 2019.

Peattie, K. (1995). *Environmental marketing management: Meeting the green challenge*. London: *Financial Times* and Pitman Publishing.

Rating Place Co-Developing a Rating Tool Workshop 1, Sydney. (2018). *Place agency & place leaders Asia Pacific in partnership with Sydney Olympic Park*. Retrieved from https://placeagency.org.au/rating-place/. Accessed 25 Feb 2019.

Rockström, J., Steffen, W., Noone, K., Persson, Å., Chapin III, F. S., Lambin, E., … Foley, J. (2009). Planetary boundaries: Exploring the safe operating space for humanity. *Ecology and Society, 14*(2), 32.

Scannell, L., & Gifford, R. (2010). Defining place attachment: A tripartite organizing framework. *Journal of Environmental Psychology, 30*(1), 1–10.

Schlebusch, S. (2015). Planning for sustainable communities: Evaluating place-making approaches. *Agriculture, Forestry and Fisheries, 4*(4), 59.

Schultz, P. W. (2002). Inclusion with nature: The psychology of human-nature relations. In *Psychology of sustainable development* (pp. 61–78). Boston, MA: Springer.

Shaw, K. (2008). Gentrification: What it is, why it is, and what can be done about it. *Geography Compass, 2*(5), 1697–1728.

Summers, J. K., Smith, L. M., Case, J. L., & Linthurst, R. A. (2012). A review of the elements of human well-being with an emphasis on the contribution of ecosystem services. *Ambio, 41*(4), 327–340.

The Living Stage. (n.d.). Retrieved from https://ecoscenography.com/the-living-stage/. Accessed 25 Feb 2019.

The University of Melbourne. (2018, March). Retrieved from https://provost.unimelb.edu.au/documents/chancellery-academic-and-international/caiprot/Student-Life-Green-Paper-March-2019.pdf. Accessed 20 Mar 2019.

The University of Melbourne. (n.d.). *New student precinct*. Available from https://ourcampus.unimelb.edu.au/student-precinct. Accessed 24 Mar 2019.

Trudeau, D. (2016). Politics of belonging in the construction of landscapes: Place-making, boundary-drawing and exclusion. *Cultural Geographies, 13*(3), 421–443.

Young, R. F., & Wolf, S. A. (2006). Goal attainment in urban ecology research: A bibliometric review 1975–2004. *Urban Ecosystems, 9*, 179–193.

14

The ART of Engagement Placemaking for Nature and People in Cities

Melissa Nursey-Bray

Introduction

Urban spaces require the engagement of citizens to create and shape them into unique signifiers of connection, residence and activity in cities and regions. In an increasingly urban and climate change-challenged world, there is a necessity to build connections between spaces, people and environment. Australian cities built on Indigenous country also need to find modes of engagement that reconcile the tensions caused by historical yet enduring invasion of space and place. This chapter explores the idea that placemaking via art is one mechanism by which connections can be forged and bridges built between these tensions, and become, in and of itself, a mode of community engagement. Via documentary and case study analysis, the chapter presents the proposition that art as placemaking can lead to powerful community engagement and become a tool that generates narratives around

M. Nursey-Bray (✉)
Geography, Environment and Population, University of Adelaide, North Terrace, SA, Australia
e-mail: melissa.nursey-bray@adelaide.edu.au

© The Author(s) 2020
D. Hes and C. Hernandez-Santin (eds.), *Placemaking Fundamentals for the Built Environment*, https://doi.org/10.1007/978-981-32-9624-4_14

and connection to urban ecologies and hence integration between people and place in cities. The question might be asked, why would this matter? This chapter is based on the argument that we live in a world dominated by the attention economy, the ultimate result of which is a scarcity of attention and thus lack of public engagement with issues of the day. This chapter argues that we need to find ways to create an understanding of 'paying attention' as an ecology rather than economy and that the use/deployment of public art in various forms is a process of paying attention—with making people pay it or getting people to make it and so get others to pay attention. As such, art via placemaking becomes a sophisticated means of community engagement. The chapter begins by presenting an overview of placemaking and its relationship to public art. The chapter then profiles three modes of art as placemaking. Firstly, public art competitions and exhibitions are considered, and the ways they engage people with nature, place, community pride, start key conversations and via fundraising build community assets. Secondly, the ways in which public art can be used as modes of resistance—getting people to 'pay attention' to social issues is explored and the ways in which it can become part of the history of place, inviting locals to see layers in their place. Finally, the chapter examines the utility and role that art plays in urban regeneration projects.

Placemaking and Art

Placemaking is a term, now popularly used in both philosophical and applied ways to infer the physical and emotional coalescing of the relationship between people and place. It can be used to strengthen this bond, and as a collaborative process by which cities can be built as places of identity, memory and practice. When placemaking has community engagement at its heart, it becomes a process that can result in the creation of public spaces that facilitate community well-being in important ways. This is the 'glue' that can engage what are now increasingly mobile, transient and multicultural societies within cities.

Placemaking historically draws its origins from a reaction to modernism, a nostalgic response to places now lost: a reaction against the destruction of unique local identities that resulted from 'standardizing and sterilizing environments or creating fantastic environments out of tune with their surroundings' (Jordaan, Puren, & Roos, 2008, p. 92). Thus, understanding a place helps prevent a loss of its history and enables planners to maximise identity, belonging, groundedness and the well-being in the community, thus making it safe from future destruction as people come to love and identify with that area.

Shaw and Montana (2016) citing Ryan (1995, p. 1) note that placemaking serves multiple functions including invoking engagement, rootedness, it is a process that can make people stop and become involved, it offers rich experience, and creates a sense of belonging, evokes pleasure or contemplation. They argue that what originally started as a concept focussed on sense of place evolved to also incorporate community development, and via shared activities, such as art.

In Australia, many local councils have their own version of what placemaking means as this following definition from Charles Sturt Council in South Australia highlights:

> Place Making: the act of reimaging everyday spaces into places where people love to gather and connect. Place making is a process where local communities, business and other stakeholders work in collaboration to deliver revitalisation of shared spaces and the public realm. It results in the creation of places that: - are accessible and well connected, - attract people and are enjoyable to be in, - sustain local businesses, and - generate a sense of attachment and community. (Charles Sturt Council, 2019)

Placemaking, however, is also about policy and embedded in the politics of space and time. In a case study of Berlin, Bain and Landau (2019) find that key to placemaking is ensuring that place narratives are created with the community rather than for them, otherwise they won't work. The conjunction between space and time which often underpins the idea of placemaking can be understood as the creation of grounded territories, as in 'places' or 'bundles' of space-time trajectories drawn together by individuals through cognitive and emotional processes (Massey, 2005, p. 119). Harvey describes placemaking as 'the carving out' of 'temporary permanences' from spaces (1996, p. 241) and as an iterative, evolutionary process of defining not just boundaries or territories, but the rules and norms against which socio-spatial practices are understood.

Placemaking thus is more than an exploration of the physicality of a place but should encompass its socio-spatial relations. The coproduction of a place-narrative invites the public to collectively imagine the transformation of places, something that can only be activated via enduring collaboration. Being able to create fora where a sense of place is created is an important factor also (Blum-Ross, 2013).

Placemaking can also function as a mode to increase and enhance resiliency practices at local levels (Coaffee, 2013). In a case study of fashion in Finland as a form of placemaking, Chun and Gurova (2018) assert the importance of a dynamic interplay between all actors and the symbolic constructions of places to enable effective placemaking. This is in line with Jacobs (1961) work where she argues that place and placemaking need to take account of ways of life, and that placemaking thus is part of everyday life (Lefebvre, 1991), with urbanity essentially about processes of daily encounter in place.

Placemaking strategies have also been used in the context of urban renewal projects, yet some questions have been asked as to whether or not placemaking strategies mask social justice and inequities in practice or are a 'language without deeds' (Fincher, Pardy, & Shaw, 2016; Shaw & Montana, 2016; Sofield, Guia, & Specht, 2017). Placemaking as community engagement is in this case not only the end product but a means to an end. It enables the community to define its own priorities and to have a voice that can get heard by government and official place makers, thus acting both as a physical strategy to improve a place, but as a social agenda and a conduit for political action.

In this context, it is an opportune time to be considering how the arts can be used as part of placemaking engagement strategies. According to a survey released by the Australiai Council (2016) entitled Connecting Australians, the arts play a role in the lives of 98% of the Australian population. That is, the majority of Australians from all walks of life—different ages, genders, cultures and backgrounds—participate and engage with the arts on some level. While this figure is consistent with previous surveys, one major change is the national impact of new technologies on the experiencing and making of arts practice. For example, the survey found that 97% of all Australians aged between 15 and 24 engage with the arts online and 81% of Australians overall, up from 49% in 2009 and 73% in 2013. The major areas of engagement are listening to music (97%), reading books (79%) and going to live events (72%). More people see the arts as a way of improving cultural understanding and tolerance, with an increase from 36% of the population in 2013 to 64% in 2016. There is also an increase in those who believe the arts are more truly reflective of Australia's cultural diversity—from 64% in 2013 to 75% in 2016.

Art then has the potential to engage the community in and of itself in and as a placemaking process, and this capacity is starting to emerge in the literature. Miwon Kwon, in her essay, 'For Hamburg: Public Art and Urban Identities', distinguishes three different paradigms of Public Art that could be schematically described as placemaking: (i) art in public places, (ii) art as public spaces and (iii) art in the public interest (or 'new genre Public Art'). The latter is often temporary, city-based and focusing on social issues rather than the built environment that involve collaborations with marginalised social groups. An example of public art in Cape Town, South Africa (Minty, 2006), shows how contemporary art projects that engage critically with history, geography, memory and transformation create spaces for dialogue and/or challenges by and for the community about urban inequities embedded within the city. The inclusion of public art can be a catalyst for social inclusion to act as an antidote to the conflict that often attends regeneration projects (Sharp, Pollock, & Paddison, 2005). The creation of 'creative spaces' can encourage participation and empowerment with urban planning agendas (Pollock & Sharp, 2012).

At its extreme, Puleo (2014) argues that art plays a role in post-disaster placemaking. Using the post-recovery phase for the 2010 Haiti earthquake, community engagement in art forms assisted in individual and collective healing and recovery from the trauma caused by the earthquake (Puleo, 2014). In this case, it facilitated 'memory, perception and anticipation, allowing the mixing of past, present, and future that is essential to placemaking, particularly following a catastrophe when social and material modes of placemaking are often disrupted and destroyed. Individual and collective memories of a place's past as well as imaginations of its future become legible through the production and performance of art' (Puleo, 2014).

In rural China, Wang (2018) examines the importance of art to provide a sense of belonging in regions that are being emptied, hence art is used as a form of engagement, encouraging a sense of belonging within the community and hence a sense of desire to stay. In Beijing, art is used as an agent to build place/power geometries (Zhang, 2018) while Chang (2008) states that 'public art in urban areas offers a window on a city's soul' and that in Singapore its power and powerlessness inform place identity and inspires community aspirations. Sharp asserts that community regeneration agendas via art in the five spaces of Glasgow reflect not only a conscious move from the city centre to more marginal areas, but the opportunity for the community to set their own agendas (Sharp, 2007). As an expanding corpus of literature around geography and art demonstrate, art can also inspire critical community engagement; these studies point to the expanded role of art to encourage community encounters with space, identity and human-environment relations (Cant & Morris, 2006).

Set against this background, the next sections of the chapter will reflect on three examples where art has been deployed as an engagement model to make places and create a connection to them. The first of these is a reporting on the use of place-based public art fairs, exhibitions and shows to help build community engagement and place identity in relation to connection to the environment. The second examines the deployment of art as an engagement strategy to create modes of place-making informed by resistance and the third examines placemaking in the context of urban revival and regeneration projects.

Coastal Place Engagement with Community via Public Art

The trend towards densification as well as the cultural phenomenon that is known as the 'Sea Change' has seen unprecedented coastal development in Australia over the last twenty years. This pressure on coastal regions has also spawned much cultural diversity and activity with local populations keen to build local economies and to attract visitors to their shores. Many communities are also increasingly worried about climate change, sea level rise and the impacts of greater populations on the aesthetic, environmental and amenity values they cherish about these places. Creating and confirming attachment to coastal places helps engage local communities and binds them as communities of practice to make and build those places.

In this context, public art forms, whether by public monuments, gardens, sculptures, murals, art galleries and so on, are increasing in popularity and volume, but one example of how it is used for coastal placemaking in Australia is via the annual Sculpture by the Sea exhibitions. These exhibitions are a key means by which the 'coastal' public are often engaged on the topic of nature and by which they are actively enjoined to participate via participation in place-based art exhibitions, which require people to become active observers, judges or entrants. These exhibitions have had multiple effects on placemaking—they bring people to a particular place and encourage pride in local seascapes, and in the process of visiting the exhibitions start to build memory and identification with and for that place, which when repeated over a number of years, confirms the importance of that place. Further, over time, individual connections build to become active and constituent elements of the whole placemaking exercise.

In Australia, there are now three high-profile Sculpture by the Sea exhibitions. The first of these is the Sculpture by the Sea based in Bondi, Sydney which features a coastal walk to Tamarama, and along which multiple sculptures are situated. Held since 1997, this annual display now attracts over 500,000 visitors and hosts the work of over 100 sculptures presented by artists from all over the world. Many of the artists create works with specific intent to raise awareness about or enjoin the public in their messaging through art. For example, one work Karda—Megalania, a massive woven-grass installation by Elaine Clocherty and Sharyn Egan examines extinction and major climatic changes the planet has experienced. Bondi artist Rossi notes that the works which most appeal to her are those which respond to place: 'There is a greater connection to the land if you actually create something within it' (Rossi, 2018 cited in Moon, 2018, paragraph 28). Rossi also adds of his own work: 'I like creating works which belong and react to their surroundings. Maybe it has something to do with the fact that I immigrated to Australia from Italy twenty years ago…In the same way as the work, we react to the place in which we live' (paragraph 11).

In Cottesloe beach, in Perth, another Sculpture by the Sea exhibition regularly attracts over 240,000 visitors and over 70 art pieces. Established in 2005 and held along the Indian Ocean coast in March every year, this exhibition also binds the public in a sense of pride and belonging. For example, in the Cottesloe exhibition, 2018, thirty-two of the artists were from abroad, including entrants from Japan, China, Denmark, South Korea, India, Spain, Singapore, Sweden, England, Iran, Israel, Indonesia, Germany, USA, New Zealand, Thailand and Slovakia. Grishin (2017) notes that exhibitions like these have 'the rare ability to demystify art and to make it publicly accessible. Commercial art galleries are frequently like temples of art, where the viewer feels the need to show reverence to that which is in front of them. At Cottesloe, sculpture can appear as fun – a family thing – where visitors may own the experience and can freely express an opinion. It is a huge free community event' (paragraph 5) 'people have embraced the idea and it has now become a crucial part of the fabric of Western Australia's cultural life' (paragraph 7). As a process, the evolution of this exhibition highlights how placemaking can build community and engage them, build culture and memories with each other.

Finally, in 2019, the Sculpture by the Sea exhibition in Brighton South Australia celebrated its tenth year with over 160 pieces contributed by 110 artists. The annual exhibition attracts more than 20,000 visitors and the sale of the sculptures go towards fundraising for the Brighton Surf Lifesaving Club. The link between the surf life-saving club at one of Adelaide's most popular beaches and the artistic community helps reinforce the attachment to Brighton as a place and pride in the city overall as a creative city. They also help engage the community in key activities such as beach cleanups, coastal management and education.

Art as Resistance/Social Action: [Re]-Forging/Acknowledging Indigenous Connection to Place

The use of public art to bring communities together and make them think about key issues is one pathway used to engage them in various ways. Another is the way in which art can be used to educate and protest ideas or circumstances. In Australia, this is exemplified by the tensions inherent in the relationship between Indigenous peoples and urban planning. Cities in Australia are built on Indigenous Countrys, an original theft that still impacts on everyday life; from an Indigenous perspective, cities remain the locations that most embody the continued colonist occupation of traditional territory. As such, it is not easy to conceive of Indigenous rights and any form of title in what are now dominant non-Indigenous regimes. Yet, up to 75% of Indigenous Australians live in cities, and cities thus have a 'persistent footprint' of Indigeneity as they are located on traditional lands/Countrys (Howitt & Lunkapis, 2010, p. 110; Howitt et al., 2013). This reality cannot be extinguished, whether or not it has been recognised under Western law. The notion that Indigenous and Western planning systems can coexist remains problematic and is a persistent issue for Indigenous peoples hoping to gain some control over their resources and influence the development of their cities.

There nonetheless persists two common discourses about Indigenous peoples in cities: (i) that they are 'lacking', as in they are socio-economically disadvantaged and suffer from many ills, from domestic violence, diabetes to incarceration and (ii) that urban Indigenous peoples are not the 'real' Indigenous peoples. Both these constructions lead to denial of the possibility of a dynamic contemporary Indigenous culture in urban areas (Browne, Laurence, & Thorpe, 2009). Indeed, Larissa Berendht, an Aboriginal woman from Sydney, notes there is a conception that 'real' Aboriginal communities only exist in rural and remote areas. Or as Barry and Porter (2012) powerfully state: 'the discourse of tradition, one that activates static notions of "traditionality" and then presumes that such tradition cannot authentically survive modern development, expunges Indigenous presence from the spaces of modern urban development'. This is a process that, in asserting the 'authentic' Aboriginal identity as remote and country based, erases cultural identity in urban settings (Walker & Barcham, 2010). As Gibson (2012, p. 204) adds, 'Put simply, the further Aboriginal people are seen to live from the bare earth and the closer they are to towns, cities and the built environment, the further they are from being perceived as "real Aborigines"'.

This stereotype is reinforced by the tendency of urban planners to include Aboriginal people in activities relating to green spaces, bush tucker gardens and other elements such as putting up Indigenous flags but not in wider urban policy discussions. This bifurcation of urban space and engagement about it, means that generally, planners do not engage Indigenous peoples in active planning per se (Cardinal, 2006; Nursey-Bray & Beer, 2018):

> … when Indigenous people are accommodated as another group within planning, their claims are reduced to a needs-based dimension, where planning can 'service' those needs by simply becoming a neutral provider. It locks the relationship into a paternalistic one of need and service-based outcomes. It also fails to recognize the much more substantive and fundamental challenge that Indigenous claims make to planning, which is the assertion of a substantively different form of property and use rights, knowledge forms, human-environment relationships, and mechanisms of law and governance in relation to space and place. (Porter, 2013, p. 290)

In this context, Indigenous street art has been and continues to be a powerful tool to reclaim, intervene and decolonise urban spaces. This art, whether it is commissioned or a form of graffiti, asserts Indigenous presence and by engaging the public in the art form, also reminds them that Australia was and remains Indigenous land. As Mokak (2017) asserts:

> Public Indigenous art is often personal and political, challenging the viewer and forcing its onlookers to ask questions and start conversations. Defying the usual grounds of the white walled galleries of major art institutions, the streets offer an inclusive and accessible space for the public to

freely engage with contemporary Indigenous art and promote discussion about past and current Indigenous issues. (Mokak, 2017, paragraph 4)

As a form of engagement, it is a form of land reclamation in cityscapes that in its insistent presence 'snaps', members of the public to attention; it offers a means by which to re-negotiate the moral geography of the creative city (Mcauliffe, 2012) and to disrupt the ways the community conventionally understands urban places, to reconstruct them as Indigenous places. As Mokak (2017) further observes: 'Whether it's a small tag or a large-scale mural, Indigenous graffiti is a powerful tool used to reclaim, intervene and decolonize urban spaces'. Ultimately, the deployment of art as a form of engagement and resistance by Indigenous peoples, is also a healing practice, one that asserts Indigenous culture as dynamic, and that they are not 'lacking', thus attempting to overcome the stereotypes they face in urban environments.

There are multiple examples of Indigenous art as placemaking engagement. For example, the Greater Shepparton City Council in partnership with Rumbalara Co-Op and Yorta Yorta Nation Aboriginal Corporation have established a project specifically designed to raise awareness about and celebrate the local Aboriginal culture and history. As a major Aboriginal Street Art project, walls all around Shepparton were painted by key Indigenous artists to recall and remember people and stories important to them. One of these is a mural by well-known artist Adnate, that honours the late William Cooper, and Australian Aboriginal Activist and community leader, while other paintings address the challenges facing young Aboriginal men and women today, including deaths in custody and substance abuse.

Graffiti is another form of expression and engagement, with Dena Curtis noting that: 'Graffiti offers a platform for these artists to celebrate their culture, language and stories in a public forum and in a place that can't be ignored'. In Redfern community, Sydney wall murals also pay tribute to and enjoin the community to think about Indigenous presence in cities. For example, as early as 1983, one piece entitled 40,000 years was created on the Lawson Street rail-bridge by artist Carol Ruff. Her intent was to create a tribute to Aboriginal history in South Sydney and to remind the community of the perseverance of Indigenous culture despite the changes they have experienced. This mural is now being restored, thus enabling members of the public particularly those who come in and out of Redfern train station to engage with this work and its message. Adnate has also painted a 10 storey piece of Aboriginal Elder Jenny Munro, in the heart of Sydney; Ms Munro, an Aboriginal activist fought against State Government plans to relocate public housing tenants in Waterloo as part of plans to develop a new metro station and she founded the Aboriginal Tent Embassy in Redfern, protesting for 15 months against new development on the Block which culminated with the Federal Government agreeing to build new affordable housing for Indigenous families.

Adnate's work is a good example of how artists aim to create art as a forum to engage community attention and raise their awareness about Indigenous issues. As he reflects:

> The main drive behind a lot of my work is about creating awareness and unfortunately a lot of Indigenous communities and Indigenous people as a whole really get pushed under the carpet....I create these massive murals in cities like Melbourne and Sydney and I end up travelling all over the world. I've painted Aboriginal portraits in Singapore as well, on big buildings and everywhere...It really creates an awareness and highlights and makes people question and go, Oh yeah, true. These people are really significant. (Adnate cited in Collins, 2016)

Art in these contexts has power via its placemaking capacity to engage the public on issues that are often swept under the carpet and make visible the original inhabitants in colonial landscapes.

Maddox et al. (2016) argue that graffiti helps the public understand there are voices of dissent out there not always captured in other means and that graffiti helps express people's connection to the rest of the world. As such, graffiti can provide opportunities for empowerment, emancipation and self-determination and a form of community engagement that equally values Indigenous knowledge, and capacities where the community is engaged enough to construct its Indigenous heritage as a source of pride rather than contestation (Maddox et al., 2016).

The use of Indigenous art forms, whether via graffiti, murals or the work of prominent artists like Adnate, they all perform a singular function—which is to engage community with their active presence and give the lie to the fallacy that Indigenous people do not live in cities. As Porter (2013) notes, this means Australian cities have to account for Indigenous presence, in spatial, cultural or political terms (Porter, 2013). What was discursively constituted was consequently perpetuated in the material form cities took, in their design and construction, and in the laws that governed the use of their spaces. The deployment of art in these ways also subverts the traditional idea of Aboriginal people on Country, where 'place' is understood to signify a special connection between people and their land, a visual image that emphasises the 'remote' Aboriginal at the expense of the lived urban reality (Gibson, 2012).

Public Art, Community and Urban Renewal

Finally, the deployment of murals and other forms of public art are constantly used to encourage placemaking and connection between people and place and ground urban renewal projects. Renewal, also known as regeneration or gentrification, is a vexed issue, almost always attracting discussion around issues of equity, social justice and poverty. In this context, many developers seek to use art to help make the development more competitive, and since the 1980s public art been increasingly advocated as a means by which a sense of place and identity can be forged in these renewed areas, and where social exclusion, social change and economic development can all be facilitated (Palermo, 2014).

Regeneration and gentrification policies in places like the UK including Coventry Phoenix Initiative in Coventry, Blue Carpet and other initiatives in Newcastle upon Tyne, Up in the air and Further Up in the air in Liverpool and Sovereign Housing in Bristol have all consciously tried to enhance and build strong collaborative relationships with their local communities via art. Developers have been interested in creating processes of engagement not just in creating the work of art (Palermo, 2014).

All these initiatives try to enhance the environment by creating a strong relationship and collaboration with the communities living there. The premise here is that by development strong place attachments with and by the local communities that more authentic or sympathetic (and hence more successful) renewal or gentrification schemes will be:

> In choosing public art and cultural as an engine for regeneration and gentrification of urban spaces it is necessary to not consider the public space as an empty space to be filled with whatever work of art, and to consider citizenship as an active part of the aesthetic processes. In this way, the spectator becomes 'spect-actor' and the artist 'spect-author'. (Palermo, 2014, p. 526)

Within renewal programmes, there are a range of approaches that can be undertaken relating to the use of art to engage the public. One is to raise a piece of artwork in a very visible public space, which will create a profile for that area or areas under regeneration. Another is to install provocative pieces of work, ones which will start a dialogue between members of the public on various issues. Public art can also be used to establish collaborations within the renewal project to build relations between the artist and the community, who may then become active participants in the creation of the identity of that area. Art has also been used in regeneration projects such as in the garden festivals in Stoke-on-Trent or in the UK Millennium Projects (Hall & Robertson, 2001).

Art as a form of placemaking engagement within rejuvenation schemes can thus build a sense of community be active in the building of networks and interpersonal links and hence promote social development and cohesion (Hall & Robertson 2001, p. 10).

Othman, Nishimura, and Kubota (2013, p. 363) argue for the role of memory association in placemaking—memories are hence signifiers of place: 'Place means nothing without association, without memory a place will just be another dull place'. In using art to create places in urban renewal programmes, memories are also built and hence people's attachment to them. As a brand for urban regeneration then, art is inextricably linked to placemaking. Pollock and Paddison (2014, p. 85) in a case study of the link between placemaking and public art for the Glasgow Gorbals argue that art plays a crucial role in the reinvention of the city. They caution however against being simplistic and idealistic about this relationship, sending out a call to action to be mindful of the potential to create pockets of social exclusion where community engagement is, in fact, a tokenistic nod to lull the pathway to regeneration: 'The vocabulary of regeneration, public art and participation suggest a seamless meld contributing to a meaningful construction of place, but the reality is considerably more complex' (Pollock & Paddison, 2014, p. 89).

The case study of Port Adelaide, a suburb of the southern city of Adelaide in South Australia is instructive here. Port Adelaide, traditionally known as a place of socio-economic disadvantage within Adelaide, is one of the suburbs that the State Government, as part of a State-based Renewal SA Programme, has committed to rejuvenate. The Port Adelaide Renewal Strategy aims to engineer a shift in emphasis from Port Adelaide being a historic shipping and industrial harbour to a contemporary mixed-use urban area with a sustainable local economy and regional activity centre. The Renewal Plan offers guidance on future development which is anticipated to include construction of an additional 2000–4000 homes, the formation of 'friendly inspirational spaces' for an additional 4000–8000 people and allowances to nearly double public open space. The Plan suggests that this renewal will generate 1000–1500 construction jobs and $1–2 billion in private investment over its lifetime.

This urban renewal strategy employs placemaking techniques, with the ultimate goal of ensuring that the city becomes a place 'where people love to be'. As the catch cry of the Port Adelaide Placemaking Strategy asserts: 'We will be consulting with the local community to create fantastic new infrastructure that will provide new places to meet, relax, walk and enjoy'. The deployment of art in multiple ways has been used as a catalyst to invite community engagement in and active participation around an ongoing placemaking strategy. This is evident in the commitment in the *Public Art and Place Making Policy* by the City of Port Adelaide Enfield which states: 'Council will initiate Public Art as part of its commitment to improving the overall appearance of the City and to creating vibrant, attractive and functional spaces'.

The Council also provides a *Public Art Guide Book* that showcases the public art, artists and local community whose sense of place is anchored to the art on display. There are multiple art placemaking processes actively underway, but a few merit particular mention. One initiative has been the design and installation of artwork in public places, particularly stobie poles and bus shelters. The city of Port Adelaide is now well known for the pieces of art rendered on Stobie Poles throughout the region, adding visual amenity and 'funk' factor to the city.

The Wonderwalls Programme is another way in which the urban renewal strategies are linked to art programmes and again engage the local and wider communities. The Wonderwall Programme, welcomes all artists to come and paint blank walls in the Port. Local art collectives are given the task of transforming walls into destinations within Port Adelaide's city centre. These artworks then remain as legacies and have helped enhance the visual amenity of Port Adelaide, build civic identity and engaged the wider Adelaide community with the port community as a potential place to live or invest in. Run over a weekend in March, prior Wonderwall events have attracted more than 20,000 visitors over a few days. In 2019, the Wonderwalls exhibition is run in conjunction with the Big Picture Fest and supported by the local Pirate Life Brewery. Many local places have also become key sites for exhibitions, such as the Marine and Harbour building or Harts Mill and are enthusiastically championed:

> When I used to think of Port Adelaide, I thought of dolphins, heritage buildings, and, well, that's essentially all. That is until my partner begged to differ. 'It's a hub for artists!' he claimed. I had to see it to believe it. And what I saw was satisfyingly stupefying. This humongous colourful crocodile above has been painted on the back of a large building across from the LeFevre Peninsula Primary School. It was designed and created by an international artist named Hitnes, and also a local artist named Vans the Omega. The vibrant colouring applied in this work pops out at onlookers and looks artistically inviting. The crocodile is so long, that if you want to take a photo, be prepared to use panorama. Right beside

the creative crocodile is a number of paintings that have been locally produced. They hang high on the wall, and can be appreciated from directly underneath or from the other side of the road. The images appear to show different landmarks in Port Adelaide, and represent the positive cultural diversity in the community. (Warren, commenting on the Wonderwalls 2018)

The City Council also supports the South Australian Living Artists Festival (SALA) every year, which runs for a month in August. The Port Adelaide and surrounding businesses, NGOs and local governments all work together to assist artists to put on and showcase their work. A night street party is held each year to launch the SALA programme and the community works together to create a place based and unique experience for visitors and locals alike.

Finally, the use of art in Port Adelaide is also used to engage Indigenous and non-Indigenous artists alike by supporting Tarnanthi at the Port. Tarnanthi is a State-Based Festival of Contemporary Aboriginal and Torres Strait Islander Art. The City of Port Adelaide Enfield supported a street party to celebrate Indigenous culture, with the aim to weave 'together fresh and dynamic elements, underpinned by living traditions the event showcases the area as a thriving space of united community gatherings and artistic excellence'. Smoking Ceremonies, River Stories Boat Tours, Bush Tucker, Weaving and Dance workshops, were all part of the event.

In this case, this event was another way in which communities via art—in all its manifestations—became engaged with Indigenous culture—again making it a visible in a place that represents a site of colonial occupation (Oakley & Johnson, 2013). The hosting of Tarnanthi at the Port also engaged local Indigenous people with the Port as a place—Joshua Warrior, for example, one of the performers, has strong ties to the city, having played football for the local team the Magpies (following his father and brother) and notes: 'I can't wait for Tanarnthi. We've got singers, hip hop rappers, dancers and of course comedians coming to entertain. This cultural event is going to be fantastic for the Port Adelaide and also the Aboriginal community'.

Conclusion

Via documentary and case study analysis, this chapter presents the proposition that art as placemaking can lead to powerful community engagement and become a tool that generates narratives around and connection to urban ecologies and hence integration between people and place in cities. The question might be asked, why would this matter? It matters, because as a process placemaking has power and the capacity to change cities and regions in significant ways. Creating places that mean something to people however and do so in ways that do not erase historical memories or existing place attachments is a tricky exercise. Urban development, let alone urban renewal programmes, always run the risk of creating rather than minimising social inequities and sharpen the divide between those who have, and those who do not. In Australia, this danger is complicated by the possibility of ignoring Indigenous peoples and to exacerbating what is a negative historical legacy of racially divisive power and spatial geometries in cities. As such, the deployment of art, whether it is by public exhibitions, murals or graffiti, is inherently participative, and a useful way of thinking about how to engage the community. The community, in turn, is enjoined to 'pay attention' to messages or issues or can enable the artists themselves to become active participants in the dissemination of those messages.

Visual amenity and a sense of belonging and identity can also be fostered via peoples place attachment through art. The use of art as a mode of placemaking to engage communities is not without criticism, nor is it by any means, easy to do. However, as these case studies show, the use of art does allow for a tailor-made and positive engagement between people and place. In a world where attention is in scarce supply, getting the community to 'pay attention' to their own neighbourhood and be active actors in the design of their own futures and built environments is a significant 'win' for artists and urban planners alike.

Key Learnings:

- Building skills in cultural engagement and conflict management will help build stronger and more enduring placemaking engagements.

- Art has potential to bring communities together and bring their attention to nature and culture in urban environments.
- Art can be a form of engagement that informs placemaking.
- Art can make Indigenous places visible.

References

Cant, S., & Morris, N. (2006). Geographies of art and the environment. *Social and Cultural Geography, 7*(6), 857–861.

Coaffee, J. (2013). Towards next-generation urban resilience in planning practice: From securitization to integrated place making. *Planning Practice & Research, 28*(3), 323–339. https://doi.org/10.1080/02697459.2013.787693.

Bain, A. L., & Landau, F. (2019). Artists, temporality, and the governance of collaborative place-making. *Urban Affairs Review, 55*(2), 405–427.

Barry, J., & Porter, L. (2012). Indigenous recognition in state-based planning systems: Understanding textual mediation in the contact zone. *Planning Theory, 11*(2), 170–187.

Blum-Ross, A. (2013). 'It made our eyes get bigger': Youth filmmaking and place-making in East London. *Visual Anthropology Review, 29*(2), 89–106.

Browne, J., Laurence, S., & Thorpe, S. (2009). *Acting on food insecurity in urban Aboriginal and Torres Strait Islander communities: Policy and practice interventions to improve local access and supply of nutritious food*. Retrieved January 6, 2019, from http://www.healthinfonet.ecu.edu.au/health-risks/nutrition/other-reviews.

Cardinal, N. (2006). The exclusive city: Identifying, measuring, and drawing attention to Aboriginal and Indigenous experiences in an urban context. *Cities, 23*(3), 217–228.

Chang, T. C. (2008). Art and soul: Powerful and powerless art in Singapore. *Environment and Planning A, 40*(8), 1921–1943.

Charles Sturt Council. (2019). *A place making framework*. Charles Sturt Council, Adelaide, South Australia. https://www.charlessturt.sa.gov.au/webdata/resources/files/Place%20Making%20Framework.pdf.

Chun, N., & Gurova, O. (2018). Place-making the local to reach the global: A case study of Pre-Helsinki. *Fashion Practice*. https://doi.org/10.1080/17569370.2018.1507168.

Collins, B. (2016, June 15). Giant portraits DRAW attention to Indigenous issues. *ABC News*. Retrieved from https://www.abc.net.au/news/2016-06-15/giant-portraits-draw-attention-to-indigenous-issues/7513272. Accessed 18 March 2019.

Fincher, R., Pardy, M., & Shaw, K. (2016). Place-making or placemasking? The everyday political economy of "making place". *Planning Theory & Practice, 17*(4), 516–536. https://doi.org/10.1080/14649357.2016.1217344.

Grishin, S. (2017). *The sculptors from Western Australia & Sculpture by the Sea.* Retrieved from https://sculpturebythesea.com/sculptors-western-australia-sculpture-sea/.

Gibson, L. (2012). Colonizing bricks and mortar: Indigenous place-making through art objects and artifacts. *Postcolonial Studies, 15*(2), 203–219. https://doi.org/10.1080/13688790.2012.693044.

Hall, T., & Robertson, I. (2001). Public art and urban regeneration: Advocacy, claims and critical debates. *Landscape Research, 26*(1), 5–26. https://doi.org/10.1080/01426390120024457.

Harvey, D. (1996). *Justice, nature, and the geography of difference.* Massachusetts: Blackwell Publishers.

Howitt, R., & Lunkapis, G. (2010). Coexistence: Planning and the challenge of Indigenous rights. In J. Hillier & P. Healey (Eds.), *Ashgate research companion to planning theory* (pp. 109–133). Farnham: Ashgate.

Howitt, R., Doohan, K., Suchet-Pearson, S., Lunkapis, G., Muller, S., … Cross, S. (2013). Capacity deficits at cultural interfaces of land and sea governance. In R. Walker, T. Jojola, & D. Natcher (Eds.), *Reclaiming Indigenous planning*. Montreal, Canada: McGill-Queen's University Press.

Jacobs, J. (1961). *The death and life of great American cities.* Harmondsworth: Penguin.

Jordaan, T., Puren, K., & Roos, V. (2008). The meaning of place-making in planning: Historical overview and implications for urban and regional planning. *Acta Structilia, 15*(1), 91–117.

Lefebvre, H. (1991). *The production of space* (D. Nicholson-Smith, Trans.). Oxford, UK; Cambridge, MA: Blackwell.

Maddox, D., Anderson, P., Downton, P., Fantin, E., Gomez, G. E., Goodness, J., … Shillington, L. (2016). *Creative place-making—This is the nature of graffiti.* Montreal. Retrieved from https://www.thenatureofcities.com/2016/01/20/creative-place-making-this-is-the-nature-of-graffiti/. Accessed 18 March 2019.

Massey, D. B. (2005). *For space.* London; Thousand Oaks, CA: SAGE.

Mcauliffe, C. (2012). Graffiti or street art? Negotiating the moral geographies of the creative city. *Journal of Urban Affairs, 34*(2), 189–206.

Minty, Z. (2006). Post-apartheid public art in Cape Town: Symbolic reparations and public space. *Urban Studies, 43*(2), 421–440.

Mokak, S. (2017). Decolonising urban spaces; The power of Indigenous street art. *NITV*. Retrieved from https://www.sbs.com.au/nitv/article/2017/10/06/decolonising-urban-spaces-power-indigenous-street-art. Accessed 18 March 2019.

Moon, L. (2018). Reflecting on belonging and place at Sculpture by the Sea. *Il Globo*. Retrieved at https://ilglobo.com.au/news/40694/reflecting-on-belonging-and-place-at-sculpture-by-the-sea/#.

Nursey-Bray, M., & Beer, A. (2018). Urban planning and indigenous peoples Australia. In N. Snipe & K. Vella (Eds.), *The Routledge handbook of urban and regional planning* (1st ed., p. 16).

Oakley, S., & Johnson, L. (2013). Place-taking and place-making in waterfront renewal, Australia. *Urban Studies, 50*(2), 341–355.

Othman, S., Nishimura, Y., & Kubota, A. (2013). Memory association in place making: A review. *Procedia-Social and Behavioral Sciences, 85*, 554–563.

Palermo, L. (2014). The role of art in urban gentrification and regeneration: Aesthetic, social and economic developments. *Il Capitale Culturale: Studies on the Value of Cultural Heritage, 10*, 521–545.

Pollock, V., & Paddison, R. (2014). On place making, participation and public art: The Gorbals, Glasgow. *Journal of Urbanism: International Research on Placemaking and Urban Sustainability, 7*(1), 85–105.

Pollock, V. L., & Sharp, J. (2012). Real participation or the tyranny of participatory practice? Public art and community involvement in the regeneration of the Raploch, Scotland. *Urban Studies, 49*(14), 3063–3079.

Porter, L. (2013). Coexistence in cities: The challenge of indigenous urban planning in the twenty-first century. In R. Walker, T. Jojola, & D. Natcher (Eds.), *Reclaiming indigenous planning* (pp. 283–310). Kingston, Canada: McGill-Queens University Press.

Puleo, T. (2014). Art-making as place-making following disaster. *Progress in Human Geography, 38*(4), 568–580.

Ryan, C. (1995). Introduction. In T. Winikoff (Ed.), *Places not spaces: Placemaking in Australia*. Sydney: Envirobook Publishing.

Sharp, J. (2007). The life and death of five spaces: Public art and community regeneration in Glasgow. *Cultural Geographies, 14*(2), 274–292.

Sharp, J., Pollock, V., & Paddison, R. (2005). Just art for a just city: Public art and social inclusion in urban regeneration. *Urban Studies, 42*(5–6), 1001–1023.

Shaw, K., & Montana, G. (2016). Place-making in megaprojects in Melbourne. *Urban Policy and Research, 34*(2), 166–189. https://doi.org/10.1080/08111146.2014.967392.

Sofield, T., Guia, J., & Specht, J. (2017). Organic 'folkloric' community driven place-making and tourism. *Tourism Management, 61*, 1–22.

Walker, R., & Barcham, M. (2010). Indigenous-inclusive citizenship: The city and social housing in Canada, New Zealand, and Australia. *Environment and Planning A, 42*(2), 314–331.

Wang, M. (2018). Place-making for the people: Socially engaged art in rural China. *China Information, 32*(2), 244–269.

Zhang, A. Y. (2018). Thinking temporally when thinking relationally: Temporality in relational place-making. *Geoforum, 90,* 91–99.

Printed by Printforce, the Netherlands